TAKING PUNK
TO THE MASSES

FROM NOWHERE TO NEVERMIND

TAKING PUNK
TO THE MASSES

FROM NOWHERE TO NEVERMIND

A VISUAL HISTORY FROM THE PERMANENT
COLLECTION OF EXPERIENCE MUSIC PROJECT

JACOB McMURRAY

FANTAGRAPHICS BOOKS

FANTAGRAPHICS BOOKS
7563 Lake City Way NE
Seattle, Washington 98115

PUBLISHED by Gary Groth and Kim Thompson
EDITED by Jacob McMurray
CO-PUBLISHED by Eric Reynolds
ART DIRECTION and DESIGN by Jacob Covey
PHOTOGRAPHY by Lance Mercer

Distributed in the U.S. by W.W. Norton and Company, Inc. (800-233-4830)
Distributed in Canada by the Canadian Manda Group (800-452-6642 x862)
Distributed in the United Kingdom by Turnaround Distribution (44 (0) 20 8829-3002)

First Fantagraphics printing: April, 2011
ISBN: 978-1-60699-433-7
Printed in China

PHOTO CREDITS | Front Endpaper: Crowd during Mudhoney at the Fulham Hibernian, London, June 19, 1990. Photograph by Charles Peterson. Page I-III: Ludwig 1960's reissue drum kit, played by Aaron Roeder of The Mono Men, 1989 – 1997, and burnt during the Estrus Records warehouse fire, January 16, 1997. Page IV-V: Leather jacket, worn by Billy Zoom of X, 1975 - 1984. Page VI: Black Fender Stratocaster, smashed by Kurt Cobain during the recording of "Endless Nameless" during the *Nevermind* sessions, April 1991. Page VIII: Bradley electric bass, played by Steve Gamboa of Nation of Ulysses, 1988 – 1992. Page X-XI: Gibson Ripper Bass, played by Krist Novoselic with Nirvana, 1993 – 1994. From the collection of Krist Novoselic. Page XII-1: Cable upright piano, played by Elliott Smith, 1997 – 1999. Gift of Larry Crane and Jackpot! Recording Studio. Page 224: Peavey Telecaster played by Dave Dederer of the Presidents of the United States of America. Gift of The Presidents of the United States of America. Page 234: Cash register used by the First Avenue club, Minneapolis, early – late 1980s. Back Endpaper: Ben Shepherd of Soundgarden at Lollapalooza, UBC Thunderbird Arena, Vancouver, BC, July 21, 1992. Photograph by Lance Mercer.

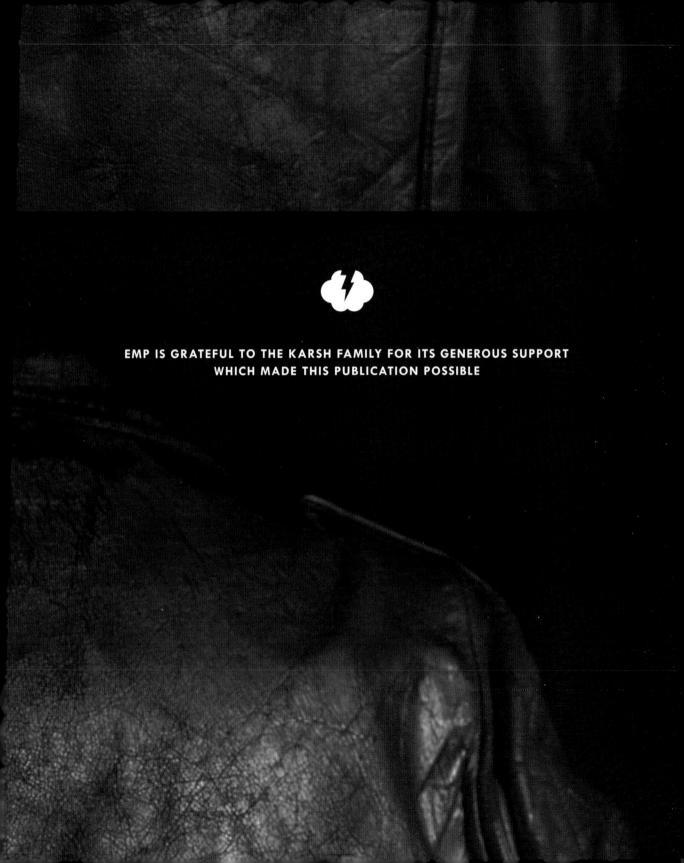

EMP IS GRATEFUL TO THE KARSH FAMILY FOR ITS GENEROUS SUPPORT
WHICH MADE THIS PUBLICATION POSSIBLE

FOREWORD
KRIST
NOVOSELIC
NIRVANA

The course of rock music has taken many stops along the way to the present day. Memphis and Detroit of the 1950s and early '60s were important starting points. San Francisco defined music during the Summer of Love and into the late '60s. New York and London in the late 1970s were homes to Punk. In the 1980s, the path lead us to Athens and Minneapolis. And the Pacific Northwest took it from there, incorporating the raw rock sounds that came out of the region in the early '60s and redefining them in the 1990s.

Rock music is an art form that thrives in reinvention. Each of these places had its own scene: musicians building on an infrastructure that took sounds from other hubs to make an identity of their own. Thus, music has always been global. And in our connected era, new sounds can come from anywhere – but their lineage can always be traced to those earlier stops along the path.

The Experience Music Project connects all points past and present. And as you look around their magnificent building, you'll see it's also about the future. It's a feast for the ears as much as the eyes. This house was built by technology, an art form itself in the form of content and information, delivered by computers, handhelds and other gizmos. And it may be pointing us to the next stop on rock's journey.

Music keeps moving but it leaves its mark on the place and people of the moment. And that's what Jacob McMurray shows within these pages. This is a document of how music shaped culture in terms of a local scene and how that scene impacted the world.

So it all comes together – as it should when the band is in top form!

— K.N.
April 2011

In late 1991, Nirvana exploded on the national music scene, transforming Seattle from a faraway backwater to the epicenter of popular music culture. Soon not only Nirvana but Pearl Jam, Alice in Chains, and Soundgarden ruled the airwaves. Seattle became a city that bands moved to, instead of away from, to make it big in the music business.

None of this success would have been possible without the rise of the underground music scene, which began in the mid-'70s with punk rock. Early punk was less about a consistent musical style (compare the three-chord power pop of the Ramones to the intricate, cerebral melodies of Television, for example), and much more about a Do-It-Yourself, or DIY, ethic and the desire to rail against the dark milieu of the post-hippie early '70s and the calcified world of contemporary corporate rock. While the major label record industry picked up on the early punk scenes in New York City and the United Kingdom, the labels ignored what was happening outside of the narrow confines of what they considered commercially viable music. For most of the '80s, the burgeoning underground rock scene outside of New York City was largely left to its own devices, allowing an unfettered flow of creativity despite the lack of resources afforded by the major labels.

During this time, Black Flag, Minor Threat, Hüsker Dü, D.O.A. and scores of other underground bands toured the country in cramped vans, spreading the gospel of punk rock. Fans launched independent record labels such as Twin/Tone, SST, Sub Pop, Touch & Go, and Dischord to put out music by their favorite bands. Other people opened venues that were friendly to the new music, published fanzines to communicate with other devotees, or started local radio shows to broadcast the music. All of this existed outside the traditional music industry, independent of the "corporate ogre," and driven solely by fellow travelers whose primary impetus was music rather than cash.

INTRODUCTION
JACOB MCMURRAY
EMP SENIOR CURATOR

Gradually, several bands, including R.E.M., Sonic Youth, the Replacements, Dinosaur Jr, and the Pixies, broadened their sound while maintaining punk roots. Year by year, song by song, they each made inroads into the mainstream consciousness, priming the public for their underground aesthetic. In the Pacific Northwest, key individuals such as Calvin Johnson of K Records and the band Beat Happening, Bruce Pavitt of Sub Pop Records, producer and musician Steve Fisk, and musician Mark Arm, among many others, acted as catalysts, helping to spark and promote the regional scene, despite the prevailing wisdom at the time that you needed to move to Los Angeles or New York City in order to "make it." For the Northwest underground, making it, for the most part, wasn't part of the equation.

The region's geographic isolation, often considered a detriment, now proved to be a boon, allowing the bands, scene and indie labels to develop their own personality, outside of the influence of major label and mainstream preferences. After all, when was the last time the nation looked to the Northwest as a music hotbed? The "Louie Louie" era of the early '60s? Heart in the mid-'70s? That might as well have been aeons ago. In 1988 when Seattle bands Mudhoney, TAD, and Nirvana on local indie label Sub Pop began generating buzz in underground circles, the region's perceived backwater status further enhanced the romantic and mythologized appeal – especially to fans in the UK and Europe, who fell in love with the idea of sweaty, flannel-wearing, blue collar lumberjacks with screaming guitars rocking out in the wilds of the Pacific Northwest. The region had the mystique of a forgotten land and that helped sell the product, something that would never have occurred in urban hubs that are eternally in the public spotlight. The downside was that the Northwest's broad musical diversity was overshadowed by a handful of bands that shared aspects of an often abrasive, guitar-heavy sound, with varying degrees of punk and metal influence. The region was far more than grunge, as the sound was tagged, but grunge is what the Northwest became known for.

By the turn of the 1990s, underground rock music throughout the US was becoming more popular, showing up on college radio and even in mainstream magazines like *Rolling Stone*. For a band like Sonic Youth to sell more than 250,000 copies of a record was *huge* in underground circles, and the majors began seeing dollar signs. A&R reps conspicuously crowded local rock shows, hoping to sign the next band with the potential of R.E.M, Sonic Youth, or Hüsker Dü. Little did they know that those metrics would soon mean nothing after the September 1991 release of Nirvana's *Nevermind*, which was selling over 400,000 copies *a week* by that Christmas, and has sold over 26 million copies worldwide to date.

Nirvana had emerged from the depressed logging town of Aberdeen, Washington, heavily influenced by underground bands like the Melvins, Scratch Acid, the Vaselines and the Butthole Surfers. But they were equally drawn to the '70s riff-heavy rock of Aerosmith or Black Sabbath, as well as the pop leanings of Big Star or the Pixies. Nirvana's ultimate appeal stemmed from the combination of these disparate musical influences, all filtered through Cobain's uncanny ability to craft melodies and catchy hooks. Moreover, his enigmatic and convoluted lyrics allowed the listener to imbue the songs with personal meaning, adding to their resonance. Furthermore, Nirvana's Gen X image belied the typical rock star stance – they wore regular clothes, gave props to other underground bands, and stuck up for the freaks, geeks, and outcasts everywhere. Instead of creating a barrier between the fans and themselves, they indicated by their affect and actions that they ultimately were one of us. Add to this a dose of pure luck, and propelled by the infectious lead single, "Smells Like Teen Spirit," and the barrier between underground and mainstream culture shattered.

Nirvana brought a punk message wrapped in a pop package, taking punk to the masses. This event changed popular music forever by instantly turning upside down the methods and assumptions of the major label record industry. Instead of largely ignoring bands coming from underground circles, the majors created internal "Alternative" departments to begin courting those bands and the independent labels that they called home. Suddenly cash was flowing into the underground network, creating opportunities where there were once none for many bands and labels, but also transforming the scene further away from its DIY roots and towards a corporate business model.

From 1991 to 1994, Seattle was the *it* town for music, but the grunge hangover soon set in, the hype died down, and new scenes began to form in other cities. And yet the Pacific Northwest was indelibly changed: music now mattered, not just to the hipsters in the scene, but to everybody. It became part of our communal fabric, and music in the region has continued to flourish with underground-influenced bands such as Sleater-Kinney, Modest Mouse, Built to Spill, the Presidents of the United States of America, Elliott Smith, Death Cab for Cutie, Fleet Foxes, the Decemberists, and myriad others.

Over the last 15 years, the curatorial staff at Experience Music Project in Seattle, Washington, has amassed a permanent collection of more than 140,000 cultural artifacts related to popular music. At least 20,000 of those are directly linked to music that occurred in the Pacific Northwest from the mid-1970s to 2000. Records, posters, stage costumes, photographs, instruments and more are included in an amazing archive of incalculable cultural wealth that contains some of the rarest and most iconic objects from the worlds of punk, grunge, and other musical genres. In addition, we have also conducted more than 800 filmed oral history interviews with musicians, artists, record label heads, venue owners, fans, and others from across the musical spectrum. These interviews have proven invaluable to all of our exhibitions, and along with EMP's artifact collection, form a central pillar of our institution. They are an element of EMP that we are dedicated to preserving and promoting for future generations.

The exhibition *Nirvana: Taking Punk to the Masses*, which debuted at Experience Music Project and inspired this book, makes extensive use of the permanent collection. Since EMP opened in June 2000, we have dedicated one major gallery to the Pacific Northwest's music scene, featuring artifacts from the Jackson Street jazz era to grunge. With the 20th anniversary of *Nevermind* in September 2011, we decided this year marked the perfect time for EMP to become the first museum to create a major exhibition that examines the worldwide impact and influence of Nirvana, placed within a context of what was happening in the Pacific Northwest and throughout the United States after the advent of punk rock in the mid-1970s. The exhibition includes more than 150 artifacts and photographs from EMP's permanent collection and a dozen generous lenders; original, interpretive films featuring performance footage and oral history interviews with key individuals, including Krist Novoselic and Dave Grohl; and interactive kiosks that allow visitors to explore the related permanent collection in depth. Given the significance of Nirvana and EMP's emphasis on the Pacific Northwest, *Nirvana: Taking Punk to the Masses*, in scope, timing, and venue, couldn't be more appropriate.

Taking Punk to the Masses: From Nowhere to Nevermind also draws from EMP's deep archives. This book features 101 primary objects from our permanent collection, with the addition of a few significant loaned objects. They are arranged, annotated and given context by excerpts from more than 100 oral histories. Together, the artifacts and oral histories provide a broad context for the evolution of punk rock throughout the '80s to the grunge of the early '90s and the indie scene that followed. The book illustrates the interweaving of a complex web of creative individuals and organizations that shifted the public perception of what music could be.

Taking Punk to the Masses: From Nowhere to Nevermind is a celebration of the independent spirit of the Pacific Northwest and the music that continues to rock the world.

— J.M.
April 2011

◉ TAKING PUNK

TO THE MASSES

"OK! Let's give it to 'em right now!" screamed Jack Ely of the Kingsmen into this microphone at the start of the guitar solo for "Louie Louie." With its simple song structure, three-chord attack and forbidden teenage appeal, this single song inspired legions of kids in garages across America to pick up guitars and ROCK. "Louie Louie" has become a touchstone in the evolution of rock'n'roll, and with over 1500 recorded cover versions to date, its influence on teenage culture and the future DIY punk underground can't be underestimated.

Ely's vocals were so rough and unintelligible that some more puritanical listeners interpreted the lyrics as being obscene and complained. This rumor led several radio stations to ban the song and the FBI even launched an investigation. All of this only fueled the popularity of the song, which rocketed up the charts in late 1963, imprinting this grunge ur-message onto successive generations of youth, by way of the Sonics, Stooges, MC5, New York Dolls, Patti Smith, The Clash, Black Flag, and others, all of whom amplified and rebroadcast its powerful sonic meme with their own recorded versions.

NEUMANN U-47 MICROPHONE, CA. 1961

"There was this great record, 'Louie Louie,' by a band from the Pacific Northwest called The Kingsmen. I bought their album and it was a great influence on me because they were a real professional band, y'know?"
— Wayne Kramer, MC5

"'Teen Spirit' was such a clichéd riff. It was so close to a Boston riff or 'Louie Louie.' When I came up with the guitar part, Krist looked at me and said, 'That is so ridiculous.' I made the band play it for an hour-and-a-half."
— Kurt Cobain, Nirvana (*Rolling Stone*, January 27, 1994)

"I was in seventh grade and ritually would watch Hugh Downs and Barbara Walters with my mother on the *Today Show*. The Who did sort of an early lip synch video of 'I Can See For Miles' and then they interviewed Townshend and Daltrey. They'd just returned from their first American tour — this was the peak of the British Invasion by and large. 'Well, what was your favorite thing about America?' They thought for a minute and said with a fairly thick accent, 'We were in this place called Seattle and we saw this band called the Sonics.'"
— Larry Reid, curator/punk promoter/manager

"I heard that one a lot, y'know, when I was six, seven, eight years old. Of course, every kid learns that pattern and tries to figure out what he's saying — what the hell is that guy saying? Is it satanic? Is it sexually-driven or what?"

— MIKE McCREADY, PEARL JAM

PARAMOUNT ★ NORTHWEST

ALICE COOPER

July 9-10   10 pm

ZE WHIZ KIDZ & DOLLY BROS

"Puttin' Out in Dreamsville!"

TICKETS: $3.00 $3.50

Available at: **BERNIES**—Aurora Village - University - University Dist. - South-center - Tacoma Mall; **SQUIRE MEN'S SHOP** — Northgate - University Dist. - Southcenter - Tacoma Mall; **IMPETUS MUSIQUE** — Capitol Hill; **MAGNOLIA HI-FI; WAREHOUSE OF MUSIC; JEANS WEST** — Downtown Seattle & Bellevue; **POSITIVELY** — 4th St., Bremerton; **CHAPTER ELEVEN** — on Pine across from the Bon.

Seattle performance art troupe Ze Whiz Kidz are one of the great hidden stories of punk rock, instilling a heavy Seattle connection to the transition between glam and punk. They were founded in 1969 by David Xavier Harrigan (aka Tomata du Plenty – pictured on this poster), who was formerly a member of the San Francisco-based psychedelic, gay drag ensemble, The Cockettes. The group featured an extensive, revolving lineup, with flamboyant names such as Satin Sheets, Gorilla Rose, Louise Lovely, Palm Springs, Cha Cha Samoa, and Rhina Stone.

Ze Whiz Kidz staged nearly a hundred gender-bending music and theater performances from 1969 to the mid-1970s, and occasionally opened for glam and glitter kings such as Alice Cooper or the New York Dolls. Tomata moved to New York in 1972 with Gorilla Rose and performed sketch theater at CBGB's and other clubs in the East Village, alongside band performances from Blondie and the Ramones. At the dawn of the punk age, Tomata du Plenty returned to Seattle and formed (along with Melba Toast and Rio de Janiero) the Tupperwares, which would soon after re-form in Los Angeles as the seminal synth-punk band the Screamers, while Whiz Kid Satin Sheets (now Satz) formed the Lewd, making a splash on the Seattle and San Francisco punk scenes.

ALICE COOPER, ZE WHIZ KIDZ, AND THE DOILY BROTHERS, AT THE PARAMOUNT NORTHWEST, SEATTLE, JULY 9 – 10, 1971

"Who else would you put on the bill with Alice Cooper, except the Whiz Kidz? Alice said at the end of the show – being as outrageous as he is – he said to us, 'You scare me!'"

— SATZ, ZE WHIZ KIDZ, THE LEWD

"We had a lot of impromptu shows. Wednesday we'd write a show. Thursday we'd call people. We'd rehearse it. And Friday we'd put it on. And by Saturday, it would be the end of the show. We had kind of a training ground in the Submarine Room, in the basement of the Smith Tower. Originally it was a gangster club. They sold sub-machine guns and a lot of drag queens were there. It had a Class H license, which was liquor, but they got busted. So the owner was sitting down there for about two weeks with nothing to do. And so I discovered this club. At the time I was only 17, but I looked a lot older, being tall. I told him I was 21. And I told him that we had a theater group, and if he let me take it over, we would bring shows in and he wouldn't have to be here. And he was real agreeable to that."

— Satz, Ze Whiz Kidz, The Lewd

"DIY in the Northwest actually precedes DIY in England or New York. The earliest punk, true, classic, DIY, scrappy, cut-and-paste punk rock posters I've ever found are actually in the Northwest. They were done by Tomata and Gorilla Rose for the Whiz Kidz. If you look at the New York scene that developed in the '70s that became CBGB's and all that stuff, their graphics more or less look like print shop graphics. It was a picture with some set type underneath it. It echoed an old show card look. It wasn't the hand-lettered, cut out, Xeroxed, collage paste-y thing that later became associated with Jamie Reid's work with the Sex Pistols. But that was the look of the Whiz Kids and The Screamers and the early punk scene in Seattle. The history of punk rock graphics goes way back in the Northwest."

— Art Chantry, graphic designer

PUNK

50¢

NUMBER 2 MARCH

PATTI SMITH AND TELEVISION PLUS...AN EXCLUSIVE INTERVIEW! BLOOD SUCKING LEECHES

New York City's *Punk* was the first magazine to devote itself totally to punk rock. By 1974, the NYC glam rock scene began to wane, and a new cadre of bands with original songs emerged. Television, Suicide, Patti Smith Group, the Ramones, the Heartbreakers, Talking Heads, Blondie and others began playing at former glam ground zero Max's Kansas City, and CBGB's.

Created by cartoonist and editor John Holmstrom, along with Ged Dunn, Jr., and Roderick Edward "Legs" McNeil, *Punk* emerged in January 1976 and made an instant impact. The goal was to cover a broad spectrum of rock and other topics, but the interest in punk music and the vitality of the New York scene dictated that *Punk* limit its scope to the local punk music community. The zine featured early work by legendary music journalist Lester Bangs, *I Shot Andy Warhol* and *American Psycho* director Mary Harron, underground cartoonist Peter Bagge, and others. Despite the rebellious name and being denied shelf space at newsstands, the magazine's circulation was up to 10,000 copies within a few months of its premiere issue and copies were being sold around the world. Until it functionally stopped publication in 1979, *Punk* was at the center of the New York punk scene.

PUNK ZINE #2, MARCH 1976

"Patti and I liked the CBGB's scene because it was small and loose. There were maybe five or six bands that hung out there — I saw the Ramones there for the first time and an early version of Blondie called the Stilettos. The owner Hilly Kristal was kind of bemused by these bands — I don't think it's what he had in mind when he named the club 'Country Bluegrass and Blues.'"

— Lenny Kaye, Patti Smith Group

"I fell in love with the Ramones at first glance. That's how I met the Stooges, I fell in love at first glance. I mean, if it takes more than five or ten seconds to figure out if you like something or not, there's something wrong with you and you shouldn't be in the taste-making end of this world. For me it's five seconds of hearing — what's left of my hearing. The Ramones had it so perfectly — they dressed alike, they had the same haircut, they had the same name, they had great songs, they had great lyrics, they were perfect. They were the perfect band."

— Danny Fields, A&R rep for the Ramones

"What really inspired me to start a band was reading about what was happening in New York. I used to read in *The Village Voice* about CBGB's and Max's Kansas City and the scene, and it sounded real exciting and open. It was all kinds of different bands playing all kinds of different music. And that's what a lot of people don't realize about punk rock. When it started it wasn't a certain style of music. It was an environment where people that made any kind of music that was outcast from the formulaic rock of the time had a venue to play. You had all kinds of bands, from the Ramones, who people associate more with punk rock nowadays, to Blondie, who was more of a pop band. The Tuff Darts were more like a bar band. And Wayne County. And Television with the long guitar jams."

— Greg Ginn, Black Flag

the
TMT
Show

Telepaths

Meyce

Tupperware

37" 22" 36"   Joy 18" 23" 36"   Candy 40" 26" 39"   Wendy 38" 22" 36"   Mioko 39" 24" 39"

.O.O.F. Hall   7:30 PM   Tickets
15 E. Pine   May 1st   3 Live Bands   Cellophane Square

This was the first show booked, promoted, and played entirely by punks in Seattle, held at the International Order of Odd Fellows Hall. At that point the scene was microscopic, and the shows were often held at friends' houses or at rented halls such as the I.O.O.F. Established clubs and bars weren't generally willing to book bands with original material, preferring to play it safe by booking cover bands that could reliably attract a steady crowd. For punks in Seattle interested in playing outside of the basement, they had to take matters in their own hands.

The Telepaths were a fuzz-laden, Bowie-inspired arty outfit, which included a member who was ancient by punk standards – 35-year-old former University of Washington professor Homer Spence. The Meyce had more of a pop sound and were Seattle's first introduction to Jim Basnight, who later reached local renown with his band the Moberlys. The Tupperwares, lead by vocalists and Whiz Kidz alums Tomata du Plenty, Rio de Janeiro and Melba Toast, had a '60s pop vibe and were backed instrumentally by scenesters Pam Lillig and Ben Rabinowitz (later of the Girls) and Eldon Hoke (the future El Duce of the infamous Mentors). With this show, the scene was born.

THE TELEPATHS, MEYCE, AND TUPPERWARES, AT THE I.O.O.F. HALL, SEATTLE, MAY 1, 1976
POSTER BY TOMATA DU PLENTY

"Admission to the TMT Show was one dollar (yes $1), about a hundred people showed up, the groups paid for the room and made their nut. This show (please correct me if I'm wrong) was the first self-promoted show in town. The bands rented the hall, got a PA and DID IT. It was as much fun or more than many of the shows now."

– Neil Hubbard, rock journalist (*Rescue*, May 1981)

"The Telepaths, Meyce, and Tupperwares had to literally go out and rent a hall to put it on. Get a PA together. Get somebody to work the door. Get some lighting. And they got a show. It had a good audience 'cause it was something fresh. It wasn't the same old humdrum crap schlock that was being forced down the kids' throats at the time."

– Satz, Ze Whiz Kidz, The Lewd

"We did that show on May Day and the Meyce opened up. That was our first real live show. It caused a good stir, there was a good turnout. And then the punk thing started really taking off."

– Jim Basnight, The Meyce, The Moberlys

LIVE PHOTOOGRAPHS OF THE TUPPERWARES COURTESY OF ANITA LILLIG (05/01/76)

Vivienne Westwood designed this outfit for the London boutique Seditionaries which she ran with her boyfriend Malcolm McLaren, manager and impresario of the Sex Pistols. With McLaren's tutelage and Westwood's clothes, the Sex Pistols became masters of media manipulation and instant symbols of punk music and fashion, setting the standard for what punk was, and largely is, to the mainstream.

Westwood and McLaren opened their London shop Paradise Garage in 1971. They began by selling vintage clothes and records, but over the next few years changed the look of the shop, its name and the clothing they sold to reflect their current interests in fashion nostalgia and avant garde culture. In 1974 they named it SEX and Westwood began creating her line of punk bondage pants and jackets, incorporating elements from S&M fashion, biker culture, and traditional Scottish design, with outrageous results. Two years later the shop was redecorated in a high-tech mode and renamed Seditionaries. Despite the change, Westwood and McLaren continued to sell the bondage pants and the now famous SEX T-shirts. Their goal: confront culture and thereby revitalize it.

BONDAGE JACKET AND ZIPPERED PUNK TROUSERS, CA. 1976, DESIGNED BY VIVIENNE WESTWOOD

"I was prepared to be a cook for the rest of my life. And then I saw some TV show, when the Sex Pistols had been out maybe three months, and were causing all this commotion, and then they said that Johnny Rotten's age was 'blank blank.' And I was like, 'I'm the same age! And I'm a cook and he's having fun! NO!' So I figured I should give it one more chance. Let's go see what we can do as musicians."

— DAVE ALVIN, THE BLASTERS

"I got into the Sex Pistols and I just loved the whole idea of them, y'know? The whole idea of someone stirring something up, because before that, everything was so complacent. It was just a bunch of rich rock stars, and that was about all you could do music-wise."

— Trudie Plunger, LA punk scenester

"You get these idiots like Malcolm McLaren, pretending they orchestrated this whole thing. He orchestrated his thing maybe, but probably not quite as cleverly as he makes out. But it doesn't matter what was going on with the real ins-and-outs of McLaren's shenanigans because we believed it in the suburbs. We believed punk rock existed through people like ATV and Mark Perry. He said, 'Here's a chord. Here's another chord. Form a group.' And we believed in the things that were being said. So, it became true."

— Billy Childish, Thee Headcoats

The Tupperwares formed in 1975 as a collision between post-glam, gay performance art and garage punk. Vocalists Tomata du Plenty, Melba Toast and Rio de Janeiro were backed instrumentally by various musicians from the scene. This shirt was handmade by Rio de Janeiro with iron-on letters, and later signed by du Plenty and de Janeiro and given to fan Stephen Vigil.

Tiring of the tiny Seattle scene, Tomata and Melba (soon to be renamed Tommy Gear) moved to Los Angeles in 1976 and hooked up with musicians David Brown and K.K. Barrett, changing their name from the Tupperwares to the more aggressive Screamers. Most important, they took the unique -- and influential – musical tack of eschewing guitars entirely in favor of synthesizers. They produced frenetic, driving synth beats and chordal snarls coupled with du Plenty's screamed vocals, which drew as much from Krautrock bands such as Kraftwerk and Neu! as early punk rock. They quickly became one of the most popular bands in the early LA scene, selling out shows at venues such as the Whisky A Go Go and the Roxy. The combination of intense songwriter Tommy Gear and irresistible frontman Tomata du Plenty was unstoppable – until they drifted away from the scene in 1980 and fully collapsed in 1981, without ever releasing a record.

TUPPERWARES T-SHIRT, CA. 1976, WORN BY RIO DE JANEIRO OF THE TUPPERWARES
GIFT OF MICHAEL CAMPBELL

PHOTOGRAPH BY STEPHEN VIGIL

"The Tupperwares were to the punk scene what the Harlem Globetrotters are to the NBA."
— Rio De Janeiro, The Tupperwares

"Tomata came back from New York and formed a punk band called the Tupperwares, and they all wore leather jackets and had Brian Jones haircuts, y'know, and they were all doing Iggy Pop covers. And for Seattle in the mid-'70s, people were freaked out! Everybody was still listening to Journey and Kansas and local bands that had names like Cheyenne and Gabriel. Heart was huge! And here's this guy coming back from New York acting the part of a punk rock dude."
— Art Chantry, graphic designer

"Within a month of coming to LA, I was at some show at the Starwood, and I ran into these two guys, Tomata du Plenty and Tommy Gear, who stood out from the crowd in that they had spiked hair, wraparound sunglasses at night, and dark clothes. Everybody else had feathered haircuts, soft yellow or light blue bell bottoms, sneakers, polo shirts, and we're listening to John Cale and Cheap Trick."
— K.K. Barrett, The Screamers

This box kept the daily earnings for the LA club, the Masque. The basement club and rehearsal space, opened in July 1977 by an eccentric Scottish expat promoter, Brendan Mullen, gave the scene a dedicated, stable venue, allowing it to grow. Soon, the Germs, Dils, Go-Go's, Weirdos, X, Plugz, and others played and rehearsed here. It was a safe haven, fostering bands that would explode in popularity by the end of the decade.

Still, the Los Angeles Police showed up frequently, claiming that the club, which was dark and rank with layers of graffiti, was a threat, shutting it down several times. The fire marshal also closed the club in January 1978. Mullen was forced to relocate the club in January 1979, and it closed for good in May. Though it lasted less than two years, the Masque provided Los Angeles with an early and vital piece of punk rock infrastructure.

CASHBOX FROM THE MASQUE, JULY 1977 – MAY 1979

"I found this basement — it was like 10,000 square feet, off Hollywood Boulevard in a building built by Cecil B. De Mille in 1926. It was a gorgeous building, and the basement was all bombed and totally trashed out. Nobody had been in it for at least fifteen years. No electricity, and I went down there sparking matches — it was this labyrinth, like in *Jason and the Argonauts* — so I'd be able to find my way back in case I got lost."
— BRENDAN MULLEN, THE MASQUE

"The Masque was in the basement of a porno theater, the Pussy Cat Theater on Hollywood Boulevard, in a really, really rotten area of Hollywood that was crawling with hookers and drug addicts and homeless people. It always stunk down there, 'cause every time there was a show, the plumbing would get messed up, and it'd end up flooding the place. It was the smell of puke and sewage and stale beer and just, y'know, smelly bodies. That was the smell of the Masque."

— Jane Wiedlin, The Go-Go's

"All the Germs, Pat and Lorna and Darby, came down to the Masque and I was supposed to audition. The room was a gutted shell of what once perhaps was a bathroom, and there was three inches of like — I don't know what this fluid was. I set my drums up in that and I just started banging on them like Mo Tucker or something, thinking they'd be impressed with how punk it sounded. And they just sort of sat there, not looking very excited. Then they went outside and talked amongst themselves for a minute, and then Darby came back and said, 'Well, you're a Germ.'"

— Don Bolles, The Germs

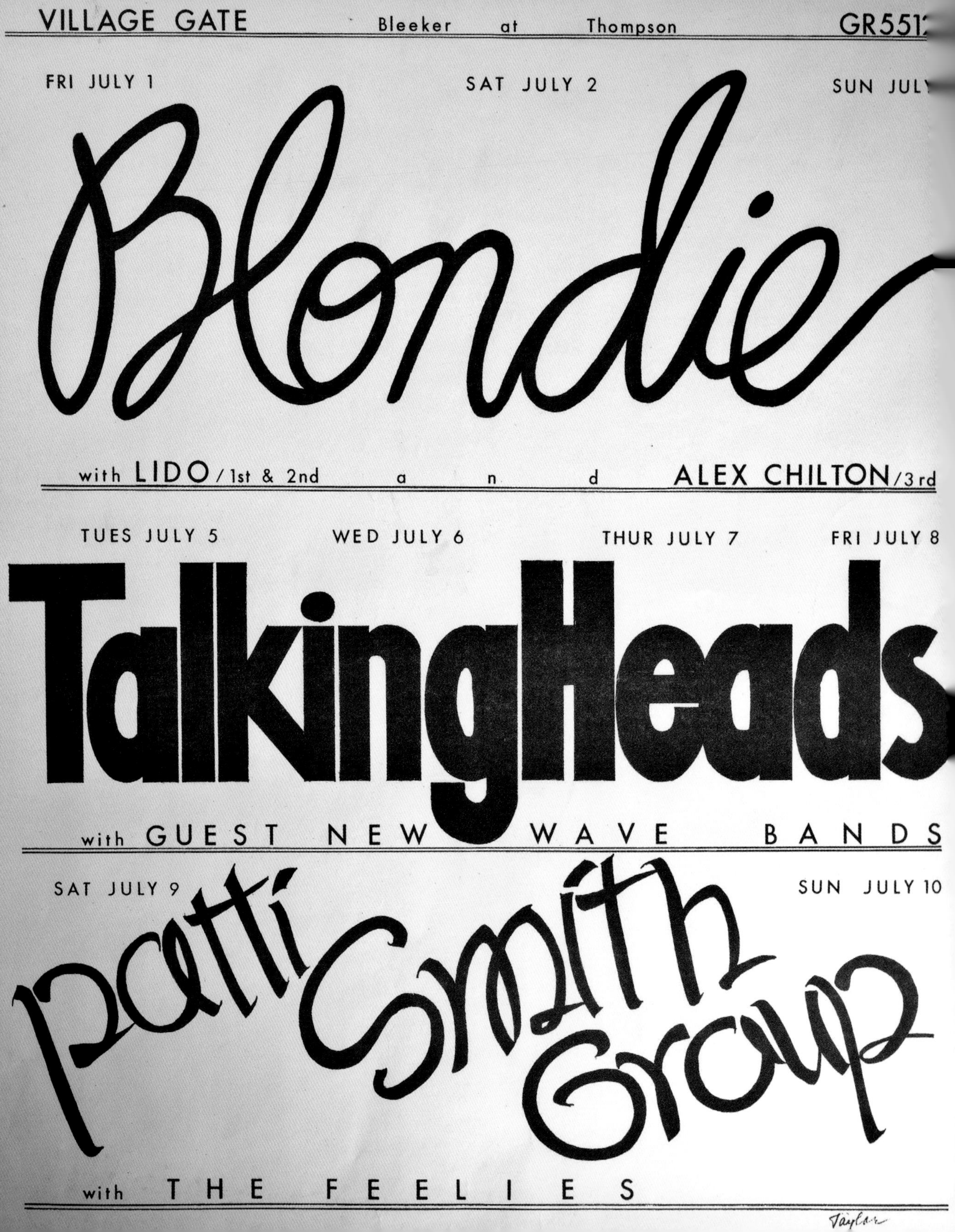

VILLAGE GATE   Bleeker   at   Thompson   GR 551

FRI JULY 1   SAT JULY 2   SUN JULY

Blondie

with LIDO / 1st & 2nd   a   n   d   ALEX CHILTON / 3rd

TUES JULY 5   WED JULY 6   THUR JULY 7   FRI JULY 8

TalkingHeads

with GUEST NEW WAVE BANDS

SAT JULY 9   SUN JULY 10

patti Smith Group

with THE FEELIES

Taylor

With this lineup of shows by the biggest bands in the city, the Village Gate, traditionally known for its jazz and R&B shows, fully embraced the New York punk scene. By 1977, the Patti Smith Group, Talking Heads, and Blondie had been defining themselves for several years. They each had a very distinctive sound, but grew out of the same insular scene of freaks and outcasts. When the major record labels began signing the New York bands, they felt that the "punk" descriptor might prove to be transitory, and began using the more marketable and appealing term "new wave," which was already used in the UK. As time went on, "new wave" became associated with more experimental acts and groups that incorporated synthesizers, while the more guitar-driven, garage-inspired bands retained the "punk" label.

Regardless of the marketing spin, Blondie and Talking Heads became chart-topping pop stars and Patti Smith and the Ramones became eternally cool rebels – the stars of the early New York scene (much like the Sex Pistols or Clash in the UK scene) have become forever associated in the popular consciousness as the creators of punk.

BLONDIE, TALKING HEADS, AND THE PATTI SMITH GROUP, AT THE VILLAGE GATE, NYC, JULY 1 – JULY 10, 1977

"Debbie Harry was like the Patsy Cline to our Loretta Lynn. She took us under her wing, as did the Talking Heads – Chris Franz and Tina Weymouth were so friendly. We went to Debbie Harry and Chris Stein's apartment and saw all these gold records just kind of lying around and we thought, 'Why don't they put 'em on the wall?' Of course now we all have ours just shoved under stuff."

— Kate Pierson, B-52s

"Blondie was the first new wave band to get anywhere. They had infiltrated into real society, and we were impressed by that. And obviously the Go-Go's evolved more and more into just being more of a pop band than a punk band, and then the whole new wave thing happened and by '81 the world was ready to take a sort of 'less threatening' punky pop band and make them a hit. So we were the ones that did something out of our scene and it was great, but I remember at the time that it was very ostracizing. It set us apart and people said we were sellouts. We went from being like this hard core punk chick to being America's sweetheart."

— Jane Wiedlin, the Go-Gos

"A lot of the people who started in new wave bands like Talking Heads and Blondie came out of art school. They were either theatre majors or painters or sculptors. So there were a lot of ideas flowing around and just the idea of deconstructing music, that was something that was in the air in all of the arts at that point in time. In New York there was an awful lot of stuff going on and if you didn't live inside the City, you had no inkling to it."

— LEE RANALDO, SONIC YOUTH

ALLEN GINSBERG
NUNS CRIME

No.1 $1

Search and Destroy

JOHNNY ROTTEN

Taking its name from a song by punk godfather Iggy Pop, the San Francisco punk zine *Search and Destroy* made its debut in June 1977. Created by ex-Blue Cheer alum V. Vale with a $100 loan from Beat poet Allen Ginsberg, *Search and Destroy* quickly became one of the most outspoken and informed sources of information about the San Francisco punk scene. In March 1979, stating only that its mission had been accomplished, after 11 issues it ceased publication.

The zine (or fanzine) was developed in the 1920s in the early science fiction fandom community, as a way to share information among the converted. Punks embraced it for the same reasons. Zines dovetailed perfectly with the era's DIY ("do-it-yourself") aesthetics and the easy access to affordable photocopy technology. At the time, there wasn't any infrastructure dedicated to relaying information about the growing punk scene, and the zine became that vital mode of communication. *Search and Destroy* in San Francisco, *Slash*, *Damage*, *Maximumrocknroll* and *Flipside* in Los Angeles, *Touch and Go* in Lansing, Mich., *Forced Exposure* in Boston, *Punk* New York City – all of these early examples lead to thousands of subsequent punk zines published throughout the '70s, '80s, and beyond. Without them, punk would have died an early death.

SEARCH AND DESTROY ZINE, JUNE 1977

"The greatest underground zine I've ever seen in my life was out of San Francisco called *Search and Destroy* where the definition of punk rock was much wider. Brilliant interviews with Devo, Iggy Pop, David Thomas of Pere Ubu, and what made Search and Destroy so good was that they didn't just ask the standard indie-zine shop talk questions of 'What's the scene like in your town, how long have you been together, what do you think of anarchy and nuclear war.' No. One or two shop talk questions and then Vale who ran the magazine and the other interviewers would just delve in with the weirdest stories they could coax out of you. You could open *Search and Destroy* to any page and learn something amazing."

– Jello Biafra, Dead Kennedys

"The first fanzine I ever saw was called *Hot Gorilla*, which was published in New England in 1976. That was the first place I ever saw the Sex Pistols or the Ramones mentioned, before *Rolling Stone* or the NBC news piece on the Sex Pistols throwing up in airports. And then I started seeing other magazines that were more specifically punk rock oriented. *Boston Groupie News*, *Killer Children*, *Subway News* – the quality of the writing in that magazine was so damn good, they really kind of elevated it to a new level. *New York Rocker* was absolutely colossal. Later on Tesco Vee's *Touch and Go* magazine – it was really great. And the early issues of *Forced Exposure* really upped the ante on anything I was trying to do with my fanzine. I thought that they right off the bat were doing the best fanzine in America."

– Gerard Cosloy, Homestead and Matador Records

"*Maximumrocknroll* was the most amazing thing, and the advertising was really cheap, and for small labels I thought it was an incredible contribution that *Maximumrocknroll* even existed because of its consistency. Whether or not you liked the content or not didn't matter. Y'know, you could put an ad in it for thirty dollars and you could sell all your records, y'know, nothing could replace that. You could find people all over the world who were interested in what you were doing. Now there's the internet and things like that which sort of replaces it in a way, but at the time it was the only thing like that."

– Cynthia Connolly, Dischord Records

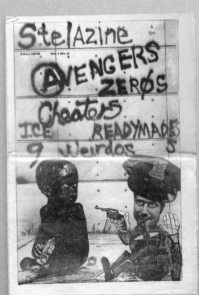

PUNK #8, 1977; TWISTED #2, 1977; SLASH #1, May 1977; SEARCH AND DESTROY, 1977; STELAZINE #3, 1978; FLIPSIDE #15, 1980; TOUCH AND GO #3, 1980; MAXIMUMROCKNROLL #1, 1980; JIGSAW #3, 1991; BIKINI KILL, early 1990s

LOS ANGELES FLIPSIDE #15   75¢

INSIDE:
GERMS
FLYBOYS
MODS

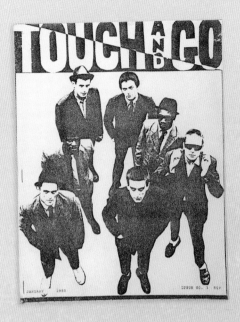

TOUCH AND GO

JANUARY 1980   ISSUE NO. 3 50¢

MAXIMUM ROCKNROLL

VOL. 1   NO. 1
MDC
MILLIONS OF DEAD COPS
MINOR THREAT
VICIOUS CIRCLE
JUVENIL JUSTICE
CHURCH POLICE
S/M NIGHTMARE
RIP RRZ?
AND
GOD FORBID
POLITICS

NORTHERN
CALIFORNIA
COVERAGE

Bi- monthly $1.00

jigsaw

No. 3 1991

"new modROCKERS and the jigsaw underground"

angry grrrl zine

BIKINIKILL   #2

GirlPower

The Wipers are one of the most important bands in the history of Pacific Northwest punk rock, directly influencing myriad indie bands and presaging grunge. They made an indelible mark on Kurt Cobain and Nirvana, who recorded the Wipers classics "Return of the Rat" and "D-7," playing them frequently in their live set. This 1969 left-handed Gibson SG with attached Bigsby tremelo was Greg Sage's primary guitar throughout the entire span of the Wipers.

In 1977, Sage formed the Wipers (whose name referred to his window washing job), just as punk rock in Portland was beginning to develop. The early local scene centered around the Revenge Club, Euphoria, the Earth Tavern and the Long Goodbye, with bands such as Sado Nation, the Neo Boys, and King Bee joining the Wipers on stage. Sage was an iconoclast, and as the vocalist, guitarist, and songwriter for the Wipers, produced a body of work of unique vision and lasting scope that has outlived any of its Portland punk contemporaries.

1969 GIBSON SG, PLAYED BY GREG SAGE OF THE WIPERS, 1977 - 1999

"If there's a transitional band between the Sonics and early grunge and punk, it's probably the Wipers, because they had that intensity down. I don't think a lot of what happened in Seattle would have happened if there wasn't something as heavy as the Wipers. Great songs, delivered with deep passion and that heavy, gutty sound that was primal punk rock."

— ART CHANTRY, GRAPHIC DESIGNER

"Portland had some amazing bands. They had the Wipers, which were probably one of the best bands to come out of the Northwest period. Greg Sage was a punk rock musical genius and he did this song called 'The Youth of America,' which was a sort of extended psychedelic workout in 1981, at a time when punk rock was getting more and more codified and the rules were becoming stricter and tighter. He was just expanding things, despite what you're supposed to do if you were punk rock at that time."
— Mark Arm, Mudhoney

"The first real show that we did was opening up for the Wipers in Olympia at an old roller skating rink or something like that called GESSCO, and like everybody else we thought Greg Sage was God, so that was pretty cool for us. I saw some photographs from that show and man, we were pretty nervous — I know I was — getting up in front of people like that. That was the first one, courtesy of Calvin Johnson."
— Mark Lanegan, the Screaming Trees

OPENING NIGHT! MARCH 4

THE ENEMY

THE MENTORS & THE TELEPATHS

AT THE BIRD
107 SPRING ST., SEATTLE

$3.00 at the door

Roger Husbands, manager for punk band The Enemy, opened The Bird in Seattle on March 4, 1978, creating Seattle's first punk club. Venues in town traditionally booked bar bands that played cover songs. Bands in Seattle's embryonic punk scene had to play at friends' houses and rental halls – it was by force of will that the scene existed at all. The Bird proved that a venue could exist on punk alone. Soon enough more venues, such as the Showbox, the Golden Crown, Rosco Louie Gallery, and others were hosting punk bands.

The Bird's band-in-residence, the Enemy, had previously been a bar band called the Fruitland Famine Band, whose guitarist Damon Titus had heard the clarion call of punk rock at a 1977 Sex Pistols show in San Francisco. The Enemy had a connection with SF-punk band the Avengers, and invited them, along with Negative Trend, Crime, UXA, and others to play at the Bird. Unfortunately it closed two months later. The Bird promoted a few shows at rented halls as "The Bird in Exile" and then re-opened in the summer of 1978 in Seattle's Capitol Hill neighborhood, before dying a final death that fall.

THE ENEMY, THE MENTORS, AND THE TELEPATHS AT THE OPENING NIGHT OF THE BIRD, SEATTLE, MARCH 4, 1978. POSTER BY FRANKO

"The Bird was certainly the first of its kind in Seattle. It was all ages, so we could actually play there. It was really great for us in the Cheaters, because there was certainly nothing else we could do. We were reading all the papers about the English punk bands, and we had the Ramones' first couple records and, y'know, Sex Pistols singles, and the Damned, and stuff like that. We thought, wow, we could actually go see this kind of stuff in our own city. And so the opening night of the Bird, we all went down there, and it was probably $3 to get in. It was no drinking or anything. I think they had bags of popcorn that you could either eat or throw at the bands, y'know, that was kind of punk and exciting. And I remember leaving the first night just thinking, 'God, if we could just play here, that would be just the coolest thing!' So we brought a cassette tape down to the guy that was in charge of booking the acts and gave him our little cassette tape that we recorded in my parents' basement. Could barely hear any music on it, but he was very nice to us and just a week or two later, it was like, 'Yeah, do you want to come down and play?'"

– Kurt Bloch, The Fastbacks and Young Fresh Fellows

"At the Bird you'd see local bands and bands from Vancouver – DOA and Subhumans, occasionally bands from LA like the Weirdos – they all were, let's face it, generally a cut above our local bands at that time, but even so, it didn't really matter who was on stage so much. It was just that you really did get the feeling that something different was going on – something slightly revolutionary. And there was a really strange buzz about the whole thing that's hard to describe. It was so fun just pogoing with your friends, and it was kind of scary too, because to me, Capitol Hill at that time was a strange, unfamiliar part of town. I had to take three buses to get there. And it was mostly older people, but everyone was always really nice to me and my friends, even though we were really corny looking, with bellbottoms, punk rock shirts – like we couldn't quite yet decide if we were heavy metal kids or punks."

– Tom Price, U-Men and Gas Huffer

Satz was a prominent part of the early Seattle punk scene, well-versed in confrontational and outrageous performance as a former member of the gay, glam, and glitter troupe Ze Whiz Kidz. When punk came around, Satin Sheets became Satz and he began exploring his new creative realm. After a number of short-lived bands, Satz formed the Lewd in 1977 and played their first show opening for the Ramones at the Commodore Ballroom in Vancouver, B.C., on August 6, 1977. The band had several line-up changes early on, including bass player Blobbo, also known as Kurdt Vanderhoof, a native of Aberdeen, WA, who would later form the seminal Northwest heavy metal band Metal Church. The Lewd released their in-your-face debut single in 1979: "Kill Yourself" backed with "Trash Can Baby" and "Pay or Die." By 1980, having exhausted Seattle venues, the Lewd moved to San Francisco, where they remained a prominent part of SF's early punk scene.

THE LEWD, AND WRAITH, AT THE GOLDEN CROWN, SEATTLE, MAY 27, 1979. POSTER BY SATZ

"I was forming bands at that time, some that didn't really exist. Satz and the 16 Year Old Virgins never played, but we had a photo. The Knobs — I think we might have played once at the Hellhole, or at the A-hole in Fremont. I might have the name wrong. Some type of hole. [The Funhole —Ed.] And then I was having so much fun with it, writing our own material, and just doing stuff that just had so much more energy to it than what was coming out of the airwaves at the time, I got serious. And so I formed the Lewd. Before long, the group just ran out of places to play in Seattle, and we were playing in San Francisco so much that we just we just relocated to San Francisco."

— Satz, The Lewd

"The poster's all cut and paste, old school. Press-type and offset printing, and right on the telephone pole. We did a photo session where we took clear tape and put it across our faces to kind of mash our features, y'know? And if we photographed it, high-contrast, you couldn't see the tape. All you would see would be just this ugly, deformed face. That wasn't us before plastic surgery. It was just tape."

— Satz, The Lewd

"The Lewd relocated to San Francisco and after about a year of doing that, I realized there were some great import albums coming in from England with names like Iron Maiden and Motörhead and I went, 'Oh, I'm going to do that.' The punk thing was fun and great and everything, but after you figure out how to play you get a little bit bored, y'know? And when you realize you're really not all that angry and that America really isn't that bad of a place and you don't really want to complain about it anymore. So after leaving The Lewd I started trying to put a band together down there, and about a year or so of never really getting anything off the ground, I relocated back to Aberdeen and started Metal Church with some people that I grew up with."

— Kurdt Vanderhoof, The Lewd and Metal Church

PHOTOGRAPH: THE LEWD IN THE U-DISTRICT, SEATTLE, CA. 1977.

Billy Zoom started out as Tyson Kindell, a kid in Nowhere, Illinois, with a jones for Jerry Lee Lewis and Gene Vincent. In the mid-'60s, he played guitar in R&B and soul bands throughout the country, finally settling in Los Angeles in the early '70s. In 1972, he re-invented himself, cutting and bleaching his long hair and changing his name to the more rebellious-sounding Billy Zoom. He began playing in roots and rockabilly bands, including his own Billy Zoom Band, amid a local resurgence of interest in rockabilly and '50s rock. By 1976, he was looking for a change and placed an ad in a local magazine, *The Recycler*, for other musicians. Bassist John Doe answered, and with the addition of Doe's girlfriend Exene Cervenka soon after, X was born. The band would quickly rise to the top of the LA scene and by the early 1980s were revered as one of the top punk bands ever.

Billy Zoom wore this spray-painted silver jacket in hundreds of live performances from 1975 to 1984 with the Billy Zoom Band and X. In addition to the jacket and shades, he sported a bleached white pompadour and a silver Gretsch guitar, successfully melding the rockabilly and the Ramones sides of his personality.

LEATHER JACKET, WORN BY BILLY ZOOM OF X, 1975 - 1984

"I had already been to New York a bunch of times 'cause my parents lived in Brooklyn, and I'd seen the Heartbreakers, the Talking Heads, and Television, and it was real obvious that that scene was already full-blown, y'know, by the end of '76. So I thought, well I'm not going to be able to weasel my way into that. I wanted to do new music from hearing Patti Smith and the Stooges and stuff like that. So California was a big change, but that was what I was looking for."

— John Doe, X

"I'd never sang and John Doe wanted to use my writing in this band he was starting with Billy Zoom. I didn't want him to take my writing away from me and start singing my words, so he said if I wanted to sing I could be in the band. My main memory of that time is walking down into

the Masque and feeling kind of historical about the whole thing from the beginning, from the very first day feeling like we were truly doing something underground and culturally significant that nobody was going to be aware of, and it was very exciting. We were pretty wild, pretty drunk, and pretty rebellious, and in our own way, very political. The punk scene was really small. It was like a secret society, and anyone fit in. It didn't matter if you were forty or sixteen, if you were a runaway or a graphic artist, or a woman or a man or black or white. Nothing mattered except that if you knew you belonged there then everyone else knew you belonged there. To me that's like the pinnacle of cultural and social activity, to have a scene that's just driven by ideals."

— Exene Cervenka, X

"I first met X at Brendan's club the Masque — they used to play there and were just getting signed to Dangerhouse Records. And they gave me one of these things called ace-tates. It's where you make like a one record thing. It's got a really cool smell to it — a really fresh smell. It had 'Johnny Hit and Run Paulene' on it. And I got that and went into my studio and started playing X a lot on the radio — like every week. My show was two nights — Saturday and Sunday from eight to midnight — so it gives even more exposure to the music. That's how X got really going — playing them on 'Rodney on the ROQ.'"

— Rodney Bingenheimer, DJ at KROQ

THE BLACKOUTS

w/MAGAZINE SEPT 8 9:00 TALMUD TORAH 1977

The Blackouts coalesced from the ashes of the Telepaths, the Bowie-laced band that formed during punk's early days in Seattle. Ex-Telepaths Erich Werner (vox, guitar), Mike Davidson (bass, replaced by Paul "Ion" Barker in 1981), and Bill Rieflin (drums), with the addition of Roland Barker (synth), became the Blackouts. Their dark post-punk salvo across the Seattle scene eclipsed the Telepaths' version of the glitter past, and the band quickly becoming one of the city's biggest punk acts.

Their sound hinged on Werner's tortured vocals and angular guitar, Barker's dark carnival synth, and Rieflin's precision drumming. Early shows, such as this one at the Talmud Torah Hebrew Bingo Hall, evoked doomed echoes of Talking Heads and Oingo Boingo. A fundamental shift occurred when Roland Barker's synthesizer was stolen at the Showbox in 1980. Instead of replacing it, Roland switched to saxophone, morphing the band in a more tribal direction. After a final show on August 27, 1982, the Blackouts moved to Boston, where they met with the musician Al Jourgensen. The Blackouts lasted two more years before they (minus Werner) teamed up with Jourgensen's synth-pop band Ministry. They helped transform the group into the popular, late-'80s industrial behemoth, paving the road for industrial superstars such as Nine Inch Nails.

THE BLACKOUTS, WITH MAGAZINE, AT THE TALMUD TORAH, SEATTLE, SEPTEMBER 8, 1979
POSTER BY TERRY MORGAN

"Within days of moving to Seattle in 1979, I saw a show featuring the Blackouts, who were then one of the preeminent bands in the city, a gentleman named Dr. Albert, and Magazine. And that show totally blew my mind. It was at the Showbox. There were definitely people with like minds in the city. You couldn't find that in Bellingham at the time."
— Jonathan Poneman, Sub Pop Records

"The Blackouts were definitely the band for a while there in the early '80s, and when the U-Men got to open for them, it was like, WOW, y'know? They would headline these shows and there'd be several hundred people there, and there was definitely a feeling that these guys could go national and become a big band. So we kind of got to know them a little bit, and they became for me what The Lewd had been a couple years earlier."
— Tom Price, U-Men and Gas Huffer

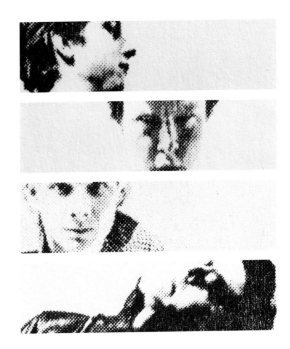

Fall 1981 The 'G' in Two Sections $1.50

ROBERT ASHLEY/CHICAGO/
CLEVELAND/PHILADELPHIA/NYC
GARY WILSON/GOSPEL/GAMES
GAMELAN /GIRLS

268 REVIEWS: RAP, REGGAE, ETHNIC, ELECTRONIC, FOLK, FUNK, JAZZ, NEW MUSIC, BLUES, COUNTRY, PUNK   INFORMATION: RADIO, PUBLICATIONS, LABELS, ORGANIZATIONS, & ARTISTS

OP was a fanzine published from 1979 to 1984. It was co-founded and edited by John Foster, the music librarian and later program director at KAOS-FM, the community-run radio station at Olympia, Washington's Evergreen State College. OP was born from the student collective known as the Lost Music Network. The "OP" of its name followed the "LMN" of the Lost Music Network. OP became a series of 26 issues, each given a letter of the alphabet, and focused on independent music, radio, and DIY and cassette culture across all genres. Issue "G" featured such varied subjects as Portland's all Girl punk band the Neo Boys, experimental musician Gary Wilson, Gospel, and Indonesian Gamelan.

At KAOS, Foster authored the "Green Line Policy," which is still in effect today. Under the rule, 80 percent of the music played at the station would be from independent sources and the remaining 20 percent could be from major label acts. Foster drew a green line on the indie records so that they were easy to identify. As disseminated over the airwaves by KAOS and in print with OP, this policy set the standard for the Olympia music scene, and reverberated outward, influencing untold numbers of radio stations, labels, musicians, and fans across the U.S.

OP FANZINE, "G" ISSUE, FALL 1981. GIFT OF JOHN FOSTER

"I wanted to find every little label and every fanzine, every little record store out there, and provide them with OP. I wanted them all to see it. This was my vision. I felt useful because we were putting people in touch with other people who had some, y'know, like-mindedness. And of course, a lot of the punk musicians wouldn't be at all interested in the bluegrass music, but that was the beauty of the thing — it was a train wreck all the time, y'know? It's all being documented. It's not just you. You're not the only hip one out there. Everyone's doing their own thing, but you can tie into it in this way, and so I insisted on putting it all together even though that was against the conventional wisdom of the day."

— John Foster, OP, KAOS-FM

"A lot of the alternative type students who were attending Evergreen wanted to play a lot of Grateful Dead, which was the alternative band of choice for many people at Evergreen. But they were on Warner Bros, so their airplay was severely limited. So there was a lot of hand wringing about that policy. A lot of people at the time did not like the aesthetic of punk and new wave — they didn't want to hear X and the Wipers and Dead Kennedys and the Avengers. But thanks to John Foster, a lot of that stuff got played and his core philosophy was really that we're a community radio station and we should be a place that prioritizes music that comes from the community. And I thought that was a good policy."

— Bruce Pavitt, Sub Pop Records

"OP magazine was the *Whole Earth Catalog* of music. It was access to tools, access to music, access to radio stations that would play your music, access to pressing plants that would press your music, access to record stores that you could call directly to get your music consigned. It was a how-to thing, so that everybody that was involved in independent music got OP magazine because they were interested in knowing how to do it for themselves. The musical politics of Olympia were pretty radical, and it really made OP magazine and KAOS and all of that just head and shoulders above anything else going on back then."

— Steve Fisk, recording engineer/producer/musician

MODERN PRODUCTIONS WELCOME

GANG OF FOUR

3 SWIMMERS / LITTLE BEARS FROM BANGKOK

JULY 10 SHOWBOX 7:30 PM

TICKETS $7.50 ADVANCE

TICKETS: CORPORATE RECORDS, EVERYBODY'S RECORDS IN BELLEVUE AND ON AURORA,
CELLOPHANE SQUARE, DREAMLAND, BUDGET TAPES & RECORDS IN WEST SEATTLE.

Art Chantry moved to Seattle from Bellingham, WA in 1978 to pursue a career in graphic design. Finding the design aesthetic of the corporate world stale, Chantry gleaned inspiration from the underground theater, art, and punk rock scenes. His work had the urgent, cut-and-paste energy of punk flyers, thoroughly mined popular culture, and added a deep familiarity with Dadaist, Surrealist, and Pop Art forms. The results were some of the first posters in the Northwest to display punk's vitality within a purposeful design vernacular – a style that Chantry would continue to explore throughout the 1980s and 1990s, exemplified in his work with Seattle's music magazine *The Rocket*, early Sub Pop Records, and in his garage-punk graphic explorations for Bellingham's Estrus Records. Art Chantry's evolving body of work would become one of the most prominent graphic voices in the grunge era, and a prime catalyst for society's shifting view of punk design from instant litter to art.

For this poster for a legendary show at Seattle's Showbox with the British post-punk band Gang of Four, Art Chantry appropriated an old Soviet stamp image, and using a Xerox machine, press type, an Xacto knife, and a waxer (to adhere the bits), created one of his most indelible designs.

GANG OF FOUR, 3 SWIMMERS, AND LITTLE BEARS FROM BANGKOK, AT THE SHOWBOX, SEATTLE, JULY 10, 1981. ORIGINAL ARTWORK BY ART CHANTRY

"Chantry's an historian. His knowledge of the past, in graphic design, is extraordinary, and he can do it right. He's very good at appropriately appropriating, and he does it with humor. Like, when he appropriates something, there's usually a sideways comment in there somewhere. There's a little bit of a knife in there, and I love that."

— Ed Fotheringham, illustrator

"The Showbox had a spring-loaded dance floor and at the time pogoing was more in vogue. At the Gang of Four show, there were maybe 200 or 300 people up front all bouncing up and down, and the floor is going with it, and the band is up there. And they just put on this incredible, incredible show. After the show, I went up to the U District to this house, and all the lights were out. And the next thing I knew, I had my arm around the guitar player from the Gang of Four and we were all dancing to the Supremes. It was kind of a watershed moment in my life."

— Charles Peterson, photographer

"What was happening with these punk posters was a kind of a cultural Dada movement. It wasn't really spearheaded by a handful of intellectuals living in Europe. It was ordinary people that came to that same point on their own, en masse. Some of them knew the connection, some of them had no idea what was going on. It was just what worked. It had the right feel, y'know?"

— ART CHANTRY, GRAPHIC DESIGNER

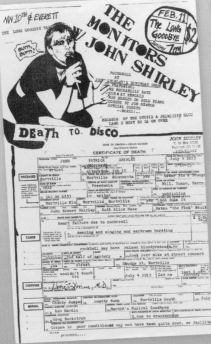

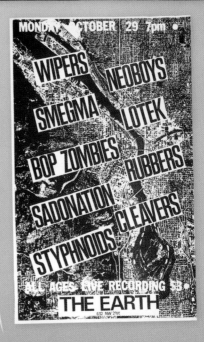

MENTORS, Ice-9, Terror Wrist, Formica & the Bitches, and Mysterious Pulse, at the Revenge Club, Portland, OR, April 1, 1978;
CHINAS COMIDAS, the Feelings, at the Ethnic Cultural Theatre, Seattle, June 9, 1978. Poster by Carl Smool; THE MONITORS,
John Shirley, at the Long Goodbye, Portland, OR, February 11, 1979. Poster by John Shirley; WIPERS, Neo Boys, Smegma,
Lo Tek, Bob Zombies, Rubbers, Sado Nation, Cleavers, Styhphnoids, at the Earth, Portland, OR, October 29, 1979;

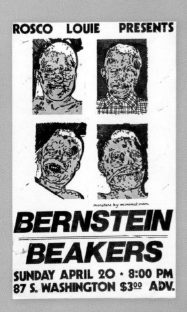

AVENGERS, Missing Persons, and the Telepaths, at the Bird, Seattle, April 7, 1978 + with the Cheaters, and Ice 9, April 8; THE FAGS, Student Nurse, at Wrex, Seattle, January 9, 1981. Poster by Helena Rogers; STEVEN JESSE BERNSTEIN, the Beakers, at Rosco Louie, Seattle, April 20, 1980. Poster by Larry Reid; THE NEO BOYS, Jungle Nausea, at Northwest Artists Workshop, Portland, OR, July 17, 1981. Poster by Mike King

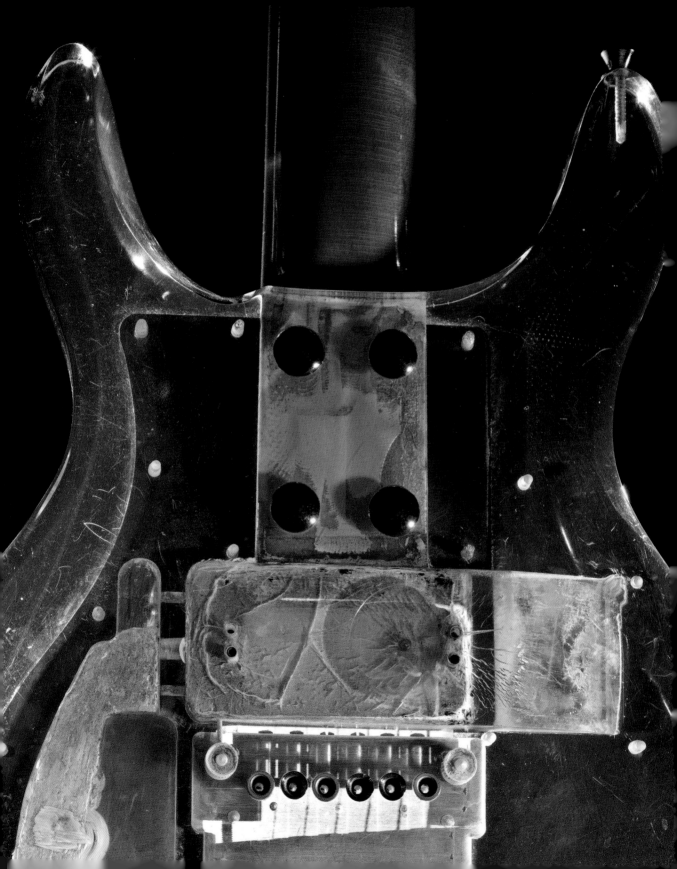

This Lucite-bodied Ampeg was Greg Ginn's main guitar during his tenure as founder, guitarist, and songwriter for seminal LA hardcore band Black Flag. Ginn and vocalist Keith Morris (later of the Circle Jerks) were inspired to form the band Panic in 1976 (which they renamed Black Flag in 1977), after seeing the Ramones play on their first West Coast tour. Ginn took the fast three-chord punk of the Ramones, added the aggressive qualities of the Stooges and The MC5, and the heaviness of Black Sabbath, and created a guitar-driven breakneck sonic assault that would become the blueprint for hardcore punk.

Black Flag quickly became known for their uncompromising work ethic, practicing for hours each day to hone their craft. Their incessant touring schedule took the band to hundreds of towns across the US, spreading the gospel of punk. Ginn's SST record label, through which he released all of Black Flag's records, quickly became one of the most successful independent labels of the 1980s. Its roster included the Minutemen, Hüsker Dü, Sonic Youth, Meat Puppets, Soundgarden, Dinosaur Jr and Screaming Trees. With his iconoclastic singularity of vision, Ginn proved to be one of the most important figures in the development of the American underground music network in the 1980s.

1970 AMPEG DAN ARMSTRONG ADA-G1, PLAYED BY GREG GINN OF BLACK FLAG, 1977-1986

"What Black Flag tried to do is play as aggressively and fast as possible, but without losing the heaviness. And that was a trick. If Black Flag had any sort of bad influence, I think it's that we influenced a lot of bands to play faster and they just rushed into it, whereas we practiced relentlessly, every night, to build up our songs faster and faster, but with the full power behind them. And I always thought it was a mistake for bands to just jump right to a fast speed and lose the feel of the music just because they want to be fast."

— Greg Ginn, Black Flag, SST Records

"Joining Black Flag was a very abrupt lifestyle change for me — going from a bank account, car, stereo, job — to a duffel bag, shoplifting food, getting rousted by cops, no money, living on people's floors, getting fleas, living in your same clothes for weeks. And every band can tell you that story. The Chili Peppers can tell you that, R.E.M. can tell you that."

— Henry Rollins, Black Flag

"Black Flag's *My War* was a really influential record. I remember Buzz from the Melvins busted that one out in Aberdeen. We would listen to side 2 of *My War*. There's only three songs on that side of the record. It's just really slowed down and heavy. It's just like Sabbath, grinding guitars. It was just really... it's grunge is what it is."

— Krist Novoselic, Nirvana

One of the appealing aspects of punk rock and the evolving indie underground was that there was an opportunity for women to fully participate on an equal basis. By contrast, in mainstream rock of the day, women were typically portrayed as sexualized objects, arm candy for male rock stars, or passive musicians. Of course, some women in punk were portrayed in these modes, and the testosterone-fueled aggression of some punk bands proved to be a very real barrier to gender equality. But by and large, because there were no written rules in punk, women could write their own.

With this iconic photograph, Chris Stein of Blondie captured the reigning queens of punk and new wave at the turn of the '80s. Debbie Harry of Blondie was the face of new wave. Guitarist Viv Albertine, who helped create the Slits' raw, reggae-inflected punk, was the archetypal riot grrrl. Siouxsie Sioux epitomized punk's foray into goth. Pauline Black was second-wave ska's princess with her band The Selector. Poly Styrene of X-Ray Spex combined teenage rebellion with a punk day-glo whimsy. And Chrissie Hynde would garner huge mainstream success with the punk-inspired Pretenders. These women would provide inspiration for thousands of others to pick up an instrument, produce a record, write a zine, and participate in the underground.

DEBBIE HARRY, VIV ALBERTINE, SIOUXSIE SIOUX, CHRISSIE HYNDE, POLY STYRENE, AND PAULINE BLACK, LONDON, 1980. PHOTOGRAPH BY CHRIS STEIN

"I was lucky enough to photograph that assembly of seminal female rockers due to someone from a music periodical whose name escapes. One thing that I remember was that Kate Bush was invited to the gathering and didn't attend. We never had a clear answer as to why not but someone brought a life-size cutout photo of her in her stead. The event was brief and I don't have much left of it beyond the pictures."

— Chris Stein, Blondie

"When I started out in music there was Debbie Harry and Patti Smith and me, and then there were all the women all around the country, like Penelope from the Avengers who didn't go on to be as famous, or notorious, or make as many records. But there were a lot of women in the punk scene doing music, and they were playing instruments and singing. And that was quite novel at the time. And most of those women were more modeled after Patti Smith and the Runaways than anything else I think because those were the only women that had come out doing that. The Go-Go's were the first girl group that came out that were very kind of cutie pie, y'know, 'We Got The Beat' and all that kind of stuff, and had somewhat of a feminine side but they also had that punk rock side still which was purposely kind of scruffy and what not."

— Exene Cervenka, X

"I think one of the most important contributions that punk made was to give women the opportunity to play, to go out there and to just not feel as though they had to compete with men, but that they were bringing something of their own that was different. And I think because it was so far removed from the kind of rock that the mainstream rock world was doing, that it was accepting. The audience was much more accepting of things that were different and women were not intimidated by the feeling that they had to live up to certain expectations."

— Alice Bag, The Bags

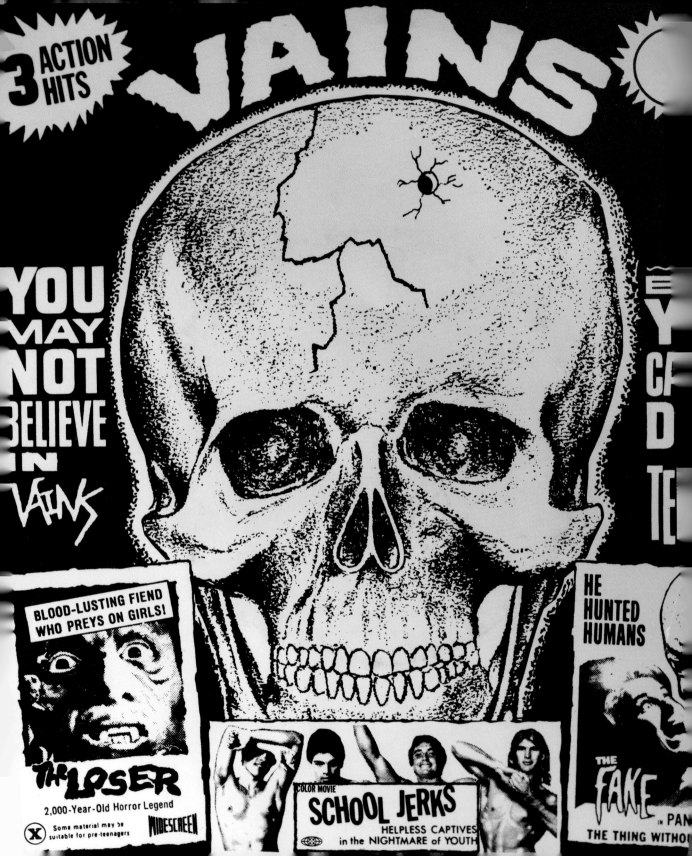

The Vains were a short-lived, snotty punk trio from Seattle featuring Criss Crass, Andy Freeze and 16-year-old Nico Teen -- a.k.a. Duff McKagan, future bass player for '80s heavy metal gods Guns N' Roses. McKagan grew up in a musical household and played several instruments. He was one of many teenagers in Seattle in the late 1970s drawn to the punk scene, and he jumped in headlong, playing bass in the Vains, guitar in the Living (with future Mother Love Bone drummer Greg Gilmore), and drums for the Fastbacks (whose guitarist Kurt Bloch released this Vains single on his No Threes record label). By the early '80s, McKagan was playing in hardcore bands the Fartz and 10 Minute Warning, which would be one of the first Seattle bands to slow down hardcore's breakneck pace and focus on Black Sabbath-inspired proto-grunge heaviness. In 1984, like many musicians before him, he decided there was no future for him in music if he stayed in Seattle, and moved to California. By the next year, he soared to new heights playing bass in Guns N' Roses, whose 1987 debut album, *Appetite for Destruction*, would go multi-platinum and become the quintessential '80s heavy metal record.

"SCHOOL JERKS" / "THE FAKE" + " THE LOSER," SINGLE BY THE VAINS, 1980

"I really liked Guns N' Roses when 'Sweet Child O' Mine' came out in the summer of '88. I just loved it and I went and bought the record and I was in some grocery store, teaching school at the time, reading this magazine, *Circus* or *Cream* or something and it said, 'Guns N' Roses Profile' and, 'Bassist Duff McKagan.' I looked at the picture and went, 'What the fuck?' I remember this guy from seventh grade when he would stand next to the record player and play air guitar and strike rock poses for hours, y'know? And now all of a sudden he's sold 10 million records."

— Dave Dederer, the Presidents of the
United States of America

"When I first moved to Seattle in '83, I was working in the kitchen of a restaurant along with a local musician. His name was Duff McKagan, and Duff had been hanging out with the Fastbacks, and he was involved with a number of different groups in Seattle. He was a real scenester and a real rock 'n' roller. I remember seeing him put pecans on a heavily-iced cake and he looked up to me and he said, 'I'm going to move to LA and become a rock star.' And I said, 'Well, good luck Duff. Why don't you just hang out in Seattle and become a rock star?' And he says, 'There's no way you can make any money playing music in Seattle, so I'm gonna move to LA and make a living as a musician.' And a couple years later, he came back into town as the bass player in Guns N' Roses, and the next thing you knew,

they became pretty much the biggest band in America. It was interesting to witness that. At the time, if you wanted to make money doing music, the idea of going to LA to do it kinda made sense, and he proved his point. But at the same time, the vision that I was carrying, and other close friends of mine were carrying, that if you actually stayed where you lived and cultivated over a period of time, that you could do the same thing. And that's what we wound up doing with Sub Pop Records, and Nirvana and Soundgarden and everything else."

— Bruce Pavitt, Sub Pop Records

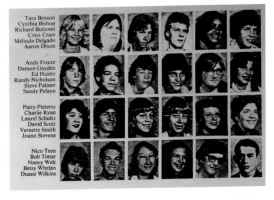

REVERSE SIDE OF VAINS SINGLE: YEARBOOK PHOTOS FEATURING CRISS CRASS, ANDY FREEZE, CHARLIE RYAN (FUTURE U-MEN DRUMMER) AND NICO TEEN.

Anonymous was less of a band and more of a musical one-off by Jim Stonecipher, Paul Tyson, and the multi-talented musician and producer Steve Fisk, who over the following decades would help shape the course of music throughout the Pacific Northwest. The Anonymous single was among Fisk's first recorded output. Side "13" (there is no A or B side) is a spastic sonic meltdown called "Corporate Food," while side "E" is a comparably mellow, but equally bizarre effort. Fisk and Co. were accomplished instrumentalists, and their efforts sound like a tongue-in-cheek, warped-Wonderland reflection on punk of the day.

Fisk was a student at Evergreen State College, an early DJ at KAOS-FM in Olympia and regular contributor to OP magazine. Since the mid-1980s, he has been a prolific musician, releasing solo efforts and records with bands such as Pell Mell and Pigeonhed. He has been most influential as a record producer, working with hundreds of bands, including Screaming Trees, Beat Happening, Steven Jesse Bernstein, Soundgarden, and Nirvana. Fisk is among a small group of individuals whose artistic explorations amid the region's underground zeitgeist helped to prime the pump for the grunge explosion to come.

"SNAKE ATTACK" / "CORPORATE FOOD" SINGLE BY ANONYMOUS, 1980
COVER ART BY DANA SQUIRES

"Steve Fisk, as we all know, is a musical genius in Seattle. One of the world's great cynics and another one of those visionary-type people. Don't know how he ended up so weird. He grew up in Southern California in one of those tract houses and he just took it from there and became his own human."
— JOHN FOSTER, KAOS-FM AND OP MAGAZINE

"The real band on 'Corporate Food' was the lost Oly prog group Conch. It was featured on Jello Biafra's *Let Them Eat Jellybeans* comp, which was a huge prop for me, my band and Olympia music at the time. 'Snake Attack' wasn't a proper band — just a synth groove with me and Seattle performance artist Heidi Drucker singing and Jim playing guitar with a rock. At the time releasing music recorded at Evergreen was forbidden by the administration. For me to get the right to commercially release these songs, let alone start an indie label for college credit, was unprecedented and indicative of the role the college was to play in the town's nascent music scene. Putting the two tracks out as a 'band' was one of many silly marketing ideas that came out of the KAOS/OP magazine think tank."
— Steve Fisk, recording engineer/producer/musician

Devo's classic single "Whip It," from the 1980 album, *Freedom of Choice*, was one of MTV's earliest hit videos, and featured the band members wearing red "energy domes." Thanks to the video's popularity, the hats soon became indelibly associated with Devo and their appealingly bizarre brand of sonic de-evolution. Devo formed in Akron, Ohio in the early 1970s from various music and art collaborations by Kent State University students Gerald Casale, Bob Lewis, and Mark Mothersbaugh. The concept of "de-evolution" was a central premise, reflecting the members' lament at the growing conformity in contemporary American society. The Kent State shootings of 1970, which occurred while the members of Devo attended the school, were a prime motivation for forming the group and contributed to their decidedly non-conformist musical direction. With their precarious combination of frenetic, synth-driven, catchy freak-pop and future-age counterculture visual messaging, they were an instant hit with the punk and new wave crowd bored with the standard major-label rock fare. Starting with their 1976 debut single "Mongoloid," / "Jocko Homo," Devo held up an intelligently skewed mirror toward American culture. Along the way, they dared pop music fans to challenge their own intolerance to difference.

ENERGY DOME WORN BY MARK MOTHERSBAUGH OF DEVO, CA. 1980. GIFT OF DEVO

"I remember going skateboarding with some friends and they had this really bad homemade quarter-pipe but I would travel miles to go there. They had like three records. They had Jimi Hendrix *Crash Landing*, a Led Zeppelin record and Devo *Are We Not Men?* Someone gave one of the brothers a Devo record for his birthday as kind of a joke and they put it on, sort of like 'Hey, check out this weird music,' and by the end of the summer that was the record that we were listening to over and over and over again and the Hendrix and the Zeppelin records had been usurped. I think that was definitely my entrée into the world of underground music."

— Mark Arm, Mr. Epp, Green River, Mudhoney

"At that time everybody there was like one band in every city in the United States. In Ohio, Akron had Devo, and then Cleveland was Rubber City Rebels, and Chicago didn't have a band yet. Boston had a few bands. San Francisco had a few bands like the Nuns and Crime. New York had a bunch of bands. You'd come in these towns and meet whoever was in the local band — everybody was just starting out with these little scenes. It was just unbelievable."

— Peter Case, the Nerves, the Plimsouls

"We developed the red hats as a way to unify our look on stage, and quite honestly to put something on where we knew we'd be objects of derision. We decided to call our red hats 'energy domes.' And we told people, of course facetiously, that we wore them because you lose so much energy out of the top of your head where the soft spot used to be when you were a baby. That we wanted to collect it and put it back in."

— GERALD CASALE, DEVO

Paul Revere and The Raiders
MARK

THE POSIES

BITTER END

SUMMER

METAL CHURCH

I support JELLO

K

The Rocket

BLONDIE IS A GROUP!

PERE UBU

ROCK is COMING

SURF AND DESTROY

save us geza!

THE MISFITS FIEND CLUB

the childrens SLASH MAGAZINE edition

SCREAMERS

The Enemy

GERMS

POINTED STICKS
MUZAK FOR THE HARD OF THINKING

BUZZCOCKS

WORMER ANT

TG

OUR MUSIC! REGGAE SOUL ROCK'n'ROLL JAZZ FUNK AND PUNK! ROCK AGAINST RACISM

THE READY-MADES

B52'S B52S

WIRE

GO-GO'S

SNAKEFINGER

1̲.̲00̲   1̲.̲00̲

s u b p o

25¢ U.S.POSTAGE   25¢ U.S.POSTAGE   25¢ U.S.POSTAGE   PLAYWRIGHT   STATES

p o p

s u b

p o p s u b

Bomp!
Greg Shaw
P.O. Box 7112
Burbank, Ca.
91510

Lost Music Network Box 2391 Olympia, WA 98507

L M N p o p s

Subterranean Pop, later shortened to *Sub Pop*, was a zine created by Evergreen State College student Bruce Pavitt to document the developing American indie underground, specifically scenes that were under-documented, such as the Pacific Northwest. From 1980 – 1983, Pavitt produced nine issues (with three in cassette format), with the help of Calvin Johnson and other like-minded souls in the overlapping circles of Olympia's Evergreen State College, KAOS-FM, the Lost Music Network, and *OP* magazine. The zine was distributed through the mail to fans, record stores, and radio stations across the US. This copy of issue #4 was sent (with a note from Calvin Johnson) to Greg Shaw, founder of the influential *Bomp!* fanzine/record label/record store in LA.

In 1983, Pavitt moved from Olympia to Seattle, where *Sub Pop* transitioned into a column in the city's music paper, *The Rocket*. Sub Pop became a record label in 1986 with the release of *Sub Pop 100*. The following year, Pavitt joined forces with local KCMU radio DJ Jonathan Poneman (at the urging of Soundgarden's Kim Thayil, who grew up with Pavitt in Illinois) to release Green River's posthumous *Dry As A Bone* EP and Soundgarden's debut single, "Hunted Down"/ "Nothing to Say." The grunge explosion had begun.

SUB POP ZINE #4, JUNE 1981

"When I came to the Northwest and saw groups like the Beakers and the Blackouts in Seattle, I realized there was very little media attention on many parts of the country.

My fanzine really tried to highlight these different regions, and showcase the music that was coming out of them. At the time, if you wanted to read about punk and new wave music, you could get *Search and Destroy*, which came out of San Francisco, you could read *Slash* that came out of LA, or you could read *NY Rocker* that came out of New York. Those scenes were very commented upon, but the rest of the country didn't exist. So what motivated me was a desire to share with people this music that was being ignored."
— Bruce Pavitt, Sub Pop Records

"Bruce moved to Olympia from Chicago primarily because he was bored of Chicago and he liked what was going on in Seattle and he specifically liked KAOS and the independent music policy and that resonated with a lot of the philosophical rants that he was doing back then. He immediately became friends with everybody and had a really cool radio show and he decided to start the *Sub Pop* fanzine. He was a very motivated, very fun, very exciting person to hang out with and a really cool guy to do radio shows with. We had a couple of bad bands together — Bruce was actually a very interesting front man. And he could dance really well, and he was always making up his own haircuts really quickly, so I was like, 'Oh, you did that? Wow. Okay.'"
— Steve Fisk, recording engineer/producer/musician

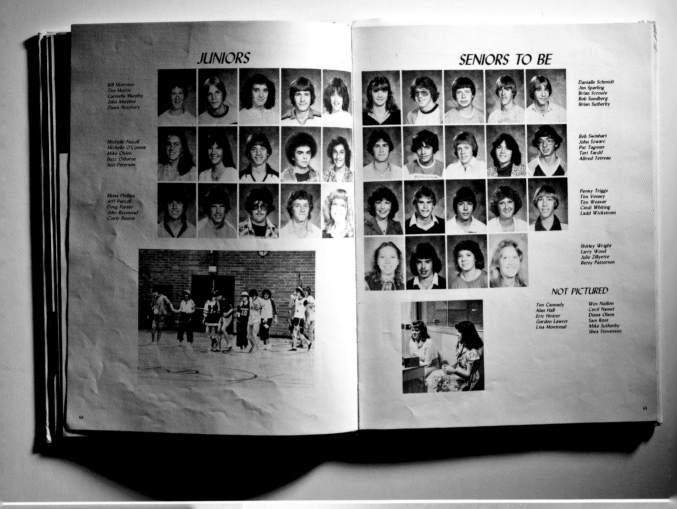

JUNIORS

Bill Morrison
Tim Morris
Carmella Murphy
John Morphie
Dawn Neathery

Michelle Nuxoll
Michelle O'Connor
Mike Olden
Buzz Osborne
Suzi Peterson

Mona Phillips
Jeff Purcell
Doug Purser
John Raymond
Cindy Reams

SENIORS TO BE

Danialle Schmidt
Jim Sparling
Brian Scroufe
Bob Sundberg
Brian Sutherby

Bob Swinhart
John Szwarc
Pat Tagman
Teri Tardif
Alfred Tetreau

Penny Triggs
Tim Vessey
Tim Weaver
Cindi Whiting
Ladd Wickstrom

Shirley Wright
Larry Wood
Julie Zillyette
Betsy Patterson

NOT PICTURED

Tim Cannady
Alan Hall
Eric Heater
Gordon Lawter
Lisa Montreuil

Wes Naillon
Cecil Namet
Diana Olson
Sam Ross
Mike Sutherby
Shea Stevenson

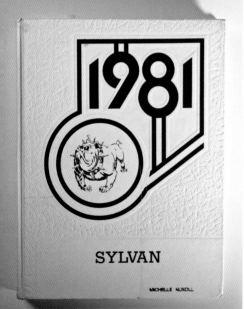

1981

SYLVAN

MICHELLE NUXOLL

CLASS OF 1985

Cobain, Kurt
Cokeley, Scot
Coker, Janet
Cole, Donna
Cuzick, Joann

Darrin Kent

Kathleen Kise
Shannon Ligh
Melinda Look
Darrin Loutha
Matt Lukin

In 1981, Kurt Cobain was finishing 8th grade at Montesano High School. He would attend classes there until partway through his sophomore year, when he moved to nearby Aberdeen and began attending Weatherwax High School. During his time at Montesano High, he played the drums in the school band (as pictured in this yearbook) and his musical interests began expanding to include the growing hardcore punk scenes in Washington, especially in Olympia and Seattle. In December of 1982 he recorded his first demo recording of songs, now lost to the ages, entitled *Organized Confusion* on his Aunt Mari Earl's 4-track tape recorder at her home in Burien, WA.

His affinity for punk rock grew when he began associating with upperclassmen Buzz Osbourne, Matt Lukin, and Mike Dillard – all featured in this yearbook – who started a hardcore group called the Melvins in 1983. Cobain hung out with them during band practices at drummer Dale Crover's house, who had replaced Mike Dillard. Soon Cobain was part of the Melvins' scraggly entourage, dubbed "Cling-Ons." Led by the singular vision of guitarist, vocalist, and songwriter Buzz Osbourne, the Melvins were one of the very few punk bands in the Aberdeen area, and would have a huge impact on Kurt Cobain, directly shaping his early musical explorations.

MONTESANO HIGH SCHOOL YEARBOOK, MONTESANO, WA, 1981

"In 1982, I met Buzz Osborne and Matt Lukin and they were in this band called the Melvins and I was working at a Taco Bell. There was this kid, Bill, who was expelled from Aberdeen High School because he lit up a pipe bomb. He was nuts. He knew these dudes from Montesano. Bill worked at the Taco Bell and he put a 'ch' at the end of 'Bell' on his hat. It said 'Taco Bellch' on it. So these dudes came in with like, y'know, these wristbands and they were into punk rock music. And back then, there was a cultural chasm – if you were into punk rock, you were really weird. And you could get beat up by the establishment people who were into good ol' boy music and driving around in Camaros or whatever. And punk rock people were on skateboards or … I drove a Volkswagen bus. So there was Buzz and Matt and the drummer Mike. And Buzz was a punk evangelist. He would just go around and like preach that punk rock is the way, man. This is the new sound. I recognized him because I got a hold of *The Vidette*, the Montesano school newspaper. And there was a column by Buzz Osborne about why punk rock is superior to conventional rock and roll."

– Krist Novoselic, Nirvana

"Kurt was 15 years old when he did the *Organized Confusion* demo. That was during Christmas vacation. He came up and recorded it on my Teac reel-to-reel. I showed him how to use the mixer and the recorder, and I said, 'Well, if you wanna use my Roland CompuRhythm' – it's a little computer rhythm machine – 'You're more than welcome to use that.' He is like, 'Oh, no way. I wanna keep my music pure.' So he grabbed his mother's pink Samsonite suitcase, emptied it out and, he said, 'You got any drumsticks?' I didn't, so I went to the kitchen and grabbed some wooden spoons. It was interesting to hear him do the music. It was loud and my husband and I would be sitting in here in the living room, listening to Kurt. It was kinda funny because doing multi-track recording, he'd do the music first and then he'd just do the vocals with the headphones on, so all you'd hear is this, 'WAHHHHH!' and 'UHH!' – y'know, screaming, and I'd smile at my husband and say things like, 'Yeah, don't you think someone's gonna think we're beating him or something in here?"

– Mari Earl, Kurt Cobain's aunt

Punk's aesthetic valued a do-it-yourself ethic, and many fans customized or created anew parts of their wardrobe to match their personal identities. This process inadvertently – and ironically – also created something of a formalized uniform, which was what punk had, in theory, railed against. Articles like this painted leather jacket acted as visual symbols, communicating membership in the punk tribe, and warnings to those outside the clan.

The original owner, "Mohawk Mike" from Charlottesville, Virginia, bought a plain black leather jacket and gradually painted his artwork onto it, adding the metal studs, chains, and skeletal imagery to create a visage in keeping with punk's confrontational side. He gave prominence on the jacket's front and left sleeve to favorite Washington, D.C. bands S.O.A. and Minor Threat. The back he devoted to the UK bands Subhumans and Broken Bones, and the right sleeve featured a spectrum of punk, post-punk, hardcore, and metal bands.

PAINTED LEATHER JACKET, WORN BY "MOHAWK MIKE," EARLY 1980S

"My mother was absolutely mortified every day when she saw me walk out of the house. My parents had a basic rule, which was: If we are out in public together, walk 20 feet behind us. Because the people in the fashion magazines who kind of cop the underground styles, they're a lot fancier looking than a shitty little crusty punk from Worcester, Mass. There was a lot that was edgy about my look; there was nothing that was becoming about my look."

— Megan Jasper, Sub Pop Records

"There was no real definition of what was punk and what was not. You would have people in bands that were wearing crazy, wild clothes, and bright yellow shirts and pink pants and a green necktie. And then you had the tough-guy punk rockers that were wearing leather jackets and had ripped up Levi's or pegged legs."

— Kurt Bloch, Fastbacks, Young Fresh Fellows

"You see people with crazy hair and piercing and tattoos and clothing, it was a flag, it was a banner, a badge you wore on yourself and identity. If somebody was looking a certain way, you knew they were rooted in the same kind of music you were, which was something different, something about change."

— Mike Roche, T.S.O.L.

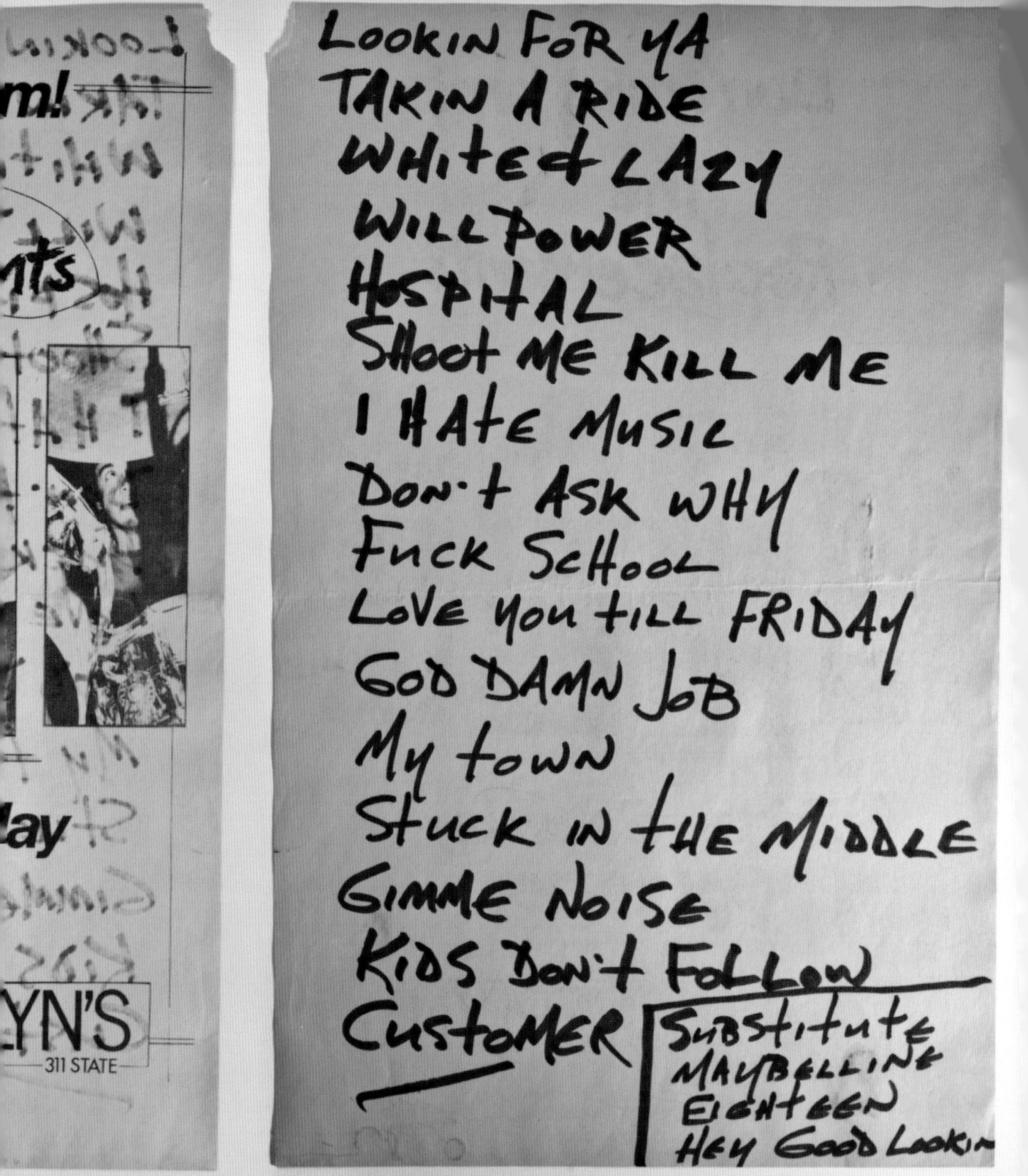

LOOKIN FOR YA
TAKIN A RIDE
WHITE & LAZY
WILLPOWER
HOSPITAL
SHOOT ME KILL ME
I HATE MUSIC
DON'T ASK WHY
FUCK SCHOOL
LOVE YOU TILL FRIDAY
GOD DAMN JOB
MY TOWN
STUCK IN THE MIDDLE
GIMME NOISE
KIDS DON'T FOLLOW
CUSTOMER

SUBSTITUTE
MAYBELLINE
EIGHTEEN
HEY GOOD LOOKIN

YN'S
311 STATE

These set lists show songs played by the Replacements on the tour before the April 1983 release of their album *Hootenanny* – an album that exposed the band to a national audience beyond their native Midwest. They were well known for covering songs, sometimes tongue-in-cheek, sometimes for entire shows. On these two nights they mixed their own music with such staples as Bill Haley's "Rock Around the Clock," the Who's "Substitute," Chuck Berry's "Maybellene," Alice Cooper's "Eighteen" and Hank Williams's "Hey Good Lookin'."

The Replacements formed in Minneapolis in 1979 and throughout their career played classic guitar rock filtered through a ragged punk lens. Vocalist Paul Westerberg's throaty yowl was backed by the rock of guitarist Bob Stinson, bassist Tommy Stinson, and drummer Chris Mars. Their performances were frequently notoriously drunken affairs that often tilted out of control before the finale. The band's heart-on-the-sleeve honesty and decidedly non-arty sound would attract legions of kids to the underground who were otherwise not interested in new wave or art-school post-punk.

HANDWRITTEN SETLIST FOR THE REPLACEMENTS AT MERLYN'S, MADISON, WI, OCTOBER 29-30, 1982

"The Replacements were just totally amazing. I saw them on the *Ma, I Forgot to Take Out the Trash* tour. Bobby Stinson, the brother who played guitar before he got chucked out, was still there. And it was, as soon as they started, just one big pile of bodies all over the place."

—ALEX SHUMWAY, GREEN RIVER

"The Replacements were like a four-ring circus. They were a great band live because each one of them was such a character. You had Bob Stinson who would dress in diapers or a tutu and play these amazing wild solos. They would play 'Rock Around The Clock' at light speed, and he was obviously still trashed out of his mind but he would still play the solo note for note. Paul Westerberg was sort of this punked out Rod Stewart-type figure, obviously a very cool guy – the suburban thug with the poet's heart. And he was riveting on stage too. Tommy Stinson was the Mexican jumping bean and always dapper in his own funky way, and Chris Mars I remember was always just in the back, grimacing with his eyes bugging out just trying to concentrate on playing as steadily as possible."

— Michael Azerrad, music journalist/biographer

"The Replacements was a huge influence on a lot of us 'cause they were such a great band built around great songs and kinda this chaotic persona and their live show was like that too. They're sort of a pre-grunge band that sort of epitomized a lot of the ethos of grunge. I guess you could summarize it by saying, you wore the same clothes on stage that you wore in real life. You didn't have a costume change just 'cause you were on stage. Your life was spent on the road in a van and you made records on the cheap and put on great, energetic live shows that were very raw and visceral and played with the human body, y'know? And I remember seeing the Replacements and just really thinking that that's the best live band I've seen yet."

— Barrett Martin, Skin Yard, Screaming Trees

FLIPPER

ALBUM

GENERIC FLIPPER

Flipper was formed in San Francisco in 1979, quickly making a name for themselves with their chaotic, heavy weirdness, epitomized by their 1980 single "Sex Bomb": seven minutes of ramshackle, no wave skronk groove with the single lyric, "She's a sex bomb, baby. Yeah!" Their debut full-length, *Album – Generic Flipper*, was released on Subterranean Records in 1982, and broke punk's trend toward "Loud Fast Rules!" It was one of the first albums to bring the heaviness of Black Sabbath into punk, and along with Black Flag's *My War*, slowed punk's breakneck speed and paved the way for grunge.

In addition to their spiritual role in the evolution of music to come, Flipper had a very specific influence on the members of Nirvana. Kurt Cobain wore a hand-made t-shirt with the Flipper logo throughout Nirvana's Nevermind tour and on *Saturday Night Live* in January 1992. Nirvana's Krist Novoselic credited *Album – Generic Flipper*, with helping him understand for the first time the power of punk rock. The band must have made an impression, since Novoselic took over bass duties with the band from 2006 – 2009.

ALBUM – GENERIC FLIPPER, LP, 1982

"Buzz Osbourne lent me his *Generic Flipper* record and I put it on and go, 'What is this? It's just really weird. It sounds bad. Like where was this recorded, like on a cassette player?' I was laying on a waterbed, and then on the third time, laying on this waterbed, listening to *Generic Flipper*, I was like, 'Wow, this is amazing! This is total art.' You can do anything you want. You can take it or leave it. And that was my epiphany about punk rock."

— Krist Novoselic, Nirvana

"I think as the success and the money started to roll in, I think that a lot of bands kind of felt guilty about their success and really took a lot of pains to try and pay back to the community. Like Nirvana took Urge Overkill out on their tours right after *Nevermind*. Kurt Cobain would wear Flipper T-shirts and would plug the Vaselines."

— Michael Azerrad, music journalist/biographer

"My main reason for wanting Mark Arm to play guitar was so he wouldn't hop around like he did in Green River and climb everything and stuff. Plus he was like Flipper's guitar player, y'know? Either one finger barre chord type stuff or this great feedback noise."

— Steve Turner, Mudhoney

FLIPPER AND OTHERS AT 1839 GEARY, SAN FRANCISCO, FEBRUARY 29, 1980

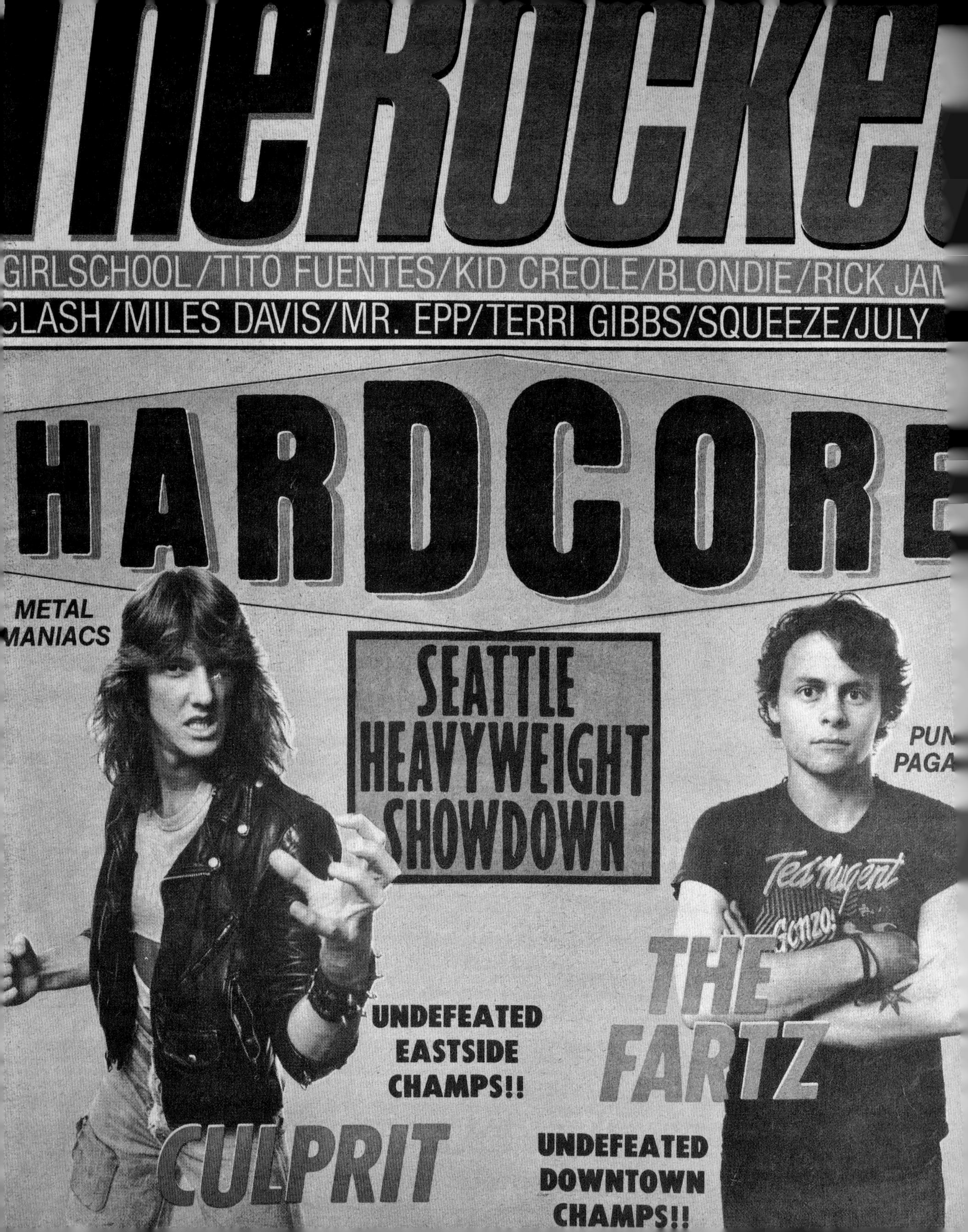

THE ROCKET

HARDCORE

METAL MANIACS

SEATTLE HEAVYWEIGHT SHOWDOWN

PUN PAGA

UNDEFEATED EASTSIDE CHAMPS!!

THE FARTZ

CULPRIT

UNDEFEATED DOWNTOWN CHAMPS!!

In the early '80s, the Seattle area was a hotbed for heavy metal. While urban punks chose jackhammer hardcore beats over virtuosity, suburban metalheads worshipped the technical prowess of Iron Maiden and Judas Priest. This issue of *The Rocket*, Seattle's music monthly played up the somewhat facile differences and perceived beef between the "metal maniacs" and the "punk pagans." Culprit and the Fartz were huge in their respective communities during the early 80s. Culprit was lauded in the Northwest as the Next Big Thing and toured with Metallica; the Fartz were one of the most renowned hardcore bands in Seattle and had signed to Alternative Tentacles, the San Francisco record label owned by Jello Biafra from the Dead Kennedys. But in the ensuing years, the musical distance between punk and metal would diminish with bands such as Green River, Soundgarden, and the Melvins melding aspects of the two, creating a new amalgam that would be soon dubbed "grunge."

THE ROCKET, JULY 1982. COVER DESIGN BY BOB NEWMAN

"There was a division between metal and punk rock in Seattle, but I didn't pay any attention to it. Those bands from the Eastside kind of dressed up and would basically be an arena rock band in a teeny little venue. And I guess some of us thought that was kind of funny, like 'Ha ha ha, look at that, they're trying to act like Queen' or something. I remember seeing a band called Myth — Geoff Tate from Queensrÿche's first band and at the Lake Hills Roller Rink and the drum riser was so big that the drummer was almost hitting his head on the ceiling. But I thought it was great. And then those bands started listening to bands from Seattle and some people started intermingling and then you had other bands that wouldn't be so weird, like Metal Church. So it never seemed that weird to me. It's all just based in hard rock, y'know?"

— Kim Warnick, Fastbacks

"To me, metal and punk rock was almost kind of hand in hand. I didn't see as huge of a difference as maybe some people did. I mean, the look was obviously slightly differ-ent — you had the long hair and the gun belts and stuff like that, whereas punk rock was definitely a different kind of look. But it sort of started merging itself, y'know? I'd see guys that were totally into the whole metal scene at punk rock shows and vice versa. 'cause I'd be at metal shows. And I think the similarity of the music being intense and aggressive is what really brought the two more together."

— Chad Channing, Nirvana

"At the time, in 1981, metal ruled the northwest. But there was two camps, metal and punk, and the theory is that the two camps kind of came together and hence we have grunge. But let me give a sense of what was going on at that time and what the music scene was like, the reaction of the audience, places to play, just the vibe of the city. The city itself was opening up more and more to bands with original songs. And even in the punk scene, if they weren't playing Iggy, they were developing their own songs. And whether you were into punk or metal, kids began to know your songs. And you would get reactions from these crowds around these halls that were equal to what you'd get in a 20,000 seat coliseum. And it was more intimate — there were people right up in your face, fists in the air, calling your name. It was everything we wanted to do at the time. But, also, there were only about five or six clubs that we could play. And sometimes they would have punk, and sometimes they would have metal."

— Brad Sinsel, TKO

X was at the forefront of the original wave of LA punk, producing for seminal local label Dangerhouse the 1978 single "Adult Books" / "We're Desperate" and their classic track "Los Angeles," which appeared on the label's *Yes L.A.* compilation. By 1980, X were one of the most lauded of bands from in the LA scene, and with their 1980 album *Los Angeles* and 1981's *Wild Gift*, both released on Slash Records, their profile in the American underground soared, and they began to make inroads into the mainstream.

With the release of *More Fun in the New World*, their second album on major label Elektra, the band's sound was expanding, becoming more radio-friendly, garnering a wider audience who found entry into the music through its rockabilly and folk-infused sensibilities. Exene Cervenka, the band's charismatic vocalist, created this artwork, which was used in slightly modified form for the *More Fun in the New World* album cover. With her evocative lyrics, distinctive voice, and multi-faceted artistic talents, Cervenka became something of an eidolon of Patti Smith, evolving Smith's confident punk-poet archetype through the lens of the West Coast in the 1980s – an exemplar for thousands of women in bands to come.

ORIGINAL ARTWORK BY EXENE CERVENKA FOR X'S LP *MORE FUN IN THE NEW WORLD*, 1983

"X was a direct revolt against the excesses of the '70s and the '60s, and it was very anti-cocaine, anti-limo, anti-groupie. There was a Communist element to it. We kind of had the Raymond Chandler and the Charles Bukowski thing happening. X was very literary and we were chronicling an underground, seeing a very kind of folkie scene, kind of like what Woody Guthrie would have written about. It was the people who were disenfranchised from society. A lot of the people in that scene were really intellectual which I really miss now. I miss the higher ideals, and the intellectualism of that kind of scene because now I think things are so commercialized that that almost can't exist anymore."

– Exene Cervenka, X

"After X put out two records on Slash we were courted by Joe Smith from Elektra. The Doors were on Elektra, and so was Phil Ochs, so I just thought I died and went to heaven. And that's cool. I wanted to get this music out to as many people as possible. So a major label had no stigma at that point. We had total artistic control, they can't tell us what to do, and they didn't. They were into artists. But eventually

that became a problem because they didn't work hard enough to sell records. They just wanted us like a painting on the wall. But I'd say an equal number of people gave us shit for signing with Slash as gave us shit for signing with Elektra. It was like we were supposed to make cassettes and hand them out for our whole career, y'know?"

– John Doe, X

"X was so incredible. I want to say it was maybe like 1982, and I was at the Channel in Boston and it was all-ages so it's all kids there and I had one of the best times of my fuckin' life. I just – I felt at home in a way that I'd never felt at home. I was hearing music that I loved, I thought Exene was the coolest woman in the world and this incredible role model, and I was so psyched to be around freaky kids like me that I felt just like that was my home. I was totally committed to this community, this lifestyle, and this music. It meant everything to me because it was the first time that I found something that I felt like I could really be a part of."

– Megan Jasper, Sub Pop Records

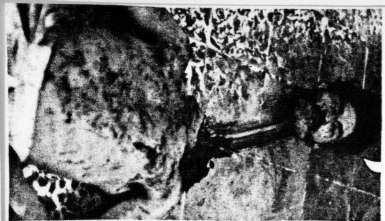

Hey Big Boy—
Why don't you get on down
Here to EL SALVADOR,
We're having some kinda fun!
But you know, it is getting
Sort of lonely without you—
We're getting tired of just playing
with ourselves—we need some
FRESH BODIES

Mr. EPP U-MEN
Limp Richards

GET DOWN & GET POLITICAL At A
BENEFIT For the Ad Hoc Committee for the July 2nd demonstration
AGAINST U.S. INTERVENTION IN
EL SALVADOR etc.

JULY 2ND At 9:30 @
LANGSTON HUGHES Cultural Center
10717 S. — 17th & Yesler
Take bus 3, 4, 27, or 48

$3.00

cum and test how
sociable your
social conscience is.

Hey Helmut,
WANNA GET
LUCKY?

JA, JA
of course,
but first we
must get
Political!!

I wonder if
he'll give me
some foreign
AIDS

Punk rock by its very nature was always political. But in the '80s, American punk became more strident still after Ronald Reagan became president. This poster, from midway through Reagan's first term, is typical for the time, lambasting Reagan's foreign policy toward El Salvador, and referencing Reagan's influence over German Chancellor Helmut Kohl and the growing AIDS epidemic.

The Seattle bands featured on the poster – Mr. Epp and the Calculations, the U-Men, and the Limp Richerds – featured members who would go on to play large roles in the music scene to come. The U-Men were revered for their swampy cow punk explosion. Guitarist Tom Price would later play in the garage punk band Gas Huffer, while bassist Jim Tillman would move on to the psychedelic grunge band Love Battery. Mr. Epp was a chaotic noise combo featuring future Mudhoney guitarist/vocalist Mark Arm. Their song "Mohawk Man" became a staple on L.A. DJ Rodney Bingenheimer's KROQ radio show. The Limp Richerds were a wall of shambling distortion, later incarnations of which also featured Mark Arm (this time on drums) as well as guitarist Steve Turner – who together would form the proto-grunge group Green River.

MR. EPP, U-MEN, LIMP RICHERDS, AT LANGSTON HUGHES CULTURAL CENTER, SEATTLE, JULY 2, 1983
POSTER BY JO SMITTY

"I'd met Mark Arm through Charles Peterson 'cause they were roommates, and I heard this song on KCMU called, 'Mohawk Man,' and I thought it was fucking brilliant – sorta like how The Fall's 'Totally Wired' was brilliant. It was funny and it was damning and just as snarky as you could be. It sounded pretty cool to me. And then Charles said that his roommate was in Mr. Epp, and I thought that they were fucking famous 'cause they were on the radio. I was like, 'You know that guy? Does he make a lot of money?' And he didn't. In fact, I think his mum was bringing him groceries on Sundays."

– Ed Fotheringham, illustrator and Thrown-Ups "vocalist"

"When we started Mr. Epp, we had no idea about anything, like we had this guitar and we didn't know how to tune the guitar. All we did was turn the saturation button up as much as possible on the Peavey and get as much feedback as we could and we thought we were Jimi Hendrix. But not the part of Jimi Hendrix actually playing a riff – the part between the riffs. Just the feedback noise."

– Mark Arm, Mr. Epp, Green River, Mudhoney

"Through the efforts of Bruce Pavitt, who had Sub Pop, a column in The Rocket magazine, the U-Men came to the attention of Gerard Cosloy, who was running the Homestead label. The U-Men signed with them and just that in and of itself – signing a record contract with a national label – was astonishing for any local band. I mean, it had been done but not in the hardcore punk milieu. Homestead at the time had had Nick Cave and the Bad Seeds, Dinosaur, Sonic Youth – a number of bands actually which became very influential on music that would be later produced in Seattle. Through the U-Men they signed Green River which would almost form the basis for what would later become known as grunge or the Seattle sound."

– Larry Reid, curator/punk promoter/U-Men manager

Mike Shaughnessy created and played this guitar with the Olympia, WA band the Wimps. He built it in August 1983 from one of his worn-out skateboards and a cheap, Norma guitar neck that he got from a thrift store. The homemade instrument actually produced a raw, gritty tone perfect for the band's lo-fi party punk. With a sound that combined Clash riffs with Jonathan Richman lyrics, the Wimps, along with the Young Pioneers, Beat Happening, and others, emphasized fun and teenage abandon over confrontation and aggression – hallmarks of the growing Olympia scene that would be amplified throughout the '80s and beyond via Calvin Johnson's K Records, influencing countless bands, fans, and musicians to come, including Nirvana's Kurt Cobain.

The Wimps played with Ze Whiz Kidz, Young Pioneers, and Beat Happening at the opening night of the Tropicana on February 25, 1984. The all-ages Tropicana was located in downtown Olympia, and wasn't even open for a full year (it closed on January 31, 1985), but that's a lifetime if you're a teen with lots of time on your hands and an interest in punk rock. It served a vital role in the Olympia scene, providing a stable venue for underground music to grow and thrive.

SKATEBOARD GUITAR, PLAYED BY MIKE SHAUGHNESSY OF THE WIMPS, 1983

"Olympia was where the culture was, because it seemed that while in Aberdeen at the time there were some bands that played original music, it was more kind of '70s rock, or bands that played covers, and to me the interesting music was punk rock music. And Olympia had the infrastructure with the Tropicana in downtown Olympia. There would be shows there and it was not even an hour drive, so it was really easy. You could even take the bus to Olympia from Aberdeen."

— Krist Novoselic, Nirvana

"We played in one of our first shows with Beat Happening and Girl Trouble in Olympia at the Tropicana. I think it was probably the first all-ages show we ever did. It was just amazing. I have such great memories of that show. That was like 1984."

— Scott McCaughey, Young Fresh Fellows and Minus 5

"I was interested in coming to the Evergreen State College. The music I was interested in at the time was very similar to what was going on there, and what was going on in Olympia was very exciting, as far as the Lost Music Network, KAOS Radio, *Sub Pop* magazine, and OP magazine. I was aware of some of the bands there like John Foster's Pop Philosophers, the Beakers, the Macs, and of course the Blackouts from Seattle, and so I think that was part of the interest: part was music, part was education, and it was far away from Chicago. I figured there were probably better musical opportunities as well because it was a smaller town that was actively involved in that aspect of independent punk culture, whereas Chicago at the time was a lot of bar bands and blues. And it was so big. It was hard to get any sort of central thing going on, or to participate in it."

— Kim Thayil, Soundgarden

The Replacements played Seattle for the first time in 1983 at the Metropolis. The show was documented by photographer Charles Peterson, whose images of Soundgarden, Nirvana, TAD, Mudhoney, and others are one of the primary visual signifiers of the grunge era. These photographs of guitarist Bob Stinson and the crowd at the Replacements show illustrate how small the scene was in the early 1980s. Pogoing near the front of the stage are (left to right, listed with their best-known bands), Dana Collins (The Accüsed), Sergio Avenia (Deranged Diction), Heather Lewis (Beat Happening), Mark Arm (Mudhoney), Alex Shumway (Green River), Gary Allen May (Supreme Cool Beings), Steve Turner (Mudhoney), and Ed Fotheringham (Thrown-Ups). The Replacements playing Seattle was an EVENT, and everyone was there.

The Metropolis was started by Hugo Piottin, an artist-friendly jack-of-all-trades. It was open for just two years, but it had a huge impact on music in Seattle, mainly because it was all-ages and a stable venue. This access and consistency allowed teens that were interested in alternative music and culture a regular destination to see punk bands and hang out, all within a city that at the time largely ignored the cultural needs of its youth. The Metropolis was the creative epicenter for many that would go on to be major players in the grunge era.

THE REPLACEMENTS AT THE METROPOLIS, SEATTLE, NOVEMBER 30, 1983
PHOTOGRAPHS BY CHARLES PETERSON

"The Metropolis is now a teriyaki joint that I go and eat lunch at occasionally. I had been eating there forever, and then one day I was sitting there, and I looked at the brick wall, and I was like, 'Oh my God, this is the Metropolis!' That's the wall that the bands played against, y'know?"

— CHARLES PETERSON, PHOTOGRAPHER

"The Metropolis was the only place you could go being a 15-year-old to see bands like Hüsker Dü or the Bad Brains or Channel 3. Every place else was over 21, and you were fucked. If the Metropolis wasn't there, we would all have been just hanging out in front of the 21-or-over place and making trouble. Not only that — it sort of stirred the pot, if that makes sense, because the whole scene was basically incestuous. One person from one band would go to another band, would move to another band, y'know, and they were fucking each other's sisters and starting another band. And it was all from the Metropolis. I mean, if there was no Metropolis, there wouldn't have been any of that stuff that came after. No grunge, no nothing."

— Alex Shumway, Green River

"I remember in the Metropolis days, Krist Novoselic would come into town with the Melvins guys. I knew Buzz Osbourne and Matt Lukin really well and every once in awhile they'd have this tall dude with them at a Metropolis show. And then later on it was like, 'Oh, that tall dude who's the Melvins' friend is in a band.'"

— Mark Arm, Mr. Epp, Green River, Mudhoney

"I went with Buzz and Matt to the Metropolis in downtown Seattle, and Matt had this '67 Chevrolet Impala that was a nice emerald green. We piled in — you could fit six people in this big, big car. What was the band? I know I met Mark Arm there and he did a stage dive and that was the first stage dive I ever saw in my life."

— Krist Novoselic, Nirvana

This "crucifix guitar" was used for the cover photograph of Metal Church's 1984 eponymous debut album. To give the instrument the appropriate weathered look, the $200 Gibson Explorer copy was tied to a bicycle and dragged around the block, then buried in the garden for a few days. The cover was inspired by a drawing by a friend of the band featuring a graveyard filled with guitar headstones. Metal Church employed photographer Saulius Pempe, who had worked with guitarist Kurdt Vanderhoof when he was in the Seattle and San Francisco punk band The Lewd, to create the brooding cover photograph.

Metal Church formed in 1980 after Vanderhoof after he tired of playing bass in the Lewd. Excited by the sonic possibilities of the heavy metal scene, Vanderhoof moved back to his hometown of Aberdeen, WA and formed a band called Shrapnel (soon renamed Metal Church) with several childhood friends. The band's 1984 *Metal Church* album was released on the Ground Zero label run by metal fans Willie MacKay and Jeff Gilbert, and quickly sold over 50,000 copies. Its success illustrated the widespread popularity of heavy metal in the Pacific Northwest, and garnered the attention of Elektra Records, which would reissue the album the following year.

PROP GUITAR USED FOR METAL CHURCH'S EPONYMOUS DEBUT ALBUM, 1984

"Our first record was on Ground Zero records, put together with Jeff Gilbert and Willie MacCay, and one day Willie McCay is at his record store in West Seattle, and Elektra Records calls, and is asking him how much money he wants for Metal Church. Kim Harris, who was managing Queensrÿche, was standing right next to Willie McCay, our manager, and Willie covers the phone and says, 'They want to know how much money for Metal Church,' and Kim is going, 'Ask the moon and then you can always come down,' and Willie says — inexperienced Willie, y'know I love you man, but good God! — he goes, 'Well, I've got about $5,000 into the band right now.' Kim is screaming at him, 'NO! NO! 150, 200,000, quarter million!' Willie's like, 'No, no, no. I need at least $5,000. So I guess ten would be okay.'"
— David Wayne, Metal Church

"The first metal band that I really started to like was Metal Church and their first album. I've always had some good times in the metal scene. It was great. It was real exciting to see a band that was metal, so unabashedly metal, start getting somewhere, and we were like, 'Wow, Metal Church.' We got that first album, and totally thought it sounded like a million bucks, it was a great sounding record."
— Kurt Bloch, Fastbacks and Young Fresh Fellows

Kurt Cobain created this mixed-media untitled work in Mr. Robert Hunter's art class during his 1984-'85 senior year at Aberdeen's Weatherwax High School. His work featured the distinct Reagan-era theme of impending nuclear annihilation. Cobain airbrushed a post-apocalyptic skyline and overlaid a pencil illustration of two aging punk rockers – an "American Gothic" couple of the wastelands, one with a badge touting the "Nuclear Mutants of America." Cobain's signature and thumbprint sign the work.

Cobain had long exhibited a talent for creating visual art, particularly drawing and painting. As he delved further into punk rock in the early 1980s, he identified with the disenfranchisement that many kids of the day felt, a feeling that was echoed in much of the underground music that he was listening to. His creative expressions became more unconventional as Cobain grew older, exhibiting a dark sense of humor and a keen interest in Americana kitsch and human anatomy – all of which would inform the music and lyrics he would create in Nirvana.

UNTITLED BY KURT COBAIN, CA. 1984 - 1985

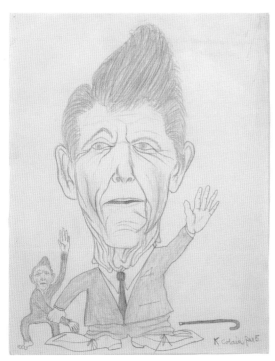

UNTITLED BY KURT COBAIN, CA. 1984. COURTESY OF THE KARSH FAMILY COLLECTION.

"Kurt went to Aberdeen High School for a while and he was like a class or two below me. I was kind of aware of him at that time. He was a great artist. He was insightful. You can see some of the art he did – if he would have just stuck with painting and sculpture! I have this pipe he made me and [laughter] I never used it. It's this writhing, weird, tortured spirit person. It's like a ghost. He was always creative and he was always compelled. He was a very hard worker."

– Krist Novoselic, Nirvana

"Kurt was a creative genius. Not only did this guy have an amazing voice, but what we saw was somebody who was an amazing performer, somebody who had a lot to say in interviews about gender issues, all sorts of things, somebody who was a brilliant songwriter, but also conceptually he was a very creative artist. When you think about the cover of *Nevermind*, it's iconic, it's considered one of the classic rock covers in history. He art directed that. You look at the first Nirvana video, 'Smells Like Teen Spirit,' where you have the cheerleaders with the anarchy symbols – that was Kurt. So really, what we were witnessing was the unfolding of a creative genius."

– Bruce Pavitt, Sub Pop Records

BLACK FLAG AND DEAD KENNEDYS at the Mabuhay Gardens, San Franscisco, CA, October 10, 1979. Poster by Raymond Pettibon; CIRCLE JERKS, Minor Threat, at the 9:30 Club, Washington DC, June 11, 1981; *T.V. O.D.? Try the New Maximumrocknroll*, Tuesdays, 8-10 pm, KPFA 94 FM, ca. early 1980s; D.R.I., Rejectors, at Graven Image, Seattle, WA, July 1, 1983. Poster by Kevin Clarke;

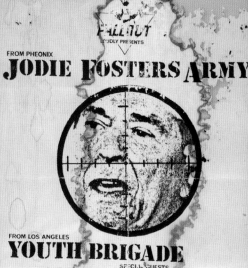

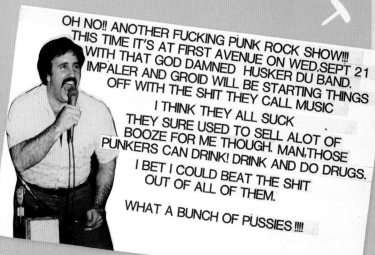

MINOR THREAT, Government Issue, Social Suicide, E.N.B., at Wilson Center, Washington DC, February 25, 1983; JODIE FOSTERS ARMY, Youth Brigade, Sun City Girls, at Graven Image, Seattle, August 10, 1984. Poster by Larry Reid; ORIGINAL ARTWORK for Hüsker Dü, Impaler, Groid, at the First Avenue, Minneapolis, MN, September 21, 1983

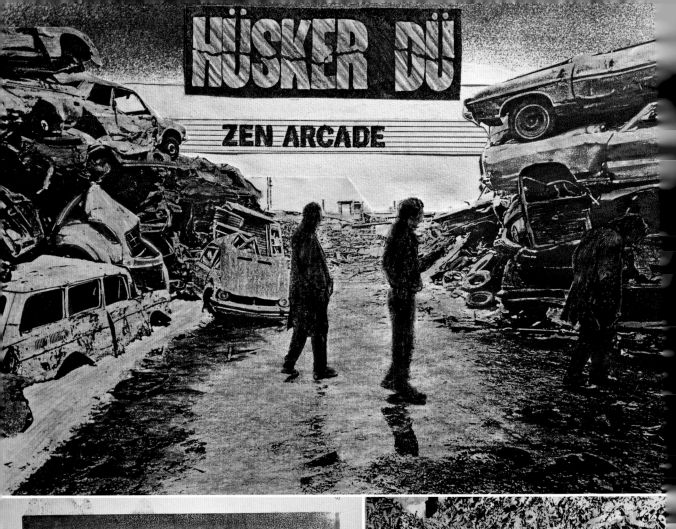

HÜSKER DÜ

ZEN ARCADE

SOMETHING I LEARNED TODAY
BROKEN HOME, BROKEN HEART
NEVER TALKING TO YOU AGAIN
CHARTERED TRIPS
DREAMS REOCCURRING
INDECISION TIME
HARE KRSNA

3
SOMEWHERE
ONE STEP AT A TIME
PINK TURNS TO BLUE
NEWEST INDUSTRY
MONDAY WILL NEVER
   BE THE SAME
WHATEVER
THE TOOTH FAIRY
   AND THE PRINCESS

2
BEYOND THE THRESHOLD
PRIDE
I'LL NEVER FORGET YOU
THE BIGGEST LIE
WHAT'S GOING ON
MASOCHISM WORLD
STANDING BY THE SEA

4
TURN ON THE NEWS
REOCCURRING DREAMS

The cover of Hüsker Dü's double album, *Zen Arcade*, released in 1984 on SST, was designed by drummer Grant Hart, based on a photocopy of a photograph by Mark Peterson of the band in a Minneapolis-area junkyard. Adopting the moniker Fake Name Graphx, Hart manipulated the photocopied image, using colored pencils and an Xacto knife to collage the final cover design. *Rolling Stone*'s David Fricke noted in a 1986 piece on the band that *Zen Arcade* was "American punk's *London Calling* [by The Clash], fleshed out with the fearless eclecticism of the Beatles' *White Album*."

Hüsker Dü formed in Minneapolis in 1979. With the release of their 1982 debut album, *Land Speed Record*, they proved themselves staunch devotees of hardcore punk, having been influenced by bands such as Black Flag, Vancouver, B.C.'s D.O.A. and Seattle's the Fartz. As time wore on, songwriters Hart and guitarist Bob Mould would incorporate more melodic elements into their music. *Zen Arcade* shows the band at a moment of musical expansion, capturing a sense of confusion, inertia, and aspiration in mid-1980s America. The double album garnered widespread critical praise, and placed Hüsker Dü in a long line of bands essential to the development of Alternative Rock.

ORIGINAL COVER ART FOR HÜSKER DÜ'S *ZEN ARCADE*, 1984, BY GRANT HART

"I think we intimidated some people, and not only that but I think we got to like it. And in that I think we found our mania for excess which was perhaps best displayed on *Land Speed Record* which is one live set that was an amalgamation of everything corrosive that we had composed, put into one 26 minute set and delivered at the end of our first national tour, west of the Mississippi. We brought that sound back to Minneapolis after hammering it out on the road, seeing what other people were doing in other towns — influential bands like D.O.A., Minutemen, Black Flag, Discharge, Circle Jerks — those types of bands were having an influence on us. We were not yet coming into our own. We were copy cat killers, we were applying that hardcore ethic to the songs that we had composed, and then brought that ethic to Minneapolis."

— Grant Hart, Hüsker Dü

"When I first saw Hüsker Dü, it was overwhelming. They played so fast and so loud, I mean it really was over-whelming. I don't use that word lightly. It was just so intense, like a tornado coming off the stage. And it was also kind of intoxicating and almost hypnotic sometimes because it was such a blur. You just got overloaded. When Bob Mould would sing it was like a baby screaming. It was like this real primal scream, and he was one pissed off guy. And for all us malcontents in the audience he was our mouthpiece. And then Grant Hart would sing slightly sweeter songs, and that was our other side. It really was this very yin and yang type of band. Everything was there."

— Michael Azerrad, music journalist/biographer

"When that whole grunge thing started supposedly in Seattle — I mean, think back, the Hüskers were grunge before anybody was. There wasn't an alternative department in a record company until what, '88, '89? There wasn't even a label to put on the music at the time."

— KARL MUELLER, SOUL ASYLUM

CALL IT
NIGHT
NOW IS TIME

DREAM
HAPPY
SOMETIMES
WAIT
AMERICA
BIRTHDAY
RUTS
SEE & SAY
WHAT WILL SAY
SAYS WHO

In 1984, the Fastbacks opened for the UK hardcore band GBH at the Mountaineers Club, along with local hardcore band March of Crimes (which featured a young Ben Shepherd, later of Soundgarden). This setlist features songs from the band's first three releases – 1981's *It's Your Birthday 7"*, 1982's *The Fastbacks Play Five of Their Favorites* EP, and 1984's *Every Day is Saturday* EP – all on guitarist/songwriter Kurt Bloch's No Threes Records.

Bloch formed the Fastbacks in 1979, and their brand of pop-punk was a fixture in the Seattle scene for more than two decades. The band finally called it quits in 2001, after dozens of releases and stints by nearly every drummer in town, including Duff McKagan (Guns N' Roses), Tad Hutchinson (Young Fresh Fellows), John Moen (Decemberists), Jason Finn (Presidents of the United States of America), Dan Peters (Mudhoney), and Mike Musberger (the Posies). The band's instantly catchy tunes, powered by Bloch's guitar god licks and the harmonized vocals of bassist Kim Warnick and guitarist Lulu Garguilo, earned them universal acclaim throughout the underground music sphere, while eternally managing to elude mainstream tastes.

FASTBACKS SET LIST FOR THEIR CONCERT WITH GBH AND MARCH OF CRIMES AT THE NORWAY CENTER, SEATTLE, MARCH 16, 1984

"I think the Fastbacks are one of the nuggets of Seattle. They'll get lost in the history, but they're such an important part. They have roots in the early '80s punk rock scene, and came up and hit both Sub Pop and Popllama and epitomized 'do it because you love it,' and just have fun with it. I mean, no one wrote a better hook than Kurt Bloch, y'know? That's for sure. And he also had that gift for lyrics, incredible lyrics. I don't know of another band that had been doing it 20+ years and still being great. From the beginning, I think, the success was defined differently. After Nirvana, a lot of bands seemed like they just want the record deal. Fastbacks just wanted to play music and that's something you can't bottle and sell."

— Susie Tennant, DGC representative

"Well, the Fastbacks had – this is a number I can never get right. It's either 11 or 12 or 13 drummers depending on if you want to count one guy that came back. Some bands have bass player problems, we had drummer problems. It wasn't like we were a working band making a lot of money, so maybe they just got bored."

— Kim Warnick, Fastbacks

"The Fastbacks were a great band, a really good pop band. I remember the first time hearing them do 'Set Me Free' by the Sweet and I was like, 'Oh man, I'm so glad I bought that record again.' They were great and Kurt is an amazing guitar player. Too bad about that whole drummer thing."

— Mark Arm, Mr. Epp, Mudhoney, Green River

Featuring Ex-members of
Mr. Epp, Deranged Diction, + Spluii Numa.
GREEN RIVER
THE MELVINS
GREY DOOR LOCALS
'R' GANG
FALSE LIBERTY
AUG. 11
SATURDAY · 9:00
THE GREY DOOR · $3.
'84 Jeff Ament

Green River played their second show at Seattle's Grey Door, as advertised by this poster created by bassist (and future Pearl Jam founder) Jeff Ament. Green River featured Ament, Mark Arm (vocals), Stone Gossard (guitar), Steve Turner (guitar, later replaced by Bruce Fairweather), and Alex Shumway (drums). They formed out of the ashes of Mr. Epp and the Calculations, Spluii Numa, the Limp Richerds, the Ducky Boys, and Deranged Diction, and soon were playing around Seattle. By 1985, they had released their debut EP, *Come on Down*, on Homestead Records.

A record on a national indie like Homestead was rare for a Northwest band at that time, and it helped foster valuable connections for Green River with tastemakers like Sonic Youth. In 1987, Green River released the *Dry as a Bone* EP on Sub Pop Records. Label head Bruce Pavitt described the disc as "ultra-loose GRUNGE," initiating the beginnings of an empire for Sub Pop but the end for Green River, who began to disagree on musical direction. Their final album, the posthumous *Rehab Doll*, was released on Sub Pop in mid-1988. By that point, Green River had already broken up and its members had formed two bands that would begin a new chapter in the Northwest music story: Mother Love Bone and Mudhoney.

GREEN RIVER, THE MELVINS, 'R' GANG, AND FALSE LIBERTY, AT THE GREY DOOR, SEATTLE, AUGUST 11, 1984. POSTER BY JEFF AMENT

"A couple months after playing with the Limp Richerds we kind of gave up on that and tried to start Green River. It was March '84 and I started working at Raison D'Etre with Jeff Ament in a calculated bid to force him into playing with me and Mark. We wanted to get him to play bass with us because he was the only bass player that played with a distortion box in town. So I infiltrated the restaurant and convinced Jeff to play with us, even though he just hated Mr. Epp. He thought we were clueless, which, y'know, we were."

— Steve Turner, Mr. Epp, Mudhoney, Green River

"In Green River, we were saying, 'I like Cheap Trick.' Or, 'I actually like Black Sabbath.' I think, at that point, a lot of the other bands that used to be hardcore bands, started to go more of a rock route, and we went more of a more stir-the-pot kind of route. We actually took influences from everything that we had, rather than just flipping the whole thing over. It was just a giant melting pot more than anything else."

— Alex Shumway, Green River

"All of us with the exception of Stone Gossard were deeply involved in hardcore. And his friends were kind of more the Eastside metal-type dudes, y'know — like he was friends with the kids from Shadow and he had Iron Maiden t-shirts. Stone actually turned Steve and I on to Alice Cooper, which we were totally unfamiliar with and I have to thank him eternally for that. But with Green River, we were really into following what Black Flag was doing, which at that point was around the time of *My War*. They were slowing down and I was buying some of the records that I had sold when I got into punk rock. Like I had to go find that Sweet record again, y'know, and Aerosmith. So we were kind of slowing down and getting heavier and trying out some new things."

— Mark Arm, Mr. Epp, Mudhoney, Green River

FELLOWS

DEC 84 #1 WEAR MONTHLY

STIMBO SANGSTER LIVES

WHAT'S INSIDE:
* **FELLOW** of the **MONTH**

Yvonne's FUN FACTS

the **POPLLAMA STORY**

YOUNG FRESH FRIENDS

Popllama HALLOWEEN

splab

and more...

THE BELUGA!!

Princetons Amp

autographed especially for "YOU"

Scott McCaughey

With a sound that drew as much from the Monkees and '60s teen party rock as it did from punk, the Young Fresh Fellows created pop gems for the underground scene, starting with their 1984 debut *The Fabulous Sounds of the Pacific Northwest*. The first issue of *Fellows Wear Monthly* was a tongue-in-cheek mouthpiece for the band, with band bios and articles on fellow Popllama Records bands, the Squirrels and Fastbacks. Over the next few years, the Fellows' good-humored, addictive tunes (mostly written by vocalist/guitarist Scott McCaughey) would attract a cult following and secure them a deal with Los Angeles indie label Frontier Records.

Their 1987 album *The Men Who Loved Music*, considered one of the band's greatest albums, was a college radio hit. Led by the McCaughey-penned "Amy Grant," it manages to gently mock the Christian Contemporary artist and imply a secret affection for Barry White, all set to a wah-wah funk groove laid down by bassist Jim Sangster, guitarist Chuck Carroll, and drummer Tad Huchinson. The Fellows and PopLlama labelmates the Fastbacks (whose guitarist Kurt Bloch would join the Fellows in 1988), Flop, the Posies, the Squirrels, Pure Joy, and the Presidents of the United States of America represented an alternative vision for Seattle music – one in which pop ruled.

FELLOWS WEAR MONTHLY, #1, DECEMBER 1984

FELLOWS WEAR MONTHLY, #2

recording studio, and I'll record it if you let me put it out on my label.' And we said, 'OK, whatever.' So he somehow got the addresses of like 30 radio stations across the country and did a promotional mailing, and we started getting mail. A month later we got a playlist from the college station in Bloomington, Indiana and our record was number one. We're just like, 'This is insane.' All of a sudden we realized people like this stuff. There was no reason for them to play it except for the fact that they got it and they dug it. So we started thinking maybe this is something we could actually do. And I think somehow that happened because we were in Seattle, and because we didn't care. Whereas everybody in California is kind of trying to make it, y'know, and do something really serious. And we were just screwing around."
— Scott McCaughey, Young Fresh Fellows, Minus 5

"The reaction to the first album was insane. Conrad Uno, who runs Egg Studios and PopLlama, when he heard we were going to make a record, he said, 'Well, I've got a

"The Young Fresh Fellows were probably as big of an influence on the Posies as any band could be. I remember seeing them in Bellingham at a place called the Viking Union Lounge at the college and it was the one show I think actually made me want to do what they were doing. The place was packed, they rocked, things got smashed, people were having a great time. That's definitely the show that really turned me on to wanting to do it."
— Jon Auer, the Posies

```
18.00  GAS
20.00  GAS
 6.00  Belt
20.00  GAS
29.50  MIRROR
 3.90  OHIO toll
 1.00  Ill toll
30.00  ALLOWANCES
128.40
129.00
173.00  - left over
282.00  - left with
-25.00  GAS
258 00
```

```
       245
       153
       398
      - 30    ALLOWANCE
       368
        10   GAS
        20   GAS
        25   tension
         4   tolls
        51   BATT
         9   tools
        20   GAS + oil
        12   GAS
        24   booze
        12  - OXY + BRAZ.
         2  - Muff.
```

In the early and mid-1980s there were very few formal venues willing to book punk bands. Groups like Hüsker Dü toured incessantly, to get their music out to a wider audience. Along with Black Flag, D.O.A., and others, they helped create a widespread underground music network across the US. This infrastructure contributed greatly to the spread of independent music in the 1980s. As this expense sheet shows, the band survived on a shoestring budget, doing all the booking, touring, and promoting themselves, in keeping with their DIY ethos. Most of the expenses listed here are directly related to the band's van, which covered thousands of miles, criss-crossing the nation on tour. After being cramped together for weeks on end, along with their equipment, and having only each night's gig for a respite, it's not surprising to see they set aside some cash for booze.

Hüsker Dü brought their increasingly melodic songs to towns across America, and eventually attracted the interest of major record labels. Warner Bros. released the band's final two albums, 1986's *Candy Apple Grey* and 1987's *Warehouse: Songs and Stories*, making the Hüskers and their Minneapolis compadres the Replacements the first bands to jump from the underground to the mainstream. A new day was rising, and the traditional record industry was watching.

HÜSKER DÜ TOUR EXPENSE SHEET, CA. 1984

"The Hüskers asked us to go on tour and we said, 'Yeah, sure.' We did thirty-one shows in thirty days, starting in Seattle, and wound up in Cleveland or something. We did the whole country in a month and that really taught us what it's all about. Made you realize that how much work it really can be."

— Karl Mueller, Soul Asylum

"As far as going out there and really hitting the road, I think Hüsker Dü were the first in the area, and I think that the Replacements were inspired by that. They wanted to get out of town. They didn't want to just be local heroes and so they started hitting the road as well — and often in those days we were doing it on the coat tails of Hüsker Dü. I'm sure the first time the Replacements went to Chicago we went as an opener for Hüsker Dü."

— Peter Jesperson, Replacements manager, Twin/Tone Records founder

"First show I ever saw was Dead Kennedys with Hüsker Dü when they were doing *Land Speed Record* and Dead Kennedys were doing *Fresh Fruit for Rotting Vegetables*, so it was their first show in Seattle that I know of. Hüsker Dü were just totally mind blowing. I went back to school the next day and told everyone."

— BEN SHEPHERD, SOUNDGARDEN

seattle
SCENE
found
DEAD

This poster was posted on telephone poles in Seattle in 1984, lamenting the lack of municipal support for local music. At that time, the Seattle punk scene was small, underground, and losing all-ages clubs and options for performance space. The early 1980s had been a relatively vibrant time for music in Seattle with various new wave, punk, and heavy metal acts vying for attention at numerous, if short-lived, clubs around Seattle. In 1984, the Metropolis, along with two other all-ages clubs, operated within blocks of one another, providing ample opportunity for kids to see live shows.

By the end of the year, all had shut their doors. A number of clubs closed due to fire code breaches and riots that erupted after police tried to intervene at shows. This left few clubs featuring original underground music. A benefit group was formed to raise awareness of the withering nightlife called S.O.S., for "Save Our Scene." The all-ages scene in Seattle was further hampered in 1985 with the Teen Dance Ordinance, which effectively made it impossible to run an all-ages venue. Bands then turned to bars for gigs, but most placed little value on underground music. In a few years, though, as bands such as Soundgarden and Green River began to get popular, the tide began to change, ushering in the beginning of a new musical era.

SEATTLE SCENE FOUND DEAD, 1984

"FINAL NOTICE. As you probably know by now the Met is closing down in March, mainly because this type of place and the behavior of some of its patrons aren't tolerated in this part of town. When a small minority of dumb shits trash cars, buildings, break windows and bottles, it ruins the fun for everybody. After the closure, we will be promoting other big shows, the first being GBH at the Norway Center on March 16. If trouble occurs at this show, inside or out, there won't be any more shows. We plan on bringing bands like BLACK FLAG, DEAD KENNEDYS, MINUTEMEN, & SOCIAL DISTORTION, among others. So, you can really help us out in our effort to promote good music here. Don't trash, don't write graffiti, don't break bottles, don't fight, don't sneak in, and try not to fuck up. Do have fun and enjoy the music! And thanks for your cooperation and support... THE MET"

— flyer posted at the Metropolis, 1984

"That particular summer was totally dead in Seattle. Clubs kept getting closed down and touring bands weren't coming to Seattle — it was too small of a market. What music existed was a sort of power-pop bar band sound that was popularized by the like of the Rangehoods and bands of that nature. It wasn't a very big scene in the first place, but it really felt 'over.' Bands like Malfunkshun and Silly Killers and Green River and Feast and Beat Happening played basements and parties and small one-night clubs that closed immediately. The people who went to these early shows were a handful of little kids that were so deep underground that the older scene didn't even notice them (except to sneer at them). They were 'kid shows' for the street kids and skate teams. A couple of years later these bands really took off and became the famous bands we all know now. This poster was a reaction to a very brief calm before the storm, y'know? And that storm was a hurricane. It's terrifically ironic, now."

— Art Chantry, graphic designer

"I loved 1984. For me the scene was still thriving, beer was still available, girls were still cute, and my skate still worked. It was the year I got a brand new punker jacket, and got my teeth knocked in by some jocks in front of the Metropolis — what's not to love? Was this the year the U-Men were kicking ass? Summer of LSD? Either way I don't even remember seeing this flyer. I just wanted to dance."

— Lance Mercer, photographer

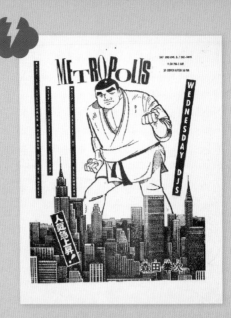

GUN CLUB, U-Men, at the Metropolis, Seattle, June 24, 1983. Poster by John Bigley; WEDNESDAY DJS AT THE METROPOLIS: Helene Silverman and Bob Newman, September 14, 1983 + Bruce Pavitt, September 21 + Norman Batley, September 28. Poster by Helene Silverman; THE REPLACEMENTS, the Accüsed, 10 Minute Warning, at the Metropolis, Seattle, November 30, 1983; ACCÜSED, Mr. Epp, U-Men, Fastbacks, at the Metropolis, Seattle, December 9, 1983; BUTTHOLE SURFERS, Ten Minute

Warning, Deranged Diction, Extreme Hate, at the Metropolis, Seattle, December 16, 1983. Poster by Hugo Piottin; TALES OF TERROR, Bundle of Hiss, March of Crimes, at the Metropolis, January 20, 1984. Poster by Tony Godbehere; THE CRAMPS, U-Men, at the Metropolis, Seattle, January 24, 1984; YOUNG PIONEERS, Wimps, John Foster, Rich Jenson, Beat Happening, Supreme Cool Beings, Legion of Honor, at the Metropolis, Seattle, January 15, 1984

maxell LN 60

A DATE 4 . 24 . 85   B DATE New : Temporal

LN **Sound Garden** 4-Track Demo   maxell

A 6 Songs for Bruce   B Zen Deity Speaks

1. I Think I'm Sinking
2. Bury My Head in Sand
3. Tears to Forget   — Hiro sings This.
4. The Storm   — Extra Added Bonus Song
5. Incessant Mace   From Chris.
6. In Vention
7. out of my Skin

Hiro Yamamoto — Bass   Sound Garden
Vocals on 3.   Recorded in our Basement
Kim Thayil — Guitar   Correspondence:
Chris Cornell — Vocals   307 N. 40th #101
+ Drums, All Instruments   Seattle, WA. 98103
on special Added Feature   632-4098 ; 789-5040
#4 By Chris.

A All songs © Sound   B Recorded April, 1985
        Garden   "It coulda' been better"

In April 1985, Sound Garden (soon to be Soundgarden) recorded this demo, *6 Songs for Bruce*, which included songs that would later appear in finished form on the 1987 EP, *Screaming Life* ("Tears to Forget") and the 1988 album, *Ultramega OK* ("Incessant Mace"). "Bruce" was Bruce Pavitt, who re-imagined his *Sub Pop* zine as a newspaper column. He eventually turned into a full-fledged record label, with the help of Soundgarden's guitarist Kim Thayil and bassist Hiro Yamamoto, who grew up with Pavitt in Park Forest, Illinois. Along with vocalist/drummer Chris Cornell, the band was soon playing around Seattle, gaining popularity in the punk crowd with their Black Sabbath-inspired, riff-heavy songs. In order for Cornell to focus solely on vocals, the band added Scott Sundquist on drums, who himself was replaced in 1986 by Skin Yard's Matt Cameron.

Jonathan Poneman, who at the time was a DJ for KCMU, Seattle's influential commercial-free public radio station, was such a fan of Soundgarden that he offered to help pay for the band to release an album. Kim Thayil, aware of Bruce's label plans, brought the two together, turning Pavitt's dream into a reality. In 1987, the nascent Sub Pop Records released Soundgarden's first single, "Hunted Down" / "Nothing to Say," and defined the new Seattle Sound.

SOUNDGARDEN 4-TRACK DEMO, APRIL 1985

"Everyone was really surprised at how immediately everything clicked. There was a creative environment that was encouraging to all of us. We all liked the material that was coming out and there was room for each of us to express ourselves musically. And so a couple times a week we'd grab a twelve pack of beer, head over to Hiro and Chris's house, and go up in the attic and play. Eventually we got a gig. There was a band called Vexed, who was opening up for a band from New York called Three Teens Kill Four. And Vexed couldn't do the gig, and they recommended these friends of theirs who only played in their attic. And that was Hiro and Chris and I."

— Kim Thayil, Soundgarden

"The first time I saw Soundgarden, I was like, 'Whoa! This is BIG.' It's filling the room. That was back between '84 and '86 when Chris played drums and sang and Hiro did a lot of singing or screaming too. But there was just something about them — these guys are really good, they're not punk rock, and they're not heavy metal, they're not Barbie metal at all, they're just their own thing. We'd all talk together after the show about who was the best of the night, and we all agreed, that first time we saw them, that Soundgarden blew everyone away."

— Ben Shepherd, Soundgarden

During the early 1980s, heavy metal in the Seattle area had a loyal following. The majority of metal bands played in the Eastside suburbs of Seattle across Lake Washington. Roller rinks were popular venues, particularly the Lake Hills Roller Rink in Bellevue, WA. A man named Craig Cooke began booking metal bands at Lake Hills as well as at nine other rinks in the area. The scene eventually died out in the mid-1980s, due to the dwindling interest in roller skating.

Shadow was one of a number of bands to play the roller rink scene at shows like the one advertised here in Lynnwood, a suburb north of Seattle. The band comprised teenagers Mike McCready, Dan Newcomb, Rob Webber, and the Friel brothers, Rick and Chris, all of whom went to Seattle's Roosevelt High School. Shadow was heavily influenced by Kiss, Def Leppard and Iron Maiden, and they soon gained notoriety in the local metal scene. In 1986, the band moved to Los Angeles, with little success. They moved back to Seattle in 1988 and called it quits. Within a few years, McCready would be invited by friend Stone Gossard to play music with him and fellow ex-Mother Love Bone member Jeff Ament in a group that quickly transformed into Temple of the Dog and paved the way for Pearl Jam.

SHADOW AT ROLL-A-WAY SKATE CENTER, LYNNWOOD, WA, JULY 16, 1985

"We played all over, y'know — they had these things called Metalfests. And we would play opening up for Culprit, opening up for TKO. And then we did our own shows occasionally. That went on for a good while, probably three years. We actually played one show and Green River opened up for us. That was our last show as a five piece. Then Rob left and went to LA, and Danny hung on for a little while, but he kind of lost interest and went back to college. Rick and Chris and I went on for another good three, four years. We actually made the huge jump of moving down to Los Angeles to try to make it, because we couldn't make it up here at the time, because the Seattle scene at the time — y'know, like Green River and all that was just starting to happen. There still wasn't anywhere to play."

— Mike McCready, Shadow, Mad Season, Pearl Jam

"Other than Culprit, there was Mace, which became eventually Queensrÿche. We'd done several shows, predominantly in the Lake Hills area 'cause we were Eastside guys. Shadow was another one — all those guys used to hang around the band quite a bit."

— Brad Sinsel, TKO

"There was a ton of talent out here, so I think everybody inspired each other musically. The musicians and the kids were partying and they just loved what they were hearing. You could go up to Lake Hills for a couple of bucks and go

see some great bands, and then not have to worry about alcohol and things like that because in Seattle that's where the scene was, you had to be 21."

— Bud Burrill, Culprit

This Sweda Model Q cash register was used at Minneapolis' premier live music venue, the First Avenue, during the 1980s. The building was constructed in the 1930s as a Greyhound bus station, and in the early 1970s, became a live music venue called Uncle Sam's, later shortened to Sam's. At the beginning of 1981, it was renamed the First Avenue.

The club was essential in promoting the careers of virtually every underground band from the Twin Cities, including Hüsker Dü, the Replacements, Soul Asylum, Babes in Toyland, and many others. Prince, too, regularly played at the First Avenue, and it was featured heavily in his film, *Purple Rain*. Consisting both of a large room, known as the First Avenue, and a smaller room called the 7th Street Entry, the twin clubs became the musical epicenter for the Twin Cities, helping the scene to flourish and become one of the decade's most prominent underground music communities.

CASH REGISTER USED BY THE FIRST AVENUE CLUB, MINNEAPOLIS, EARLY – LATE 1980S

"There were no major labels, no big agencies were involved in '80, '81, '82. It was just connecting the cities with the dots. How do you get a band from the East Coast to the West Coast, and who's doin' it without the commercial radio? Your Hüsker Düs of the world were hooking up with your Minutemen and Black Flag on the West Coast, and there was your Rifle Sports hooking up with your Big Blacks in Chicago. It was like a community coming together in the music scene."

— Steve McClellan, First Avenue manager

"I got a fake ID when I was 17. I always was trying to scam my way into shows, always trying to sneak in. So whenever I did get into First Avenue through the back door or something it was real cool, y'know? I got thrown out of the Psychedelic Furs show because they found out that I was underage. Chris Osgood would take me to the Entry, and I'd have to stand off over in the corner, far away from the bar. I think the band he was in at the time was called Speed Wiener, and Hüsker Dü was opening up for them. And that was before the Hüskers turned a million miles an hour. They had this different sound. It was kind of more a Public Image-y kind of thing. I remember Bob was playin' this Mosrite guitar that I'd been lookin' at for years on the wall of the guitar store. It was this crazy purple Ventures guitar. And there it was, Bob Mould was playing it."

— Dave Pirner, Soul Asylum

DEEP SIX

GREEN RIVER
MALFUNKSHUN
THE MELVINS
SKIN YARD
SOUNDGARDEN
U-MEN

DEEP SIX

GREEN RIVER	10,000 things
THE MELVINS	scared/blessing the operation
MALFUNKSHUN	with yo' heart (not yo' hands)
SKIN YARD	throb
SOUNDGARDEN	heretic/tears to forget
MALFUNKSHUN	stars-n-you
THE MELVINS	grinding process/she waits
SKIN YARD	the birds
SOUNDGARDEN	all your lies
GREEN RIVER	your own best friend
U-MEN	they

In August and September 1985, recording engineer Chris Hanszek booked time at Ironwood Studios in Seattle to record Green River, the Melvins, Malfunkshun, Skin Yard, Soundgarden, and the U-Men – all bands that he and partner Tina Casale felt epitomized a new, grittier sound emerging from the Northwest underground scene. These tracks were released in 1986 as the seminal grunge compilation, *Deep Six*, on Hanszek and Casale's new label, C/Z Records.

After the rise of grunge, *Deep Six* became a prized collectible from the early scene. At the time of its release, though, sales were negligible, prompting Hanszek and Casale to pass on the C/Z banner (following one more release, the Melvins' 1986 debut, *Six Songs*) to Skin Yard bassist Daniel House. With House at the helm, C/Z went on to release albums by Built to Spill, the Gits, 7 Year Bitch, Silkworm, and Hammerbox, among others. Hanszek liked to record bands at Reciprocal Recording, a studio he opened with Skin Yard guitarist and future Nirvana recording engineer Jack Endino. By 1992, the new sound that *Deep Six* announced had become the *it* sound for the nation.

DEEP SIX COMPILATION, 1986

"Deep Six was cool. When that came out, I was stoked. Soundgarden was great on there. I even thought Skin Yard was good on there even though it had a saxophone."

— LANCE MERCER, PHOTOGRAPHER

"By '86, '87, a lot of the younger people that had been going to the Metropolis started playing music that was a little more metal influenced, so it was kind of a punk/metal hybrid. And, we're talking about bands like the Melvins and Soundgarden, Malfunkshun, Green River, Skin Yard, Feast, and there seemed to be a general consensus that slower, heavier music was kind of cool. I had been observing all these different regional scenes around the country, and I finally got to a point where I was like, 'Wow. There's something interesting going on in the city.' The *Deep Six* compilation came out on C/Z and documented a lot of that. And it was a very distinctive sound, so I started checking out more of these shows."

— Bruce Pavitt, Sub Pop Records

"When the *Deep Six* record was getting together, I knew that there was something going on here. We liked bands like the U-Men, and we would in our minds associate with them or Vexed or the Crypt Kicker 5 or Green River. But for all we knew the U-Men didn't know we existed, but they were a band we liked to go see live. And we felt that through part of that community we had a similar audience, friends that were like-minded."

— Kim Thayil, Soundgarden

KANE HALL

$4 AT THE DOOR
(FOR DIRECTIONS CALL 543-2985)

U of W CAMPUS

formerly "SLEZE"

ALICE 'N CHAINS

SAT.

8 PM

and introducing

DREAMER

MAY 16

KANE HALL

U of W CAMPUS

$4 AT THE DOOR
(FOR DIRECTIONS CALL 543-2985)

Layne Staley began playing in heavy metal bands around the Seattle suburb of Lynnwood in his teens. By 1985, he had graduated high school and joined the hair metal band Sleze, which changed their name a year later to Alice 'N Chains. The quartet, featuring Staley on vocals, Nick Pollock on guitar, Johnny Bacolas on bass, and James Bergstrom on drums, played glam speed metal covers and originals such as "Lip Lock Rock," "Hush, Hush," and "Ya Yeah Ya."

Staley met guitarist Jerry Cantrell at the Music Bank, a rehearsal space in Seattle, about the time that Alice 'N Chains was disbanding. The two got along well, and Staley asked Cantrell to join the funk band he was playing in, which Cantrell agreed on the condition that Staley in turn join his band Diamond Lie, which featured Mike Starr on bass and Sean Kinney on drums. By 1988, Staley joined Diamond Lie full time, which soon adopted the new moniker of Alice in Chains. By 1989, the band's dark, blues-inflected metal got the attention of Columbia Records, giving the band access to a national audience, and honing the band's unique voice as one of the top grunge bands of the 1990s.

ALICE 'N CHAINS AND DREAMER AT KANE HALL, UNIVERSITY OF WASHINGTON, SEATTLE, MAY 16, 1987

"Layne was probably my favorite singer. He just had this incredible tone and timber to his voice, even when he spoke. He was just a unique guy and his voice is just one of those voices of a generation that just took you to a different place when you heard him, y'know? They say the eyes are the window of the soul — I think with Layne it was his voice. I mean, you could just hear every bit of emotion in that guy's voice. It was an amazing vocal power. Seriously. It got down to your bone marrow. That guy was just such a special man all around."

— Mike Inez, Alice in Chains

"A buddy of mine, who played with Layne in an earlier version of Alice in Chains, invited me up to a party in Alki that Owen Wright and Tim Wolfe from Mistrust were having. I got to know Layne there and he was just really cool, and we really hit it off."

— Jerry Cantrell, Alice in Chains

ALICE 'N CHAINS, VARIANT CAUSE, AND RUFF TOIZ AT THE BACKSTAGE, SEATTLE, AUGUST 5, 1987

Chicago's Big Black played the final show of their career at the Georgetown Steamplant, an imposing concrete building that provided power to Seattle in the early 20th century. Its giant steam turbines and monolithic architecture create an imposing sense of industrial manufacture – a setting that was perfect for Big Black's abrasive guitar and drum machine-driven proto-industrial rock.

U-Men manager and former Rosco Louie / Graven Image gallery owner Larry Reid worked some bureaucratic magic, convincing the city and the Boeing Company to let him use the space for the event. Poet Steven Jesse Bernstein, a mainstay of the scene, opened and former Blackouts keyboardist Roland Barker set the tone with industrial atmospherics. A crowd of Northwest scenesters, including a young Kurt Cobain, attended. Big Black ended the show by smashing their instruments and igniting a huge brick of firecrackers – an apt dénouement for one of the most influential bands of the '80s underground. Big Black's influence stemmed from the uncompromising DIY ethic of founder Steve Albini, who also was quickly becoming one of the most sought-after recording engineers, creating stark, honest recordings with Big Black, Slint, Pixies, Urge Overkill, Breeders, TAD, Fugazi, Shellac, and Nirvana.

BIG BLACK, ROLAND BARKER, AND JESSE BERNSTEIN, AT THE GEORGETOWN STEAMPLANT, SEATTLE, AUGUST 9, 1987. POSTER BY LARRY REID AND SUSAN PURVES

"The last Big Black show was set up in Seattle by a guy named Larry Reid. Somehow or another he talked the Boeing company into letting us use a disused power generating facility as a venue, and it was on Boeing field. I cannot imagine something like that happening now with all the blockades and security and that kind of stuff. But he convinced them that this would be a good idea and so there was a stage constructed and a PA assembled and we played the show. There were planes taking off over our heads throughout the show. It was a great environment — there were these giant tools everywhere, like you'd see a wrench just leaning up against the wall and the wrench was six feet long, it would take three people to lift it. Like a circuit breaker the size of a Volkswagen, that kind of thing. It was really visually arresting."

— Steve Albini, Big Black

"The final Big Black performance was really a celebration of the contributions of Big Black and Steve Albini, not just in the music world but in the world of DIY self-production. Many of the musicians that would later go on to create the Seattle sound and really popularize punk rock on a broad level were there and at the end of the show Big Black, as is their wont, blew up a brick of like 4,000 firecrackers that I got them, smashed their instruments in just this cacophony of insanity. Bruce Pavitt wrote a review of that show in his *Rocket* column and I believe the entire review consisted of 'Big Black at the Georgetown Steamplant was the best show ever.' In very large type. I thought it was very fitting, this 20-word review of what was a very phenomenal show that I believe helped to inspire things that would happen later in the Northwest."

— Larry Reid, curator/punk promoter/U-Men manager

27 REASONS WHY WASHINGTON STATE IS A COOL PLACE TO LIVE

A.D.R.D. Talk is Cheap demo
ACCUSED More Fun Than an Open Casket Funeral LP (Combat)
BEAT HAPPENING Look Around 45 (K)
BEERGARDEN Swallow the Green Room demo
BUNDLE OF HISS Push demo
CAT BUTT Journey to the Center of Cat Butt demo
CHEMISTRY SET Fields demo
THE FASTBACKS and his Orchestra LP (Popllama)
FEAST cassette box
GIRL TROUBLE Tarantula 45 (K)
THE GO TEAM Your Pretty Guitar cassette
GREEN PAJAMAS Book of Hours LP (Green Monkey)
GREEN RIVER Dry as a Bone EP (Sub Pop)
H-HOUR Production demo
MELVINS Gluey Porch Treatment LP (Alchemy)
MY EYE SO Much Going On 45 (C/Z)
ROOM 9 VOICES. . .On A Summer's Day LP (C'est La Mort)
S.G.M. Strunk cassette
SCREAMING TREES Even If and Especially When LP (SST)
64 SPIDERS cassette
SOUNDGARDEN Screaming Life EP (Sub Pop)
SWALLOW Shooting Dope Gives Me a Boner demo
TAD Daisy demo
THE THROWN UPS Smiling Panties 45 (Amphebian Reptile)
U-MEN Solid Action 45 (Black Label)
WALKABOUTS Psyclone 45 (Necessity)
YOUNG FRESH FELLOWS The Men Who Loved Music LP
(Frontier)

Bruce Pavitt moved to Seattle in 1983, transitioning his Olympia, WA fanzine into a column in *The Rocket* dedicated to under-represented music scenes across America. In this column, Pavitt hypes the Northwest scene, giving 27 reasons for becoming a Northwest music locavore. Besides promoting releases from established Northwest greats such as the Fastbacks, Accüsed, Beat Happening, Girl Trouble, the Melvins, Green River, Room 9, U-Men, Screaming Trees, Young Fresh Fellows, and Soundgarden, Pavitt also lists several demos from bands that would soon have full-fledged releases on his Sub Pop Records label. At the time, Pavitt worked, oddly enough, at elevator music giant Muzak with Mark Arm (Mudhoney), Tad Doyle (TAD), Chris Pugh (Swallow), Tom Mick (Feast), Grant Eckman (Walkabouts), and others. It's hard to imagine some of the heaviest music from the Pacific Northwest originating from the slumberland of Muzak, but the workspace functioned as a vital melting pot – an exchange of ideas and connections, and a test bed for the growing Seattle scene.

SUB POP: 27 REASONS WHY WASHINGTON STATE IS A COOL PLACE TO LIVE, CA. 1987. DESIGN BY ASHLEIGH TALBOT

"It was just one of those situations where somebody gets a job somewhere and they start inviting their friends because the benefits are good and you've got health insurance and the pay's not too bad, and you can listen to whatever music you want. And in a lot of ways, it helped to solidify the scene in that you had a group of people who were working together side by side, every day, for months at a time, developing a certain camaraderie, a certain trust, a certain understanding of each other. I remember when Mark came into Muzak with a demo tape of his new band, Mudhoney. He played me 'Touch Me I'm Sick,' and I thought, 'This is a really good song.' Tad told me that he was working on some demos, and he played me a demo called 'Daisy' which eventually became one of the first 45s out of Sub Pop, along with 'Touch Me I'm Sick.' So in essence, because we were working together, Muzak served as almost a de facto office space for the label before it really decided to launch. Very ironic, I must say."

– Bruce Pavitt, Sub Pop Records

"Reading Bruce Pavitt's Sub Pop column in *The Rocket* was a great way for someone who felt as culturally deprived as I (living in my little backwards farming community of Ellensburg) to feel slightly enlightened or 'in the know' without having to spend all the money or do all the trial-and-error research that it would require to settle on just what the best releases of the month were."

– Mark Pickerel, Screaming Trees, Truly

"Bruce Pavitt was writing a guest column in *The Rocket* magazine called Sub Pop. It was in the back, and was just reviews of interesting indie records that had come out, not necessarily from the Northwest. John Poneman was working at KCMU and also working freelance as a show promoter. I was already working with a lot of the bands who ended up on Sub Pop. In fact, some of the recordings were made before there was a Sub Pop. I was making recordings for these people, and Bruce and Jon put their heads together and said, 'Well you know, there's these recordings being made. Maybe some people would buy these. Why don't we start a record label and we can put out a Green River record, maybe put out a Soundgarden record, see if anybody cares.' And that's how things started."

– Jack Endino, record engineer/producer/musician

The K cassette revolution is exploding the teenage underground into passionate revolt against the corporate ogre.
Send for our free newsletter: K Box 7154 Olympia, Wash. 98507 U.S.A.

THE GO TEAM
YOUR PRETTY GUITAR
It's autumn. There are red leaves outside and everybody's playing football, except Steve and Calvin. They are playing their guitars. These ten minutes of clarity, grace and charm is the result.

SOME VELVET SIDEWALK
From Playground 'til Now
Here are the early days fo punk rock curled up in a fetal position, screaming in agony and whispering sweet nothings in your ear.

SUPREME COOL BEINGS
Survival of the Coolest
The legendary trio of Gary, Heather and Doug produce a timeless sound on this eight song classic of the pop underground.

BEAT HAPPENING
THREE TEA BREAKFAST
Five songs recorded in various Tokyo apartments. Short and Sweet.

PELL MELL
for years we stood clear
as one thing
A monster 90 minute mix of live and studio recordings by this stalwart instrumental combo. Wait no more.

let's Sea
Our third international compilation of rockin' pop of the most faith restoring variety. Young Pioneers, Danger Bunny, Screaming Trees, Cannanes, Steve Fisk, BEAT HAPPENING, the Few, Mecca Normal, White Sisters, Half Japanese, Streator, Fastbacks, Velvet Monkeys, Manta-Men, Snake Pit, Lighthouse Keepers.

The Olympia scene in the mid-1980s came to life in Evergreen State College dorms, house parties and rental halls, as well as the town's main punk venue, the Tropicana, and on KAOS-FM. A prime engine for the scene was Calvin Johnson's K Records, which documented the scene, with cassettes by the Supreme Cool Beings, Rich Jensen, John Foster's Pop Philosophers, the Young Pioneers, and his own Beat Happening. By 1984, he released K's first vinyl record, Beat Happening's "Our Secret" / "What's Important," which epitomized the flavor of the Olympia scene – prioritizing honest emotion and audience connection over musical virtuosity.

This point-of-sale display was used to showcase K Records cassette releases by the Go Team, Some Velvet Sidewalk, Beat Happening, Supreme Cool Beings, Pell Mell, and others. The cassette format focus was a clarion call for DIY – anyone with desire and a tape recorder could be in on the action. As stated on the display, "The K cassette revolution is exploding the teenage underground into passionate revolt against the corporate ogre." This message would serve to spiritually link the Olympia scene with the like-minded across the globe, creating what Johnson called the International Pop Underground.

K RECORDS CASSETTE POINT-OF-SALE DISPLAY, CA. 1987

"At that time there was a band called the Supreme Cool Beings. They played a lot of parties and things here in town. They recorded some songs and we decided to make a cassette and put it out. I was involved in music in Olympia since I was a teenager, and it just seemed a natural progression from working at KAOS, the radio station, and writing for magazines and playing in bands and it just seemed like starting a record label was just the same thing."

— Calvin Johnson, K Records

"We got down to Olympia in the winter of '86 and played GESSCO, which was being operated as a forum for music and all sorts of events. And that's where I met Calvin Johnson of K Records. We'd already put out our first album and they had put out Beat Happening on K, and we traded records. And I put mine under the seat of the bus, and it was summer. We got back home and there's this weird-looking record with a cat on it in a rocket ship, and okay, let's give this a spin. And of course it's all warped and weird, and I'm like, 'What...what... what is this?' Sort of like this light, kind of dum-de-dum-dum sort of stuff, and we're like this real hard-edge, political punk band, right? I still listen to that record a lot, but at that point, the Beat Happening sensibility was a bit odd. But it was interesting to eventually find that we all had common ground."

— Jean Smith, Mecca Normal

"In Olympia, Calvin Johnson, who was a DJ at KAOS, started a group called Beat Happening and they released their first 45 on K called 'Our Secret.' It was actually produced by Greg Sage of the Wipers who came up from Portland, and it was recorded in a tiny closet right next to the KAOS office. This is how scenes breed, intermingle and move forward. You had the best producer from Portland, coming up, hanging out at KAOS and recording one of the DJs at KAOS who later went on to become a rock personality himself."

— Bruce Pavitt, Sub Pop Records

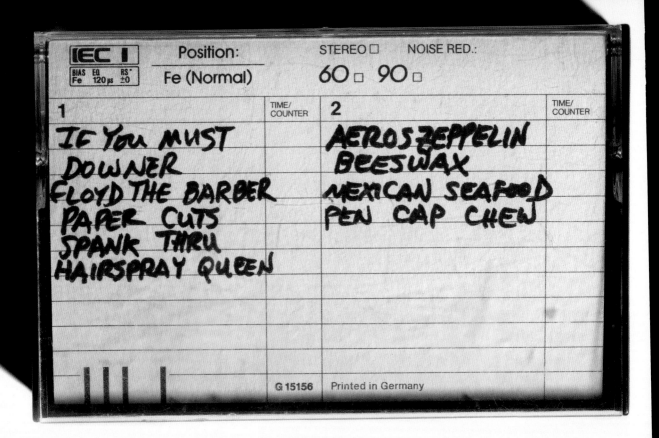

IEC I	Position:	STEREO ☐	NOISE RED.:
BIAS EQ RS* Fe 120 µs ±0	Fe (Normal)	60 ☐ 90 ☐	

1	TIME/ COUNTER	2	TIME/ COUNTER
IF YOU MUST		AEROS ZEPPELIN	
DOWNER		BEESWAX	
FLOYD THE BARBER		MEXICAN SEAFOOD	
PAPER CUTS		PEN CAP CHEW	
SPANK THRU			
HAIRSPRAY QUEEN			
	G 15156	Printed in Germany	

BASF   IH-FT

On January 23, 1988, Kurt Cobain, Krist Novoselic, and Dale Crover drove from Aberdeen to Seattle to record their first demo at Reciprocal Recording. The band had been playing under various names, none of which was yet "Nirvana" (Endino's tapes list them as "Kurt Kovain [sic] and Co."). The band was currently without a drummer, prompting Kurt to ask his friend Dale Crover of the Melvins to sit in on the sessions.

The demo cassette includes nine-and-a-half songs. "Floyd the Barber" and "Paper Cuts" were later remixed and included on Nirvana's 1989 debut, *Bleach*. The final track, "Pen Cap Chew," is incomplete because the tape ran out during the session and the group couldn't afford another reel. Jack Endino recorded and mixed the songs that day for a fee of $152.44. That evening, they drove down to Tacoma's Community World Theater and played the same set live. Before they left Seattle, Endino asked if he could make a copy for some friends – this cassette he gave a few months later to fellow Skin Yard member and C/Z Records owner Daniel House. Cobain sent copies to dozens of indie labels, but nothing happened until Endino passed the demo on to Jonathan Poneman of Sub Pop Records, who liked the songs and began pursuing the band in earnest.

NIRVANA'S FIRST DEMO RECORDING, HAND-LETTERED BY JACK ENDINO, CA. JANUARY 1988

"We rode up to Seattle in this old 1960s Chevy truck with like a camper on the back that had a woodstove in it. This dude, Dwight Covey, it was his rig. He was nice enough to drive us up and drive all our gear. And then, we went to Reciprocal Studio there in Fremont. We had heard about this person, Jack Endino. He did the Green River tape. Kurt at the time was living in Olympia and he had a job in the evenings cleaning dentists' offices and doctors' offices. He saved up his money and that's how we paid for the recording. We had rehearsed a lot and were disciplined and we busted it out. And I guess it fell in the hands of Jonathan Poneman. And that was all through Jack. He said, 'Hey, you should check out this band.'"

– Krist Novoselic, Nirvana

"Kurt, he didn't have a band name, he just said, 'Well, I want to come in and just record some songs. You know, we don't have much money, we just need to, we want to book like one afternoon and just see what we get done.' So they came up January 23 of 1988 and recorded. In one afternoon, we recorded 10 songs and mixed them. I think we, you know, they probably showed up at noon, by 3 o'clock we were done recording, and then you know, by 5 o'clock I had mixed 10 songs and they were out the door."

– Jack Endino, recording engineer/producer/musician

In the early 1990s, Seattle became a household name across the nation as Nirvana, Pearl Jam, Alice in Chains, Soundgarden, and others began climbing up the charts. "The Seattle Sound" was partially accurate, as there was a thriving scene in town that produced many of the most successful bands, but it wasn't the entirety of what was happening in the Pacific Northwest. Urban centers in the Northwest are far-flung from one another. As a result, many towns developed their own sustainable scenes. Yet these various musical loci were all in communication, all interacting and influencing one another. This poster from 1988 features the Screaming Trees, from Ellensburg, a small town 110 miles east of Seattle on the other side of the Cascade Mountains. Through record producer Steve Fisk, the Trees developed a relationship with Olympia's Beat Happening. Both bands were fans of Girl Trouble from Tacoma, 40 minutes south of Seattle. These three bands, which held similar ideals about independent music, but sounded nothing alike, were playing shows together in Mt. Vernon and Bellingham, more than an hour north of Seattle, close to the Canadian border. The interconnection among these disparate scenes contributed greatly to the vibrancy of the region.

SCREAMING TREES, GIRL TROUBLE, BEAT HAPPENING, AT EAGLES HALL, BELLINGHAM, WA, FEBRUARY 5, 1988 AND AT SKAGIT VALLEY COLLEGE CAFETERIA, MOUNT VERNON, WA, FEBRUARY 6

"I do believe in regional sounds and characteristics of regional music, and I think that there may be some characteristics that are shared by musicians or by music that comes out of an area. And I think that a lot of those characteristics are overlapping. But overall it feels like a cohesive sound. But in terms of describing those characteristics, I wouldn't know where to begin. If you were to talk about New Orleans blues versus Memphis blues, I would feel uncomfortable trying to describe the difference, although you can feel the difference."

— Calvin Johnson, K Records, Beat Happening

"The way culture works is like a pinball machine. It's like those chrome balls get stuck in a bumper and do that for awhile and then bust loose. Well that has always kind of been the Portland, Tacoma, Seattle axis. The pinballs get caught in bumpers and they bounce back and forth and become influential. For a while Olympia's influencing Tacoma and Tacoma ends up becoming important in Portland and bang, Seattle."

— Art Chantry, graphic designer

"I think most of the music from the Northwest is from people that grew up here. Most of the people doing interesting music in Olympia grew up in Olympia. The Melvins grew up in Aberdeen. They pretty much stayed there for a really long time. That's where they were working. Screaming Trees lived in Ellensburg for years and years and years before they left there. I see that in Bellingham, in Anacortes, and a lot of the places around the northwest. Tacoma. Where people are making really interesting music, they're doing it in their home."

— Calvin Johnson, K Records, Beat Happening

LEGGO MY EGO PRESENTS......
NIRVANA
ALSO KNOWN AS....
SKID ROW, TED ED FRED, PEN CAP CHEW, BLISS
BRING CANS OF FOOD AND YE'S FEE SHALL BE RE-DUCED
HEY KIDS! Dont Buy A GRAM This week-end, Come see a Revelation IN PROGRESS, it will be A Gosh DARN...
HEALING EXPLOSION.
WITH
LUSH
AND OTHER SPECIAL GUESTS YET TO BE ANNOUNCED
$5
SAT. MAR. 19
So. 56th & M St TACOMA
COMMUNITY WORLD THEATRE

Kurt Cobain, Krist Novoselic, and new drummer Dave Foster played their first show as Nirvana, with Olympia's Lush (featuring future Kill Rock Stars label head Slim Moon) at Tacoma's Community World Theatre on March 19, 1988. The band had been playing under various names, including Skid Row, Ted Ed Fred, Pen Chap Chew, and Bliss. By pure chance or divine fate, the name Nirvana was chosen, and the band never looked back.

The Community World Theatre was an all-ages venue opened by Tacoma scenester and Girl Trouble compatriot Jim May. Like many other small, vital venues that came and went in the region, it was only open for a short time, from early 1987 to mid-1988. Nonetheless, it became a vibrant venue for local underground music. Tacoma was halfway between Seattle and Olympia, so the Community World Theatre became a focal point for bands from those three cities and throughout Washington. It was a central spot where various regional scenes mixed and interacted.

NIRVANA AND LUSH AT THE COMMUNITY WORLD THEATRE, TACOMA, WA, MARCH 19, 1988
POSTER BY KURT COBAIN

"The Community World Theatre was in Tacoma, and that was Jim May and it was formerly a union hall. It was for union members and their families to socialize, and then it fell into disrepair, and y'know, the times changed and it seems like a punk club is always the last stop — what's the last thing you can do with it? Let's make it into a rock club. It was a big theater, it had a stage and seats and bands played there all the time."

— Krist Novoselic, Nirvana

"Tic Dolly Row was originally the Magnet Men, and that was Chad Channing's band, and they just asked me to sing for them which to me was a chance to be weird, so I did that. And we were playing a show at the Community World Theatre with Malfunkshun and this band called Bliss that wound up being called Nirvana. I hadn't seen Krist Novoselic since the March of Crimes and Melvins days. Krist was always on the sidelines, 'cause he was friends with all the guys in the Melvins, and so we get to the show and we're all loading in and stuff and there's really tall Krist and I go, 'Whoa, man! What's goin' on?' He's like, 'Dude, I'm playing in a band tonight, and we were wondering if your drummer would let us use his drum set.' And I was like, 'Yeah, his name is Chad, he's right over there. Just go ask him, I'm sure he'll let you.' So that's how they met Chad."

— Ben Shepherd, Soundgarden

"Jimmy May had taken over an old porno theater and opened the Community World Theatre in Tacoma, but I don't think he did anything to it. Like, I don't think he cleaned it out or anything. [laughs] That place was weird. And I just remember Kurt had these satin pants on, which was really, really funny. They were so sort of David Bowie, like 1974 or something."

— Alice Wheeler, photographer

By 1988, Soundgarden was becoming increasingly popular outside of Seattle. They had moved from Sub Pop to SST, which at the time was the pinnacle of indie achievement. In October 1988, SST released the band's debut full-length, *Ultramega OK*, which raised their profile further. Soundgarden commenced on a US tour, packing their equipment into this 1986 Chevy Beauville van. By the end of 1988, they signed to A&M – the first grunge band to sign to a major label – and began recording *Louder Than Love*, which was released in September 1989.

With A&M's backing, the Beauville was left in Seattle and Soundgarden climbed into tour buses. The *Louder Than Love* tour, while more comfortable, was a tumultuous time – original bassist Hiro Yamamoto quit and went back to college. He was replaced by Jason Everman, who had just left Nirvana as their second guitarist. Everman was let go at the end of the tour, replaced by Ben Shepherd. But the biggest blow came on March 19, 1990, the day Soundgarden returned from the *Louder Than Love* tour: vocalist Chris Cornell's roommate, Mother Love Bone frontman Andrew Wood, died of a heroin overdose. Soundgarden was bigger than they ever had been, but the Seattle scene had been dealt a huge blow.

1986 CHEVROLET BEAUVILLE VAN, USED BY SOUNDGARDEN 1988 – 1990. GIFT OF KIM THAYIL

"We knew we needed a van that was bigger to haul more gear, and that perhaps had working air conditioning and windows. And so we found this '86 Beauville in early '88. It was a good deal, so we bought it and Hiro built a futon frame in the back for sleeping. Underneath the futon we stored our luggage, and amps, and guitars. We did a tour that way all the way to New York, played Boston, a few small clubs, and a West Coast tour. Then we had a bigger tour booked by SST. It was a little more thorough. We were touring with a band called Sylvia Juncosa, she was opening for us. Now we got a U-Haul, so we put all the amps in there, but the more intimate articles like the guitars and our underwear, we put underneath the futon frame. And then we did a couple months around the US, up through the South, and Texas, and Florida, and even got pulled over in Louisiana by some local sheriffs and a few DEA agents, and they went through the damn thing on the side of the road. We just stood on the side of the road and looked at lizards."

— Kim Thayil, Soundgarden

"With *Louder Than Love*, there wasn't too much pressure on us to write a radio hit or anything. Just because the radio format at the time was still rock of the '80s, y'know? But I think that the label saw potential. They did insist that the guys that mixed *Appetite for Destruction* mix our record, because *Appetite* was blowing up at that point. One thing that really benefited us when we went to A&M was that we had an audience already. We had toured for two or three years. And we had three records out. So we had a history. And I think that really helped us in the long run."

— Matt Cameron, Soundgarden, Pearl Jam

"Soundgarden was the first really commercially successful group to come out of the scene. They had a very unique blending of commercial and alternative sensibilities. You had a singer who was a classic rock star, sang like Robert Plant, looked good, and you had a guitar player that listened to a lot of underground music and would experiment with atonality as well as heavy riffing. So when you listen to the first Sub Pop single they did, 'Hunted Down,' it's not the kind of guitar playing you would expect to hear in a commercial metal band. Plus, they had really slowed the tempo down and had a super heavy sound that was not necessarily commercial but had definite references to Led Zeppelin. It was basically Led Zeppelin meets the Butthole Surfers. Also, the ethnic makeup of the group: you had a bass player who was Japanese and a guitar player of Indian ethnicity, and that really went counter to a lot of corporate LA commercial hard rock, which was almost uniformly white males. They were kind of a new paradigm."

— Bruce Pavitt, Sub Pop Records

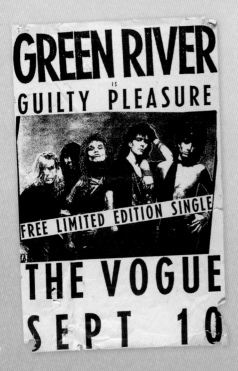

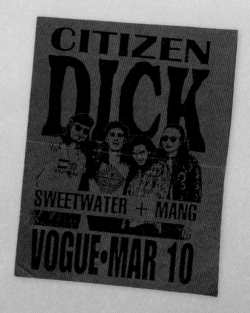

SUB POP SUNDAY: DJ Bruce Pavitt, Swallow, at the Vogue, Seattle, September 13, 1987. Poster by Lisa Orth; NIGHT OF THE LIVING U-MEN, part II; second feature *The Return of the Living Dead*, at the Vogue, Seattle, July 29, 1987; GREEN RIVER IS GUILTY PLEASURE: Green River, at The Vogue, Seattle, September 10, 1986; PROP FOR THE MOTION PICTURE *SINGLES*: Citizen Dick, Sweetwater, and Mang, at the Vogue, Seattle, March 10, ca. 1991; VALENTINES DAY: Soundgarden,

Room Nine, Bundle of Hiss, Pure Joy, Skin Yard, Vexed, Ash, plus Jesse Bernstein, Patrick McCabe, the White Boys, at the Central Tavern, Seattle, February 14, 1987. Poster by Cam Garrett; U-MEN, Hell Cows, Thrown Ups, at the Central, Seattle, January 16, 1988. Poster by Ed Fotheringham; REDD KROSS, Soundgarden, The Central Tavern, Seattle, October 24, 1987. Poster by Jim Blanchard; POP DEFECT, Skin Yard, 64 Spiders, Central, Seattle, November 13, 1986

VOCALS: Layne
BORN: Aug. 22, 1967; Seattle, WA
CAREER: 4 years

    Taking center stage for DIAMOND LIE is the energetic and
electrifying Layne. Layne's experience with various groups of
various styles has given him quite a range of vocal capabilities;
from the speed metal group SLEZE, to the punchy glam rock of
ALICE 'N CHAINS. Layne's versatility and uninhibited stage
performance prove him to be a valuable frontman.

GUITAR: Jerry Cantrell
BORN: March 18, 1966; Tacoma, WA
CAREER: 4 years

    The much devoted Jerry Cantrell is founder and guitar ace of
DIAMOND LIE. Jerry is the only remaining member of the original
DIAMOND LIE line- up, but the transiton was a positive one. This
is his first band, but his natural talent and enthusiasm keep him
a precious driving force behind DIAMOND LIE.

Guitarist Jerry Cantrell grew up in Spanaway, WA, 20 minutes south of Tacoma, listening to hard rock and heavy metal. He was inspired to pursue music by his high school choir teacher. In 1987, he founded Diamond Lie when he was 21, with some friends in Tacoma. Eventually, Cantrell drafted Mike Starr on bass and Sean Kinney on drums. He met vocalist Layne Staley when his first incarnation of Alice 'N Chains was collapsing, and Cantrell convinced him to join Diamond Lie. The band clicked, and soon changed its name to Alice in Chains.

This press kit was assembled by publicist Jenny Bendel and sent to Columbia records in an effort to get the band signed. "Their sleazy, bluesy, in-your-face, tough rock 'n' roll is unable to be matched by any other band in Seattle," the bio asserts under an obvious influence of Guns 'N Roses. The band's sorry state at the time is summed up by Bendel's note, "More quality pictures can be sent to you if you'd like, but for the time being the band is broke and a photo-copy is the best we can do. Please see what you can do so we can get these boys out of Seattle!" A year later, Alice in Chains was still in Seattle, but signed to Columbia. With the release of their 1990 debut EP *We Die Young* and full-length album *Facelift*, they became rising stars, with hit singles on metal and mainstream rock radio.

DIAMOND LIE PRESS KIT, 1988

"From the very heart of Seattle and the Ballard Music Bank comes a band to reckon with; DIAMOND LIE. The band has been together in Seattle now for about six months, and has left a favorable impression on most of Seattle's music enthusiasts. ... They bring new life to their cover tunes and put new hope in our local music scene with their originals. DIAMOND LIE's live performances are overwhelming with the electrifying music and the raw attraction of the band. They already taken Seattle by storm and have created a devoted following; keep an ear out in YOUR town for DIAMOND LIE!"

— Diamond Lie press kit

"We put out *Facelift* and there wasn't grunge, there wasn't any of that, and I remember going to Europe and there was this really small chunk of people that would be at shows — 'cause they were kinda on to the Sub Pop stuff more than they were in the States even. And they'd be like, 'the Seattle Sound,' y'know? There'd be these little pods of people and they would talk to you about people you know. You'd get this little taste of home goin' on."

— Sean Kinney, Alice in Chains

"Layne worked at this place in Ballard called the Music Bank, which was a 24-hour rehearsal studio with about 50 rooms and it ran 24 hours a day, 7 days a week, and he lived there and kind of worked there. So he invited me to basically come up and live with him, y'know? Doesn't even know me, just met me, but we hit it off and he's like, 'Man, just come up and hang with me for a while 'til you get your shit together and we'll figure it out. He knew I was actively trying to put a band together, but he had his band, his version of Alice 'N Chains, and he was also really interested in Skinny Puppy and industrial stuff and Love and Rockets — so he had two things going on already. But he's like, 'Give this drummer guy a call' — who was Sean. I called Sean and started talking to him, and he's like, 'Yeah, okay, that sounds cool.' And he's asking me about if I got a bass player or I got anybody else in mind, and I'm like, 'Well, I met this guy, Mike Starr.' He was a really solid bass player and he seemed like a pretty cool dude. And he was like, 'That's really weird, 'cause he's my best friend and I'm datin' his sister.'"

— Jerry Cantrell, Alice in Chains

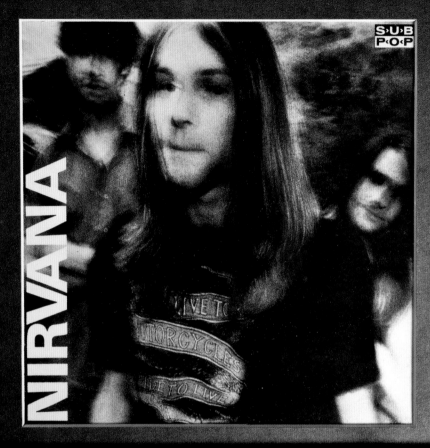

Recording engineer Jack Endino gave Nirvana's original demo to his friend Jonathan Poneman, who took an instant liking to the band. He shared the tape with his Sub Pop partner Bruce Pavitt, who felt there was potential, so they both invited Nirvana to play for them – an audition of sorts – at the Central Tavern in Seattle's Pioneer Square. Poneman and Pavitt were interested in doing a single with the band, and felt at the time that Nirvana's strongest effort was an obscure cover, "Love Buzz" by the Dutch band Shocking Blue, best known for their 1970 hit "Venus."

Backed by the original song, "Big Cheese," Nirvana's first release was issued in a limited edition of 1000 numbered copies in November 1988. It was also the first offering on Sub Pop's subscription-only Singles Club – a clever marketing ploy by Pavitt and Poneman to increase the collectability of Sub Pop's output. Which it did, handily. The "Love Buzz" single sold out quickly, and the band's profile within Sub Pop and throughout the indie community began to rise. Burnyce and Doug Channing, proud of their son Chad (who became Nirvana's steady drummer in spring of 1988), framed and displayed this copy of the single in their home on Bainbridge Island, near Seattle.

"LOVE BUZZ" / "BIG CHEESE," SINGLE BY NIRVANA, NOVEMBER 1988

JONATHAN PONEMAN: "I remember at that show, you leaning over to me and whispering, 'That's the single,' halfway through "Love Buzz."
BRUCE PAVITT: "And I also said to you, 'The drummer's got a mustache.' [laughs] But after a few weeks they had a new drummer, so it was awesome."

"'Love Buzz' is one hell of a first effort, anchored by an elegant, brooding bass line. Both cuts are resplendent in gnarly, treated vocals. Serious traces of musicianship leak through, the production is exceptionally clean, and there's even an approachable guitar solo on 'Love Buzz.' Nirvana sit sort of at the edge of the current Northwest sound – too clean for thrash, too pure for metal, too good to ignore. Absolutely worth the investment."

– Grant Alden, reviewing "Love Buzz"
for *The Rocket*, December 1988

"When I was doing things with Tic Dolly Row, there was one show where we played with Bliss at the Community World Theatre, but I don't recall meeting those guys that night. I met them at a show three or four months later, where Malfunkshun was playing. I went to that show with a friend who was going to Evergreen at the time. He knew both Kurt and Krist, and introduced me to Kurt and Krist. Kurt was like, 'Do you still have that drum kit?' 'Cause I had this North drum kit, which were weird looking kits: they fan out and look strange. They're like, 'We're playing this show soon, and it's gonna be on campus, it's an outdoor show, and we'd really like it if you'd want to come out and see it, check it out.' So I went out to the show and watched them play, and then they came to me afterwards and asked if I wanted to play drums with them. We hooked up a time to get together to jam. I think it might have been where Krist was living in Tacoma back then, and it was cool. We had a lot of fun, and after we jammed, they were like, 'Well, what do you think?' I felt like they were trying to feel me out. And we'd jam again. And the next thing you know, I'm the drummer in this band. There wasn't any DING, 'OK, you're officially the drummer for Nirvana.' It was just like, 'OK, I'm playing with them.'"

– Chad Channing, Nirvana

The Screaming Trees formed in 1985 in the small eastern Washington town of Ellensburg and featured brothers Van and Gary Lee Conner on bass and guitar, respectively, Mark Pickerel on drums, and Mark Lanegan on vocals. Their debut album, *Other Worlds*, was recorded by Steve Fisk, who subsequently introduced the band to Calvin Johnson of K Records and Greg Ginn of SST Records. Those relationships lead to both a split EP with Johnson's Beat Happening and a record deal with SST. With 1987's *Even If and Especially When*, the band began touring nationally with other SST bands such as the Meat Puppets and fIREHOSE.

This painting, by Central Washington University art student Daniel Herron, was hanging at Velvetone Studios where the Screaming Trees were recording 1988's *Invisible Lantern*. Vocalist Mark Lanegan loved the painting and asked to use it for the album's cover. The artwork revels in ominous pop psychedelia much akin to the Trees music. With this album and 1989's *Buzz Factory*, the band continued to develop a signature sound, interweaving Lanegan's hauntingly-rich vocals over the band's melodic drive. As their following grew, the Screaming Trees became increasingly connected with Seattle and the town's growing influence in the underground.

"BELEM IS HERE," PAINTING BY DANIEL HERRON, USED AS THE COVER FOR THE 1988 SCREAMING TREES ALBUM *INVISIBLE LANTERN*

"Mark Pickerel of the Screaming Trees was living in Ellensburg and I had left a few of my Anonymous singles at Ace Records over there. Mark bought the record and saw the Olympia address and just wrote me a letter and told me how much he liked the single and all about his band and their big influences and how they were into anything by Robert Fripp or Brian Eno or the Talking Heads. I thought, 'OK, I can die now. I got a fan letter from Ellensburg. The world is complete.' Probably the third day I was in Ellensburg when I moved back in '86 and I heard, 'Oh, yeah, he works at the record store sometimes, but he's at the video store now,' so without any warning or anything, I just went up and introduced myself to Mark Pickerel at the video store. And he was all excited and then immediately introduced me to Mark Lanegan and Van and Lee Conner. We got to talking about the Shaggs 'cause they were really into the Shaggs, and I think within three months Gary Lee came up and asked if they could record at the studio. And that was the *Other Worlds* sessions."

— Steve Fisk, recording engineer/producer/musician

"Screaming Trees were — especially the early Screaming Trees when they were still on the SST label — were a huge influence on me. There's a record of theirs called *Invisible Lantern* and one called *Even If And Especially When* that are just amazing records to me. I played them to death when I was still in college."

— JON AUER, THE POSIES

Jack Endino used this mixing console when he worked as a sound engineer at Seattle's Reciprocal Recording studio, which he and Chris Hanszek opened in the summer of 1986. The Ramsa was a workhorse that Endino used to mix dozens of classic records, including TAD's *God's Balls*, Screaming Trees' *Buzz Factory*, Mudhoney's *Superfuzz Bigmuff* EP and *Mudhoney* album, the Fluid's *Roadmouth*, Skin Yard's *Fist Sized Chunks*, Cat Butt's *Journey to the Center of*, and Nirvana's debut album *Bleach*, among many others.

Endino was soon inundated with projects by bands that wanted to take advantage of his intuitive talent as a recording engineer (as well as Reciprocal's reasonable pricing). Many of the bands came from Sub Pop, which placed Endino's sonic stamp on the grunge sound and earned him the semi-joking nickname, "The Godfather of Grunge."

RAMSA WR-T820 MIXING BOARD, USED BY JACK ENDINO AT RECIPROCAL RECORDING, 1988 – 1990

"Jack Endino could just make things sound great. He's a total magician. The man is a shaman. He's magic. Bands would go in, drop eighty bucks and come out with a hit 45. The 'Touch Me I'm Sick' / 'Sweet Young Thing' single by Mudhoney, which to this day I think is the best single we've ever put out, I believe was recorded for $100. And I love that. I love the fact that you can create great art by just pulling it out of thin air, and that's what Jack Endino did."

— Bruce Pavitt, Sub Pop Records

"Jack was kind of my first musical mentor. I met Jack, I think it was in 1989. I had been seeing his name poppin' up on these Sub Pop singles and I heard him doing an interview on KCMU. And something — just the way he talked about music, the way he described the power of music and the importance of independent music and how it was building in Seattle, I realized that I had to meet him in person. I didn't know what would come of it, but I just felt like I needed to talk with this guy about music."

— Barrett Martin, Screaming Trees

"My approach is basically to let bands be bands and capture that energy in the studio and try and make it sound good and make it a pleasant thing to listen to."
— JACK ENDINO, RECORDING ENGINEER/PRODUCER/MUSICIAN

Nirvana played a Halloween-themed party with Lush and Lansdat Blister at dorm K208 on the Evergreen State College Campus. Krist Novoselic rocked the bass shirtless, with fake blood dripping down his face and chest, while Chad Channing pounded the drums wearing a Germs (*GI*) album t-shirt. At the end of the performance, Kurt Cobain, spattered with fake gore as well, smashed his Univox Hi-Flyer to pieces – an archetypal move that would be repeated by the band countless times during the next half decade.

The smashing of instruments certainly created a feeling of awesome finality to their shows, but it also played with the idea of rock star cliché and excess, paralleling the primal destructive tactics of Hendrix or Pete Townshend. The key difference was that Hendrix and the Who could *afford* to smash things, whereas Nirvana were broke at the time. The destruction of their instruments wasn't a casual, throwaway gesture, but a vital component of the music.

UNIVOX HI-FLYER GUITAR, SMASHED BY KURT COBAIN AT THE EVERGREEN STATE COLLEGE, OLYMPIA, OCTOBER 30, 1988

"Lush played with Nirvana [on October 30, 1988] and we totally sucked. Right away we were completely out of sync. One of our guitar players broke a string, and he had to retune everything, because he had this floating bridge. It was loud, and the place was too full, and the audience was crushing up against us, and we had all this pent up energy, and everybody in the band was trying to talk at him all at once. And I stepped over to try and tell him my version of what he should do, and the drummer said, 'DON'T YOU SAY A WORD TO HIM.' I just snapped and kicked over his entire drum set, threw down my microphone and walked straight across the room to the back wall, where I ran out of room to walk. I turned around, and he was right behind me and he punched me in the face. I left and went to Safeway with my sister, and when we came back, Nirvana was in the middle of their set. At the end, they smashed their instruments and knocked over their amps. It was like The Who. And I always felt that the spectacle of my band imploding — that Kurt's personality, as downbeat as he always seemed, could never be upstaged. I always felt like the whole reason that they smashed their instruments was because it was the first time we had ever upstaged them in any way."

— Slim Moon, Lush, Kill Rock Stars

"For a guy who fixes things all day long, I would seek out things that are broken just to fix them and always marvel at why somebody would abuse these things. There's something about the spirit of why Nirvana was doing it that really looked like fun. I was a fan of The Who growing up, y'know, and we would go see *The Kids are Alright* play in the theater. And I remember we would go night after night, and sit in the front row, because it was closest we were going to get in Pullman to seeing The Who live in concert. So staring up at that big screen and watching Pete Townshend smash guitars was really thrilling. And even though this is Kurt Cobain in the *Bleach* era, it's a kid smashing a guitar, and he's into it. I mean you're watching him and you know that he probably can't afford that guitar, but he's so serious about the show that he wants you to remember it."

— Earnie Bailey, guitar tech, Nirvana, Foo Fighters

"3:30 AM. Dana, Here is a piece of Kurt's guitar. He smashed it as a 'Grand Finale.' If you think they played good Friday you should have seen them last night!!! Ryan [Aigner] and I played security guards to a bunch of drunk, slammin' punks. It was great! Tell you more later, Ben"

— Ben Lattin, in a letter to his sister Dana, describing the K Dorm show and the guitar fragment (not the artifact pictured here) he collected.

Released in December 1988, *Sub Pop 200* is a principal document of the '80s Northwest underground scene. It featured early tracks by bands that would go on to epitomize the grunge sound – TAD, Nirvana, Mudhoney, Soundgarden, Green River, Blood Circus, Cat Butt and Screaming Trees – but also bands that explored other musical territory, such as Girl Trouble, Beat Happening, Steve Fisk, the Walkabouts, and Steven Jesse Bernstein. In the following years, the Northwest would become inextricably linked with grunge, but the region itself was diverse in its musical attribution.

Sub Pop 200 was the embodiment of Sub Pop's half-joking goal of "world domination." The compilation was presented as a triple LP box set with a 16-page booklet featuring Charles Peterson's photography and this cover by artist Charles Burns, who would go on to become one of the most revered artists in underground comix. Burns was an alum of Olympia's Evergreen State College when Bruce Pavitt commissioned him to illustrate cassette covers for three issues of his *Sub Pop* fanzine. The stark illustrations worked perfectly with Pavitt's emerging aesthetic for *Sub Pop*. With *Sub Pop 200*'s cover Burns created a sense of larger-than-life, foreboding mystery that Sub Pop would milk to great effect in the years to come.

CHARLES BURNS ORIGINAL ARTWORK FOR THE *SUB POP 200* COMPILATION, 1988

"They were starting their label and they had the ideas for their *Sub Pop 200* Compilation. They said, 'We're going to make a big deal of this. Do you guys want to be on it?' And, like, 'Of course, y'know, who wouldn't?'"
— Kurt Bloch, Fastbacks, Young Fresh Fellows

"Bruce wanted Sub Pop to be a regional thing, yet have farther reach than that. And he saw the need for a cohesive producer, for a cohesive design, and a cohesive style of photography on the record sleeves. It was about with *Sub Pop 200* that really that all gelled for good. He had the idea of putting out a triple box set, which was unheard of at the time. I mean, I think the only thing that had come before that was The Clash's *Sandinista*, y'know, which was in the industry considered pretty much a failure. So, 'Let's put out a triple box set and put a 16-page booklet in it.' And I was like, 'Great!' Because that was going to be 16 pages of my photographs. And it worked. It really drove home the personality and the character of these bands, and the sort of the family aspect of it, and the excitement of the gigs. That's kind of really when it first came together."
— Charles Peterson, photographer

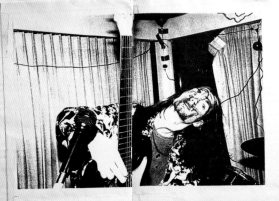

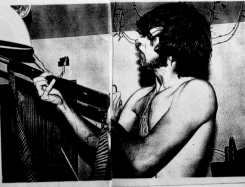

All photos: TRACY MIRANDAR

"Our biggest fear at the beginning was that people might think we were a Melvins rip-off," Kurdt admits. Yet the association has probably also worked to the band's advantage. Nirvana recorded an ear-splitting demo tape which immediately had every noise addict in town flapping his lips over the next great white hope of grunge...and it probably didn't hurt that Melvin Dale was sitting in on drums (this was before Chad joined).

SUB·POP·200

3 12" EP BOXED SET. AWESOME 16-PAGE BOOKLET FEATURING PHOTOGRAPHS BY CHARLES PETERSON. UNRELEASED HITS BY BEAT HAPPENING, STEVEN J. BERNSTEIN, BLOOD CIRCUS, CAT BUTT, CHEMISTRY SET, FASTBACKS, STEVE FISK, THE FLUID, GIRL TROUBLE, GREEN RIVER, TERRY LEE HALE, MUDHONEY, THE NIGHTS AND DAYS, NIRVANA, SCREAMING TREES, SOUNDGARDEN, SWALLOW, TAD, THROWN UPS, AND THE WALKABOUTS.

NIRVANA

They're becoming the kind of band that can turn an entire audience into zombie pod people by their sheer heaviness (this is a compliment).

NIRVANA
"Love Buzz"/"Big Cheese" (45)
SubPop

BY NOW YOU KNOW: IF IT'S ON SubPop, it rocks. And this little chunk of sound — the first from the boys with the name that belongs on KNUA — certainly lives up to that tradition.

The danger for Nirvana is that other, more notorious SubPop ensembles will make so much noise this disc could disappear. It shouldn't. "Love Buzz" is one hell of a first effort, anchored by an elegant, brooding bass line. Both cuts are resplendent in gnarly, treated vocals. Serious traces of musicianship leak through, the production is exceptionally clean, and there's even an approachable guitar solo on "Love Buzz."

Nirvana sit sort of at the edge of the current Northwest sound — too clean for thrash, too pure for metal, too good to ignore. Absolutely worth the investment.

— Grant Alden

A MATERNAL LOVE FOR CANNOT LOOK ME IN THE EYES BUT I SEE HERS AND THEY ARE BLUE AND THEY COCK AND TWITCH AND MASTURBATE

why? I SAID SO NIRVANA NIRVANA NIRVANA BLACK WINDOWS OF PAINT I SCRATCH WITH MY NAILS I SEE OTHERS JUST LIKE ME

WHY DO THEY NOT TRY TO ESCAPE? THEY BRING OUT THE OLDER ONES THEY COME WITH THEIR FLASHING LIGHTS they point at my way

AND TAKE MY FAMILY AWAY AND VERY LATER I HAVE LEARNED TO ACCEPT SOME FRIENDS OF RIDICULE MY WHOLE EXISTANCE

WAS FOR YOUR AMUSEMENT

THAT IS WHY I'M HERE WITH YOU TO TAKE ME WITH YOUR LIFE NIRVANA NIRVANA NIRVANA. NIRVANA NIRVANA NIRVANA TO NIRVANA NIRVANA

Nirvana fan and friend Tamra Ohrmund created the band's first press kit in early 1989, several months prior to the release of the band's *Bleach* album. It included their first interview and a review of one of Nirvana's early Seattle shows, by Dawn Anderson from the September 1988 issue of the fanzine *Backlash*. It also included reviews of the "Love Buzz" single and *Sub Pop 200*, as well as photos by Cobain's girlfriend, Tracy Marander, of the band playing a Halloween-themed show on October 30, 1988 – when Cobain smashed his first guitar.

Nirvana's prospects were looking up: They had a manager, the interest of Sub Pop, and a record on the horizon. The band that Cobain and Novoselic had created had transitioned from an impassioned hobby to the verge of being something so much more. It seemed like it couldn't possibly get any better than this.

NIRVANA PRESS KIT LAYOUT, EARLY 1989. DESIGN BY TAMRA OHRMUND

"Tam: Chris, Chad and I are completely pleased with your managing skills and enthusiasm. We love your very guts. Thank you. Thank you. Thank you."
— Kurt Cobain, in a note to Tamra Ohrmund, ca. late 1988

"Nirvana, consisting of Kurdt on guitar and vocals, Chris Novoselic on bass and Chad Channing on drums, is still a young band, but they're fast on their way to becoming Buddhas, or at least Bodhisattvas, of the Northwest pain-rock circuit. Since some people seem to think *Backlash* is a consumer guide (what a novel idea!), it's probably only fair to inform you that if you didn't like the Melvins, or if you did like the Melvins but think lead-belly music has run its course, you won't like Nirvana. But it's also important to stress that this is not a clone band. The group's already way ahead of most mortals in the songwriting department and, at the risk of sounding blasphemous, I honestly believe that with enough practice, Nirvana could become.... better than the Melvins!"
— Dawn Anderson, *Backlash*, September 1988

Spank thru

And As the soft pretentious mountains • glisten in the light of the trees
And the flowers sing in D minor • And the birds fly happily •
we'll be together once again my love • I need you **back** oh baby baby
I cant explain just why we lost it from the start
living without you girl you'll only break my heart
I can feel it I can hold it • I can bend it • I can shape it And or mold it
I can cut it I can taste it • I can spank it I can beat it ejacu-/
-late it Ah I've been lookin for day Glo • Always hearing
the same old • sticky boredom with A book • I can make it do
things you wouldn't think it ever could

                    • Repeat

Hairspray Queen

I WAS your mind • You were my my enemy you were mine I was your
Your enemy you ~~would~~ mind • I was your your enemy you were mine
I WAS WAS your ene •   Your ears rang (repeat)
① ⎰ AT night the wishful goddess • At night she'll wish the hardest
   ⎱ At night the Disco Goddess • at night the bitch go GAWD .
② ⎰ At night the wishful Goddess • at night she'll wish the hardest on sight
   the Disco goddess • At night the itch so modest • At light the crisco
   lochness • At right the mouthful/omelette • out sight the fishfull
   goblets • At night the witch go GAAAWD .

Aeroszeppelin

whats the season in A Right • if you cant have anything • whats the
reason in A rhyme If A ~~pla~~ plan means everything • what the meaning
in A crime • its A fan it anything • wheres the leaning in A line
its A Brand its A Brand
How A culture comes Again • it was All here yesterday
And you swear its not A trend • doesn't matter any ways
Youre only hear to talk to friend • nothing new is every day
you could shit upon the stage • they'll be fans
they'll be fans if you brand
                    (cont →)

Kurt Cobain sent these handwritten lyrics to friend Tamra Ohrmund in early 1989. Ohrmund was acting as Nirvana's manager at the time, creating promotional materials for the band soon after the release of the "Love Buzz" / "Big Cheese" single and the *Sub Pop 200* compilation. Ohrmund would later sing vocals with Cobain on "Scratch It Out" / "Bikini Twilight," a July 1989 single from the Go Team, the Olympia, WA musical collective created by K Records founder Calvin Johnson and future Bikini Kill drummer Tobi Vail.

Most of the lyrics here are for songs that were recorded early in Cobain's music career, some before Nirvana was formed. An instrumental of "Downer" and an early version of "Spank Thru" first appear on the 1986 *Illiteracy Will Prevail* demo, by Cobain's band Fecal Matter. The majority of the songs listed on the lyric sheets, however, were recorded during Nirvana's initial recording session on January 23, 1988 at Reciprocal Recording in Seattle with producer Jack Endino. Many of these would be reworked further and appear on the band's debut album 1989 album *Bleach*. As was typical with Cobain's creations, the song lyrics went through many iterations, with Cobain revising words and phrasing to craft his enigmatic koans that would soon fascinate listeners across the globe.

HANDWRITTEN NIRVANA LYRICS BY KURT COBAIN, EARLY 1989

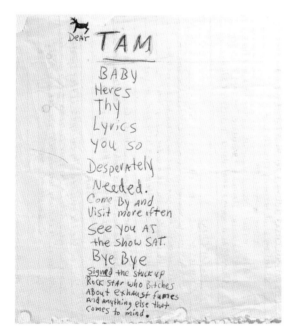

"I know exactly the first time I ever heard Nirvana. I was at Cellophane Square when it used to be at the little shop in the U District, and I was just flipping through some records and I heard something, and I was like, 'What is that?' I beelined up to the front and it was *Bleach*, I bought it and it was incredible. I had lived here and then I moved to Arizona for a couple, maybe 6 months, and that was just at the time when *Bleach* came out so it wasn't in my world before, and when I came back it was there and it was like, 'Whoa!' There's so much pop to it – and I like it when you put the edges in there and give it less of a sheen. And hooks? You never can go wrong with a great hook. I mean, that's what the music industry's made on and I can dance to it, y'know? So with Nirvana it's the combination of an incredible voice, great lyrics, great hooks, and it just has a little oomph to it, not over-produced hair metal crap, which was what was going on at the time."

– Susie Tennant, DGC Records / Sub Pop Records

"These songs that Kurt wrote so connect to the concept of dysfunction, pain, divorce. They are so pure in their emotion that new successive generations find meaning them. It's the songs. That's the key to Nirvana, and that's the reason that Kurt has this legacy. If he didn't have that body of work, it wouldn't have mattered. The art that he created was so much him, it had so much transparency in it – that's the reason that people still talk about him today. Those songs have a resonance that's far beyond his mortal life and who he was. They mean so much to people that loved them before and they mean a lot to people who discover them now."

– Charles R. Cross, music journalist/biographer/
The Rocket publisher

MUDHONEY

~~MUD HONEY~~

Cat # SP18

2 SONGS FOR
A 7" 45 RPM DISC

15 IPS, HALF-TRK, NO NR.
TONES AT HEAD : 1K, 10K, 100 Hz.

SONGS:

APPROX TIMES:

SP18 A **1. TOUCH ME**   **2:30**
   Please insribe: what does the word
   "crack" mean to you?

SP18 B **2. SWEET YOUNG THING**   3:45
   ~~Please insribe: ~~haha

opaque
BROWN
Vinyl

ENGRD BY JACK ENDINO
RECIPROCAL RECORDING
SEATTLE, WA. 98107
(206)-782-6411

Ship to: Erika Records: 9827 Oak St.
Bellflower, CA 90706 213-804-1539

This tape box contained the master recording for Mudhoney's debut single, the grunge classic "Touch Me I'm Sick" backed with "Sweet Young Thing (Ain't Sweet No More)," released by Sub Pop Records in August 1988. The heavy Sonics-Yardbirds-Stooges amalgam was Mudhoney's hallmark sound. The band formed in early 1988 after the demise of Green River. Mark Arm reunited with Steve Turner, who had left Green River earlier, and the two began rehearsing with Dan Peters, who had been drumming with Bundle of Hiss and Feast. Matt Lukin, who had just left the Melvins, completed the quartet, joining in on bass guitar. They recorded with Jack Endino at Reciprocal Recording in March 1988, after they had been together for only a few months.

With the "Touch Me I'm Sick" single and the October '88 release of *Superfuzz Bigmuff*, Mudhoney quickly became a rising force in underground circles. Early on, they earned the support of indie tastemakers Sonic Youth (who asked Mudhoney to join them on their late 1988 *Daydream Nation* tour), which helped position them as Sub Pop's most prominent band. Long before Nirvana's "Smells Like Teen Spirit" became a rallying cry for disaffected youth, the defining anthem of the new Seattle sound was "Touch Me I'm Sick."

MASTER TAPE BOX FOR MUDHONEY'S "TOUCH ME I'M SICK" / "SWEET YOUNG THING AIN'T SWEET NO MORE" SINGLE, MARCH 1988. GIFT OF JACK ENDINO

"Mudhoney: Raging primal grunginess. Ultimate gnarly, gristly, gory, grossly grainy, grimy, garage group who have shot to the forefront of British music media attention with their six-track thigh-busting album, *Superfuzz Bigmuff*, and the Sonic Youth cover of their grunge classic 'Touch Me I'm Sick.' Watch out for these boys live!"
— EVERETT TRUE, *MELODY MAKER*, MARCH 18, 1989

"'Touch Me I'm Sick' was the watershed single for the scene. It was the reference point. Mudhoney are probably one of the most important bands as far as the Northwest scene is concerned. There were other bands that had more commercial success than them, but they always got the respect, y'know? They got the cred. People forget that Nirvana came from outside of Seattle, and that bands like Mudhoney and Soundgarden were well established, well before Nirvana made it here. And so Nirvana was looking up to Mudhoney. It wasn't the other way around."
— Charles Peterson, photographer

"Mudhoney was getting international attention before any of the other bands. I really think that they were the single catalyst that brought everything into focus. Seattle really became a place to play and a scene because of Mudhoney. 'Touch Me I'm Sick' was an independent 'hit'. People were taking notice. I don't know how many it sold. Who cares? But people were definitely taking notice of it. And then, y'know, bands go to where A&R people were hanging out, and they were hanging out here."
— Ed Fotheringham, illustrator

BOMBSHELTER VIDEO AND KCMU RADIO
WELCOME FROM N.Y.C.
SONIC YOUTH
WITH SCREAMING TREES
FRI. NOV 11
AND
MUD HONEY
8PM ALL AGES
UNION STATION
4TH JACKSON
12.00 ADVANCE
CALL TICKETMASTER
628 ~ 0888
NOW
IF YOU ARE OVER 21 YOU SHOULD BRING YOUR I.D. SO AS TO PARTAKE IN THE CONSUMPTION OF BEVERAGES DIG?

Sonic Youth has had an incalculable influence on the underground scene in the 1980s. After releasing several albums on independent labels, they signed to Enigma Records and in October 1988 released *Daydream Nation*, an album considered a key influence on the "alternative rock" of the 1990s. Sonic Youth was touring for *Daydream Nation* when they played this show at Seattle's Union Station. They were pals with Mudhoney's Mark Arm and Steve Turner from their time in Green River. The following month, Mudhoney released a Sub Pop split single with Sonic Youth and they continued to tour together down the West Coast and into Texas. In the spring of 1989, they toured together again through the UK and Europe – the first European tour for a Sub Pop band.

In 1990, Sonic Youth released their album *Goo* on the Geffen Records subsidiary, DGC. Meanwhile, Nirvana had become frustrated with Sub Pop's cash-strapped operation, and Sonic Youth bassist Kim Gordon recommended DGC. Nirvana was intrigued, and DGC representatives thought Nirvana had the potential to top *Goo*'s sales of 250,000 copies. The band signed – a decision that would change rock music forever.

SONIC YOUTH, SCREAMING TREES, AND MUDHONEY AT UNION STATION, SEATTLE, NOVEMBER 11, 1988

"We were really starting to hang out with Nirvana and Mudhoney and the kind of high energy music they were making. This grunge rock really spurred us on. And I think a lot of that is reflected in *Dirty*. When I listen to that record I really hear the influences of a lot of those bands from the Pacific Northwest that we were hanging out with. Screaming Trees, I mean the list goes on and on, it's not just that it was Nirvana and Mudhoney, they were our closest friends in that scene, pretty much, but there's are tons of bands that were inspiring to us from the Northwest."

– Lee Ranaldo, Sonic Youth

"We went over to England in 1989 with Sonic Youth and opened for them for a few shows, as our first European tour. It was great. Sonic Youth were just gods over there at the time, and any band that they had open for them, you knew the doors were open. Like Dinosaur Jr a year before us. The first show in England was just like chaos, total chaos. It was in a city, Newcastle? It was in Newcastle. It was in Newcastle because we were drinking Newcastle Brown Ale, and 'cause it was

almost the only time I've ever seen Thurston Moore just drunk. It was totally nuts, the crowd was completely amped for it. During the first song me and Mark both jumped into the audience. I think Thurston might have jumped into the audience."

– Steve Turner, Mudhoney

SONIC YOUTH, U-MEN, GREEN RIVER AT GORILLA GARDENS, SEATTLE, JANUARY 19, 1985

BALANCE · TONE · EXPAND

VOLUME · TONE · SUSTAIN

BALANCE · TONE · EXPANDER

The title of Mudhoney's debut EP, *Superfuzz Bigmuff*, released in October 1988, evoked rough, dark, sexual imagery much as the band's name itself, which was taken from a Russ Meyer sexploitation flick. The music was a match: snarling, distorted garage punk that would cement Mudhoney as the seminal grunge band. The group's signature fuzzed-out sound was created in part by guitarists Mark Arm and Steve Turner's distortion pedals of choice, the Univox Super-Fuzz and Electro-Harmonix Big Muff.

The band's quick rise in prominence in the Seattle scene wasn't surprising, given the band's pedigree – with former members of Green River, the Melvins, and Bundle of Hiss, Mudhoney was a distillation of essential Northwest-ness, hit home by their focused sonic attack. After extensive touring in the UK and Europe with Sonic Youth, Mudhoney saw the previously poor sales of *Superfuzz Bigmuff* rise. The disc entered the British indie charts, prompting a renewed interest in the band and Sub Pop Records in the States. Soon the spotlight would shine even more brightly on the fledgling label and bands throughout the Pacific Northwest.

UNIVOX SUPER-FUZZ PEDAL, USED BY MARK ARM WITH MUDHONEY, 1988 – 1994 / ELECTRO-HARMONIX BIG MUFF PEDAL, USED BY STEVE TURNER WITH THE THROWN-UPS AND MUDHONEY, 1986 – 1999

"The Big Muff makes you sound like Blue Cheer. The Super Fuzz makes you sound like Brian Gregory of the Cramps."
– STEVE TURNER, MUDHONEY

"When I started playing guitar with Mudhoney, Steve was kind enough to let me use his Super-Fuzz pedal, because I had nothing. And hardly anything sounds as cool as a Super-Fuzz pedal. For a long time that was all I used. It was just on all the time. It was just by the amp – there wasn't any guitar dynamics on my part at all. It was just GO. Eventually I kind of finessed things out a little bit."

– Mark Arm, Mudhoney

"Mudhoney was it, they were the big band, y'know, and not only were they just huge in Seattle. They had the most fun shows, but they took it on the road, and they slayed England. And they kept Sub Pop in business. Everybody wanted to be in a band like Mudhoney."

– Susie Tennant, DGC Records representative

"There's people selling millions of records every day and whether they're from Portland or they're from Atlanta it doesn't effect my life any more one way or the other. What did effect my life was when Mudhoney sold 50,000 records. Because all of a sudden there was an identity to the Northwest that the Northwest never had before. And that made a difference to everybody in the Northwest. I think that before that happened, no one was aware of the Northwest. They might have heard of it. They might have seen Washington state on a map somewhere. But it never would occur to them that it was a place where something could happen. And it was only after that that suddenly it was like 'Oh, you're from up that way? Oh, I better listen to that.' That's where there was an effect. It didn't mean that we sold any more records, it just meant that people were willing to pay attention. They were willing to give it a listen. They still listen and go, 'Oh what the hell is this crap,' y'know? But they give it one listen as opposed to just tossing it in the pile."

– Calvin Johnson, Beat Happening, K Records

SUB POP

SEATTLE: ROCK CITY

...ONEY ARE THE STANDARD
...LE'S NEW GENERATION OF
...CHANTS, BUT THERE IS A
...BANDS READY AND WAITING TO
...RES. EVERETT TRUE PROVIDES A
... CONSUMER'S GUIDE TO
THE SUB POP ROSTA.
PICS: ANDY CATLIN

...IN THE FAR NORTH-WEST CORNER OF AMERICA
...you'll find Seattle, sheltered by the Cascade
Mountains, cut off from anywhere by 2,000 miles of
badlands, cornfields and the Wild West.

In the heart of Seattle lies the Terminal Sales
Building on First Avenue. At the very top of this
building are the offices of Sub Pop, lifeforce to the
most vibrant, kicking music scene encompassed in one
city for at least 10 years. Names such as Mudhoney,
Nirvana and Blood Circus abound, trampling
gleefully over the grave of punk rock and heavy
metal, digging up any old spectre they can find and
spitting on the daisies. Seattle, birthplace of Jimi
Hendrix and Sonic Youth, once more equates with the
old-fashioned sentiment ROCK 'N' ROLL!

RUN by two local music fanatics, Jonathan
Poneman and Bruce Pavitt, Sub Pop has been content
to play a steady waiting game up to now, merely
releasing a wide variety of limited edition albums and
seven-inch singles based round some great rock
music. But the continued championing of Green River
(and later, Mudhoney) by Sonic Youth (culminating in
the recent Sonic Youth/Mudhoney 12-inch
collaboration "Touch Me I'm Sick"), and John Peel's
love for "Sub Pop 200", a timeless period piece
three-album collection of the Seattle sound, has
changed all that.

Sub Pop is no longer being left to languish in the
cosy backwaters. Two of its bands, Mother Love Bone
(from Green River) and Soundgarden, have signed
major record deals and a distribution deal has been
set up in Germany, via Glitterhouse. Sub Pop releases
will shortly be available over here via Tupelo.
Mudhoney are touring Britain supporting Sonic Youth
even as we speak. A Tad/Pussy Galore single is in the
pipeline. Tours for Nirvana and Swallow are set. No
longer isolated, Seattle suddenly finds itself THRUST to
the forefront of the rock world.

"My philosophy of Sub Pop is this," Bruce Pavitt
explains. "I worked at Muzak for three years with a lot
of these guys. It was a classic corporate set-up. It
started off by being easy-going, but soon, like most
businesses, it was curtailing our freedom of
expression. And when, for eight to 10 hours a day,
your personal freedom is being restricted, when
you're being punished for being creative, then you're
not living in a free, democratic country. You're living in
a fascist dictatorship. Sub Pop is a business set up to
encourage freedom of thought."

Bruce's and John's relationship with the bands on
the label is based on a feeling of conspiracy and
humour. The bands and record label hang out
together, drink beer and criticise one another. It's a
chaotic, creative environment. Sub Pop is more a
school for learning than a record label, and that's
where its strength lies.

"As far as A&R goes," Jonathan states. "You go to
see one of your friend's bands and you think, 'Yeah,

that sounds cool'. It's only occasionally that we go out
on a limb. I did with Nirvana."

A criticism which could justifiably be levelled at the
Sub Pop roster of bands is that they're retrogressive,
merely re-treading the well-worn paths their spiritual
fathers such as Blue Cheer, Black Sabbath, The Sonics
and 13th Floor Elevators laid for them.

But to me, there's nothing regressive about the
emotional impact or sheer physicality and sexiness of
seeing these bands up and in your face. This sort of
texture and exhilaration is timeless. The regressive
angle just depends on your outlook. If someone sees
that as damning, well what can you do?

"There isn't so much a Sub Pop sound," Jonathan
explains, "as a readily recognisable movement
happening in the American North-West right now
which is heavy, confrontational guitar-based rock. It's
amazing that even in the late Eighties there are still
guitar bands that can flip people out. It's not a sound
we're necessarily trying to thrust upon the rest of the
world, we're more interested in documenting it."

SWALLOW

NON-Black Sabbath commercial hard rock in the
vein of The Smithereens. Chris Pugh (guitar) worked at
Muzak alongside Jon and Bruce. Swallow originally
came out of hardcore as a B-grade Seattle band
(vaguely Black Sabbath with a little Johnny Thunders
thrown in), but now make use of a more pop aesthetic,
à la Buzzcocks. They subscribe wholeheartedly to the
two-minute pop song ideal. A new album is due out in
Britain shortly.

GREEN RIVER

SEMINAL Seattle rock metal band fronted by
Marc Arm (now of Mudhoney). Split to become
Mudhoney and Mother Love Bone. As heavy, loud,
basic and shit-kicking as they make 'em. The Sonics,
Black Sabbath and Black Flag all rolled into one
squirming mess. "Hangin' Tree" on "Sub Pop 200" was
the tour de force of their live performances.

"At the time of 'Come On Down' (the first Green
River album)," reveals Marc Arm, "all the basslines
consisted of Steve Harris triplets – 'here come the
horses over the hill'. Steve (Turner, guitarist with
Mudhoney) hated that stuff. We were writing songs
with too many different parts. I didn't think about it

back then, I was blowing myself away by being in a
junior rush, or whatever. Steve left right at the peak of
that. Then we concentrated on writing simpler songs
and things got a lot better and people started liking us.

"So some of the other members started getting the
idea they could be popular, and began to think, 'Well
I'm getting to be 24, what am I going to be doing the
rest of my life?' So Green River got into the idea of
signing to a major, and that's how 'Rehab Doll' was
recorded, with that idea in mind. But for me, too many
compromises were made. I was listening to far simpler
stuff, such as basic Stooges. In the end we split up, on
Halloween. I formed Mudhoney and the others
became Mother Love Bone and signed to Polygram.
So I guess we both got what we wanted."

BLOOD CIRCUS

COMPLETE and utter white trash, Blood Circus
are the closest Seattle get to Australian feeding time.
Motorhead meet The Wipers; minimalist grunge
metal. Oodles of hair. Blood Circus look early
Seventies, have the drive of early Eighties and lie
strictly within the region of blues-based raw heavy
rockers. As San Francisco's Puncture magazine puts it:
"How do you feel when you're six feet underground?
Low down and dirty."

MUDHONEY

RAGING primal grunginess. Ultimate gnarly,
gristly, gory, grossly grainy, grimy, garage group who
have shot to the forefront of British music media
attention with their six-track thigh-busting album,
"Superfuzz Bigmuff", and the Sonic Youth cover of
their grunge classic "Touch Me I'm Sick". Watch out for
these boys live!

"The line 'Touch Me I'm Sick' is about when you see
people who're sick, who have cancer or something,
which isn't even contagious, but you still automatically
stand back a little," says Marc Arm. "I thought it up one
day and thought it was real funny. One critic said it
was an indictment of our audience, like they're afraid
of me. Huh?!

"'Here Comes Sickness', from the new album, is
almost a holdover from Green River days. Like, you
know, the kind of girl who's cute and will F*** anybody?
It's like, you wanna touch but you know you should
stay away. It's a euphemism for that kind of girl – like,
sickness, go away, ugh!"

NIRVANA

BASICALLY, this is the real thing. No rock star
contrivance, no intellectual perspective, no master
plan for world domination. You're talking about four
guys in their early twenties from rural Washington
who wanna rock, who, if they weren't doing this,
would be working in a supermarket or lumber yard, or
fixing cars. Kurdt Kobain is a great tunesmith, although

still a relatively young songwriter. He wields a riff with
passion. Nirvana deal a lot with Calvin Johnson (Beat
Happening) type themes — innocence and the
repression of innocence. Nirvana songs treat the
banal and pedestrian with a unique slant.

"We grew up in Aberdeen. It was real scary;
redneck, helltown, backwoods, like a village or a big
city for lumberjacks" says bassist Chris Novoselic. "You
see Jack Nicholson in Easy Rider talking about the
Rednecks? About how if they see something different
they don't go running scared, they get dangerous.
Aberdeen's like that. But they were so bone-headed,
why shouldn't we be different from them?"

TAD

A MOUNTAIN of sound. The heaviest man in
all creation. The rockiest gnarliest dude you'd ever
want to wake up next to. Totally crushing, an
enormous talent. From the backwoods of Idaho and
trained as a butcher. If you're talking about conviction
and immediacy, then you're looking at Tad. When you
watch Tad live you get the feeling someone's just
turned a faucet on, and suddenly you're being
deluged with all the rage and frustration and anger
and hurt inherent in a 1,000 dead end lives. Tad
makes early Swans seem half-hearted.

"There's a certain frequency, 27 hertz or something,
which'll make people shit their pants," say the band.
"We're still searching for that frequency. Our guitar
almost does it, it kinda does it, so people shit their pants
in their heads. Everybody thinks everybody's sick
when it happens and everybody's really embarrassed
when it happens, so at our shows everybody's running
to the bathroom at the same time."

GIRL TROUBLE

GENERIC garage/trash four-piece who are
something apart. Ouija buzzsaw guitars, trainspotter
crash thrash mentality, and an indigenous outlook
which lifts them above 99 per cent of Cramps re-run
...They hail from Tacoma, Washington, an

In 1989, Sub Pop's Bruce Pavitt and Jonathan Poneman knew that the bands that they were cultivating had very little chance of getting played on mainstream radio, reviewed in mainstream publications, or booked into big venues. The UK was a different story. It is geographically smaller, and had respected BBC radio DJs like John Peel who raved over indie releases. Most importantly, it had major music publications like *Melody Maker*, *New Musical Express*, and *Sounds* that covered the community, allowing underground bands to reach greater heights.

In collusion with UK publicist Anton Brookes, Pavitt and Poneman hatched a seemingly crazy plan, which proved to be incredibly prescient when, in early 1989, they flew UK music journalist Everett True to Seattle. They introduced him to their friends in Mudhoney, Swallow, Screaming Trees, Soundgarden, Beat Happening, TAD, Girl Trouble and Fastbacks, along with folks from the scenes in Seattle, Tacoma, Olympia, Ellensburg and elsewhere. True was a quick convert and returned to England to write this influential profile. The *Melody Maker* story portrayed a primal and mythic Northwest scene, populated by backwoods butchers and flannelled blue collar losers with screeching guitars – exactly the type of exaggerated hype Sub Pop was looking for.

MELODY MAKER, MARCH 18, 1989

"When we brought Everett True over and introduced him to some of these groups, he was really impressed. And he did very in-depth coverage / hype about what was going on in Seattle. Next month, John Peel from BBC One reviewed our *Sub Pop 200* box set and said it was the most distinctive regional sound from America since the Tamla Motown. He wrote this in the *London Times* that has a circulation of two million."

— Bruce Pavitt, Sub Pop Records

"Nirvana: Basically, this is the real thing. No rock star contrivance, no intellectual perspective, no master plan for world domination. You're talking about four guys in their early twenties from rural Washington who wanna rock, who, if they weren't doing this, would be working in a supermarket or lumber yard, or fixing cars."

— Everett True, *Melody Maker*, March 18, 1989

"This British guy came over and did interviews with tons of bands, everything that Sub Pop was even affiliated with — all the bands on *Sub Pop 200*, if I'm correct. So there was like this huge two page fold out spread that had all these little pictures. It was basically announcing to England and the world that there was this weird place called Seattle where just the greatest music on Earth right now is being made."

— Mark Arm, Mudhoney

Photographer Charles Peterson donated this desk to Seattle's Sub Pop Records, which used it as its reception desk between 1988 and 1999. As Sub Pop grew from a few employees to dozens, inhabiting several floors of the Terminal Sales Building, countless bands along with innumerable hipsters and indie cognoscenti passed by this bestickered piece of furniture. Many added their personal mark, turning this thrift store chunk of wood into a visual history of grunge and indie rock, as seen in the 1996 documentary *Hype!*, which covered the Seattle grunge scene of the early 1990s.

"Hype" was an appropriate term, since Sub Pop's modus operandi was to make the label seem bigger than it really was, through a mix of strong graphic identity, striking product photography (primarily from Charles Peterson), and consistent recording production values (from Jack Endino), all packaged into a highly-collectible product. Sub Pop's explicit goal of "world domination" was absurd, given that the Northwest in the 1980s was perceived to be a cultural backwater, especially for music. But by the early '90s, Sub Pop had indeed achieved World Domination: many of the bands it helped to cultivate had become superstars, and Seattle was the center of popular music.

SUB POP RECEPTION DESK, 1988 – 1999

"One of the real keys to Sub Pop's success is that the groups we worked with had tremendous live shows. Again, the press in America wouldn't write about them, the radio stations wouldn't play them, so your only option really was to get these bands in front of people and blow them away."

— BRUCE PAVITT, SUB POP RECORDS

"What I was trying to nail down with my early work for Sub Pop was a look that was distinct, clean, incredibly bold and forceful. That's where Charles Peterson's photography came in. I mean, he was unequaled. Being able to use Charles' photography just made the job so simple, y'know? Bold, even off-putting typography that didn't necessarily clash with the image, but complemented it. Bright colors that were out of style. Anything that was pretentious. And in a way it ended up playing right into the Sub Pop vision of promoting the label and not the band, which I thought was a brilliant thing to do. It established the label, and then the band took over. But once you had that good house-keeping seal of approval, aka the Sub Pop logo, at that point it was solid gold."

— Art Chantry, graphic designer

"It was really about the label. When I bought that stuff, I had no idea who the Lonely Moans were. I just bought it because it had the bar across the top and it had the logo."
— Jeff Kleinsmith, Sub Pop Records

"Bruce and John of the Sub Pop honchos were, if nothing else, masters of hype and propaganda, and without a penny to their name really built the label up on word of mouth alone."

— Kurt Danielson, TAD

1986 GIBSON LES PAUL Custom guitar, played by Bruce Fairweather with Green River, Mother Love Bone and Love Battery, 1986 - 1997; FENDER SQUIER II Stratocaster guitar, played by Roisin Dunne with 7 Year Bitch, 1992 - 1997

1981 GIBSON LES PAUL Custom guitar, played by Joe Spleen with the Gits, 1986 - 1993; 1978 GIBSON RD standard guitar, played by Ron Nine with Love Battery, 1990-1994

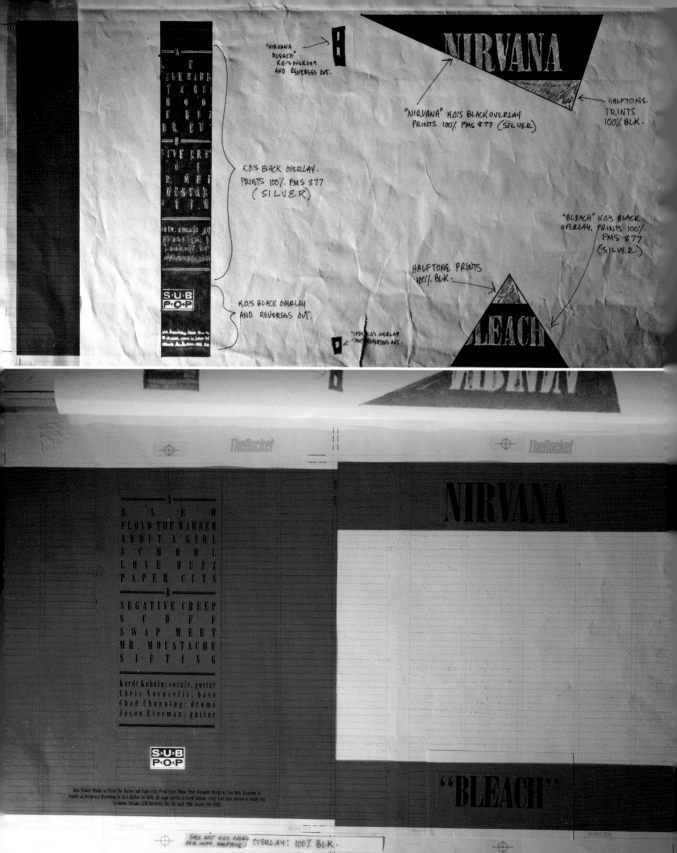

"NIRVANA" "BLEACH" K.O.'S OVERLAY AND REVERSES OUT.

"NIRVANA" KO'S BLACK OVERLAY. PRINTS 100% PMS 877 (SILVER)

HALFTONE PRINTS 100% BLK.

K.O.'S BLACK OVERLAY. PRINTS 100% PMS 877 (SILVER)

"BLEACH" KO'S BLACK OVERLAY, PRINTS 100% PMS 877 (SILVER)

HALFTONE PRINTS 100% BLK.

K.O.'S BLACK OVERLAY AND REVERSES OUT.

"SP34" K.O.'S OVERLAY AND REVERSES OUT.

TheRocket

NIRVANA

A
B   L   E   W
FLOYD THE BARBER
ABOUT A GIRL
S   C   H   O   O   L
LOVE   BUZZ
PAPER   CUTS
B
NEGATIVE CREEP
S   C   O   F   F
SWAP MEET
MR. MOUSTACHE
S   I   F   T   I   N   G

Kurdt Kobain: vocals, guitar
Chris Novoselic: bass
Chad Channing: drums
Jason Everman: guitar

SUB POP

"BLEACH"

BASE ART K.O.'S OVERD FOR INFO, HALFTONES   OVERLAY: 100% BLK.

After the release of Nirvana's "Love Buzz" single, Sub Pop agreed to issue an album. Nirvana recorded with Jack Endino in December 1988 and January '89. Thirty hours of recording time cost $606.17, which was paid by Jason Everman, who would soon become the band's second guitarist. The resulting *Bleach* album was released on June 15, 1989 and featured Melvins-esque dirges like "Paper Cuts" and "Sifting," alongside anthemic rockers such as "School," "Blew," and "Negative Creep." The beautiful "About a Girl," brought the pop elements underlying many of the band's songs out into the open.

This layout for the *Bleach* cover was created by graphic designer and musician Lisa Orth at the offices of *The Rocket*, where she also worked. The cover conformed to Sub Pop's design aesthetic: a stark field of color with bold type and a striking photograph. The photo, by Kurt Cobain's girlfriend Tracy Marander, was reversed-out as if it were a film negative. It featured the band (including Everman, though he didn't perform on the album) playing at the Reko/Muse Gallery in Olympia, WA on April 1, 1989. Orth asked *The Rocket*'s typesetter, Grant Alden, to set the band's name in whatever was already installed in their typesetting machine. And thus Nirvana's logo was born, mostly by accident.

ALBUM COVER LAYOUT FOR NIRVANA'S *BLEACH*, 1989. DESIGN BY LISA ORTH

"It was a typeface called Onyx which is a Compu-graphic bad design of Bodoni Condensed — really hunky, ugly, and those Compugraphics, if you didn't use the right kerning programs you had really bad letterspacing. And so Grant Alden basically just sat down, slammed it out, charged Lisa Orth 15 bucks, which she paid out of pocket, and that is where Nirvana's logo came from."

— Art Chantry, graphic designer

"There was definitely a chemistry between Kurt and Krist and those bass lines were very strong, and they worked in a certain way to sort of pull it all together. I mean, if you take those bass lines away, you just have a bunch of guitar riffs. You put those bass lines on, and then you have Nirvana. So at the same time, without that voice, you would just have a hard rock band doing a vaguely '70s inspired riff-rock. You put that voice on, and then it's — what is it? Is it punk rock? Is it the Beatles? What is it exactly?"

— Jack Endino, recording engineer/producer/musician

"Nirvana's *Bleach* — for me the greatest thing is those songs are heavy and they are punk rock but they're also melodic and have elements of the Beatles in them — not that they sound like the Beatles, but the songs are written really, really well. They're quick and concise, to the point, the melodies are incredible. Simple, though. I mean, I try to write these melodies that seem like, 'Wow, this is a timeless concept,' but then I'll listen to like a Kurt Cobain melody and it's just amazing. Kurt Cobain and Paul McCartney, they just had this melodic sensibility. But *Bleach* had both elements, the heaviness, which was what I was really into, with the hard pounding drums, and a melody."

— Jeremy Enigk, Sunny Day Real Estate

Sub Pop Exclusive Recording Agreement

1. This contract is for an exclusive recording agreement between <u>KURT COBAIN, CHRIS NOVOSELIC,</u> <u>CHAD CHANNING, JASON EVERMAN</u>, from here on known as "artist" and SUB POP LTD., from here on known as label.

2. Artist agrees to record exclusively for the label under the conditions outlined in this recording agreement. Any adjustments and/or changes in this agreement shall be made solely between the label and the artist.

3. Art ist agrees to record exclusively for the label for the duration of an initial one year term and <u>TWO OPTION YEARS</u>. This agreement shall be exercised by the conditions outlined further in this contract.

3a. The initial one year term shall begin on <u>JAN. 1ST, 1989</u> and shall end on <u>DEC 31, 1989</u>. The first option year, if all obligations agreed to by both artist and label in this contract are met, shall begin on <u>JAN. 1ST 1990</u> and shall end on <u>DEC 31, 1990</u>. The second option year, if all obligations agreed to by both artist and label in this contract are met, shall begin <u>JAN. 1ST 1991</u> and shall end on <u>DEC. 31ST 1991</u>. The third option year, if all obligations agreed to by both artist and label in this contract are met, shall begin _____ and shall end _____.

3b. During the initial one year term and for each option year thereafter, artist will record and complete one normal album length master tape per term. "term", for the purposes of this contract, refers to the singular initial one year term and to each singular option year thereafter.

3c. This contract is for _____3_____ complete album length master tapes to be recorded by the artist for the label under the conditions provided for in this contract. That is: one complete album length master tape will be recorded and completed during the initial option year. One complete album length master tape will be recorded and completed DURING each option year, no earlier-no later.

4. Label agrees to provide artist with the following recoupable advances per term:
For the initial one year term, the label agrees to provide artist with a <u>SIX HUNDRED</u> <u>DOLLAR</u> advance, recoupable against royalties. (i.e. sales royalties)
For the first option year, the label agrees to provide artist with a <u>TWELVE THOUSAND</u> <u>DOLLAR</u> advance, recoupable against sales royalties.
For the second option year, the label agrees to provide artist with a <u>TWENTY FOUR</u> <u>THOUSAND DOLLAR</u> advance, recoupable against sales royalties.
For the third option year, the label agrees to provide artist with a _____ _____ advance, recoupable against royalties.

4a. In exchange for each advance (noted in article 4), artist agrees to provide label with a

This contract between Nirvana and Sub Pop Records was drafted after the group demanded a legal agreement on the eve of the release of their debut album, *Bleach*. Signed by Chad Channing, Chris Novoselic, Jason Everman, and Kurt Cobain, and countersigned by Sub Pop's Jonathan Poneman on June 3, 1989, but covering the period of January 1, 1989 to January 1, 1991, this was the band's first legal agreement. It was also Sub Pop's first contract. Until that time, Sub Pop had operated like most independent labels of the day, by handshake deals between friends.

Nirvana felt they were being mishandled, and Sub Pop's increasing financial difficulties made matters worse. With the band's growing profile, they felt that a contract with Sub Pop would bring more commitment and stability. The document featured a three-record deal, with the band receiving successive advances of $600, $12,000, and $24,000 for the albums. It ultimately proved to be a boon for Sub Pop. When Nirvana signed to DGC Records on January 1, 1991, Geffen had to buy out the contract. Sub Pop received a chunk of cash, which it desperately needed. But more important, the label received royalties on the next two Nirvana records, the first of which would be the multi-platinum *Nevermind*. Without this document, Sub Pop most likely would have shut the doors in the early 1990s.

CONTRACT BETWEEN NIRVANA AND SUB POP RECORDS, SIGNED ON JUNE 3, 1989

"We did not have an attorney. We did not have the funds to hire an attorney. This is essentially why we did not have contracts, and classically, in the late '80s, indie labels did handshake deals. It was kind of the culture at the time. Krist Novoselic of Nirvana came visiting my house one night and he asked me for a contract. That was kind of a very intense experience for me. I called Jonathan about one in the morning and said, 'Dude, you'd better come over with a contract.' And he went to the library and Xeroxed a contract, customized it, a little white-out. And they signed the contract. And that was a blessing, let me tell you."

— Bruce Pavitt, Sub Pop Records

"The decision with bringing Jason Everman on was Kurt felt like he wanted to have somebody else playing guitar so he could just concentrate more on singing, and not have to worry about it. He wanted somebody that was gonna be steady, so he wouldn't screw stuff up. And that's kind of how Jason came around. We first were going to recruit Ben Shepherd. He actually went on tour with us, and had the opportunity to come up and play the guitar and stuff with us. He never did. We had a fun tour that time, though, it was really a lot of fun. I think Ben ultimately decided, 'Kurt, you know what? You don't need another guitar player at all. You're fine. Don't worry about it.'"

— Chad Channing, Nirvana

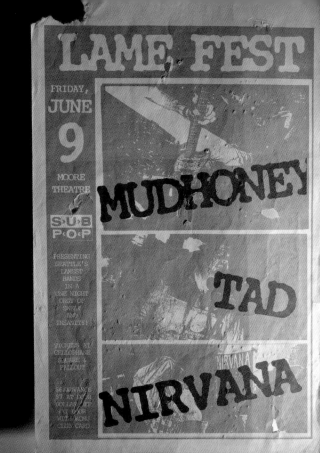

Advertised as "Sub Pop Sells Out!!! You saw it coming," Sub Pop's Lame Fest took place at the Moore Theatre on June 9, 1989, "presenting Seattle's lamest bands in a one night orgy of sweat and insanity." Three of the label's most promising bands, Mudhoney, TAD, and Nirvana, played to the largest crowd of their careers at the time by selling out the 1,400-seat venue. Nirvana, as the youngest band on the bill, opened the show, and despite poor sound, played an intense set. Battles between stage divers and overzealous security took place throughout the night, reaching a peak during Mudhoney's set when the band had to stop playing three times to calm down the security guards.

Sub Pop's Lame Fest marked a turning point in the Northwest – a bill with three local bands selling out a venue as large as the Moore Theatre was unprecedented. From here on out, bands on Sub Pop would regularly play to hundreds of people, rather than to dozens in clubs years prior. The scene was attracting the attention of people outside its traditional boundaries, and these soon-to-be legions of new fans were embracing the music and calling it their own.

LAME FEST: MUDHONEY, TAD, AND NIRVANA AT THE MOORE THEATRE, SEATTLE, JUNE 9, 1989

"Jonathan Poneman and Bruce Pavitt at Sub Pop decided to put on this thing called the Lame Fest at the Moore Theatre, which was us with TAD and Nirvana opening and I just thought they were crazy to book an all-local show at the Moore Theatre. I mean the Moore Theatre, my God, y'know? I couldn't think of any local show that would have any kind of draw there. And the show sold out. It was astounding."

— Mark Arm, Mudhoney

"It was cool to see our name up on the marquee. Part of me was like, 'Wow, that's weird.' Like at the Moore, I've seen some pretty big bands there before, y'know? It's strange to actually be standing here and seeing 'Mudhoney, TAD, Nirvana,' y'know? Wow, what a trip. Playing the Lame Fest show was really fun. It was the first time that I'd actually played a place that was really huge. I remember being on stage and it was like there was Kurt way over there, and there was Krist way over there and even Jason was playing, too, and he was like way over there."

— Chad Channing, Nirvana

"For me, I think the first show that I was able to hear the group and got it, was probably the Lame Fest show at the Moore Theatre. Nirvana was on the bill and Jason Everman played at that show. And you could really see Kurt and

hear him for the first time and hear his vocal quality. And at the end of that show he dove into the drum set, and he came back out with his guitar tangled up in his hair. He's walking around the stage with his guitar swinging – I don't even know if he tied it in knots or if it actually got caught in there. But I remember watching the show and just thinking, 'That's got to hurt!' I think there was that sense of never knowing what to expect from one of their shows after that. And feeling that you had to go and find out."

— Earnie Bailey, guitar tech, Nirvana, Foo Fighters

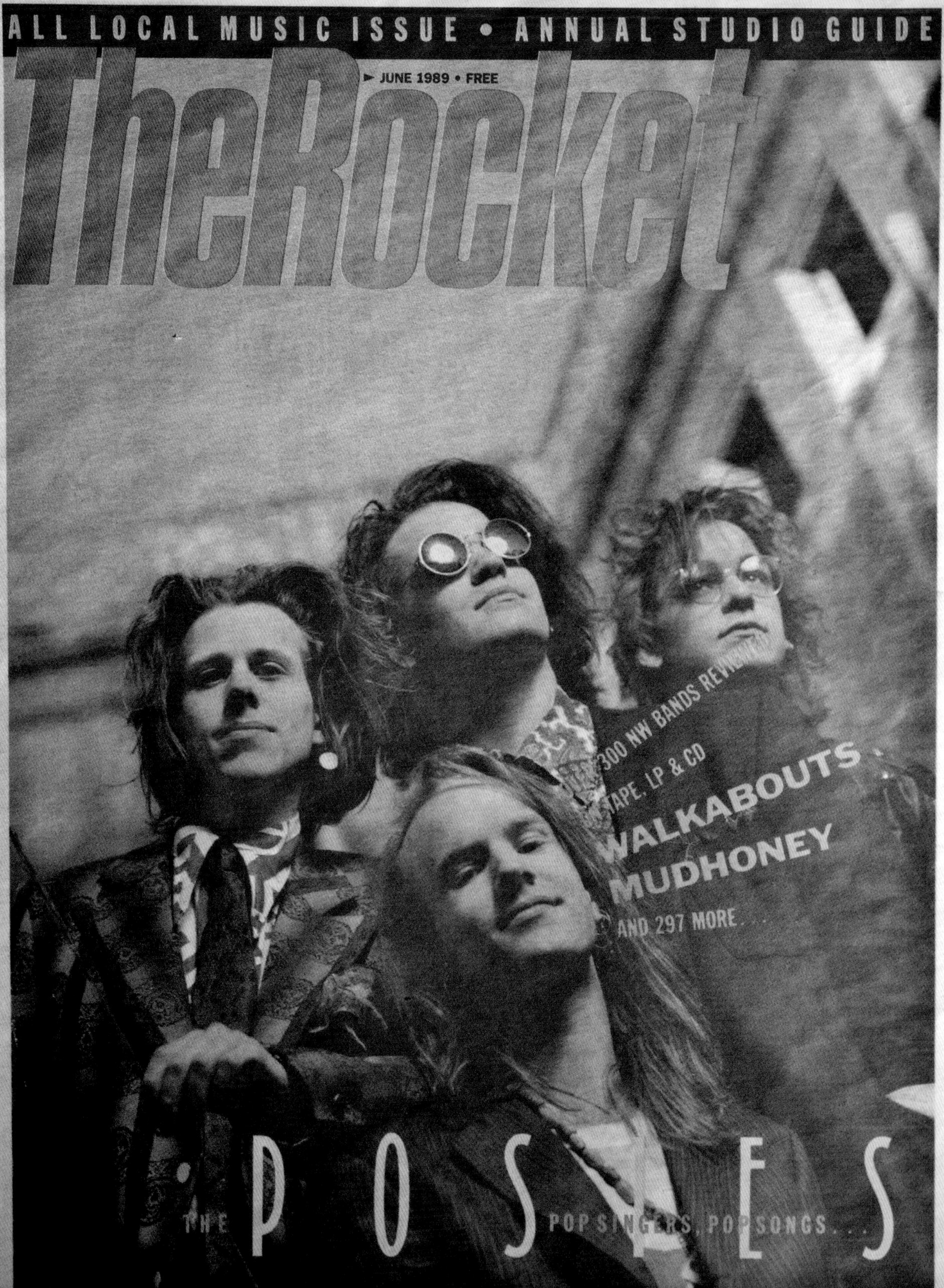

ALL LOCAL MUSIC ISSUE • ANNUAL STUDIO GUIDE
TheRocket
JUNE 1989 • FREE
300 NW BANDS REVIEW
TAPE, LP & CD
WALKABOUTS
MUDHONEY
AND 297 MORE...
THE POSIES
POP SINGERS, POP SONGS...

While Sub Pop was promoting grunge, an entirely different scene was thriving in Seattle. The Posies were the pop antidote to grunge's darkness, and despite the mythologizing of later years, pop was quite popular in the city. The Posies gained widespread attention early on, as evidenced by this cover of *The Rocket* from June 1989. Major labels could easily see the potential in the band's harmonized vocals and jangly guitar power pop. The Posies signed to DGC Records, Nirvana's future label, in late 1989, about the same time that Alice in Chains joined Columbia and Soundgarden went to A&M.

The Posies were formed in 1986 by Bellingham, WA natives Ken Stringfellow and Jon Auer. The two recorded a demo in the Auer family's home studio, which they self-released in 1988. A year later Popllama Records reissued the demo as the band's debut, *Failure*. Soon after, Auer and Stringfellow added drummer Mike Musberger (later of the Fastbacks) and bassist Rick Roberts. The band moved to Seattle and began developing new songs. Their 1990 major label debut, *Dear 23*, hit the Modern Rock charts and proved they could sustain a national audience. In 1993, they produced *Frosting on the Beater*, an album of guitar-driven power pop with the hit single, "Dream All Day," showing that the "Seattle Sound" was more encompassing that it appeared.

THE ROCKET, JUNE 1989

"When we first appeared on the cover of *The Rocket*, it was sometime in '89, it did feel at that time like that was kind of a big deal. I think that there was less precedence for it. At a certain point, it was hard to scrape up enough local bands of note to fill out the covers year round and I remember there being a lot more non-music things and national music things on the cover of *The Rocket* then. And there was also less outlets in general for music press in Seattle at the time so it was like the only game in town."

— Ken Stringfellow, the Posies

"I was on a trip with the Young Fresh Fellows when I first heard the Posies. I traveled with them in the early years as sound man and someone who wanted to be along. And we were somewhere in the middle of Utah or something, and Scott McCaughey had been telling me about this tape he got in the mail. I was driving, he was riding shotgun and he threw it in and I was just blown away by the tape that they had made and released themselves, which ended up being the *Failure* album. It was just so great. And they were fans of the Young Fresh Fellows, they were fans of the Squirrels,

they were fans of stuff that I'd put out. And so they wanted to be on Popllama. We just called 'em up and they said, 'Yeah!' It was great. In their formative years they decided they wanted to be on this silly little label. Go figure."

— Conrad Uno, Popllama Records

"When the first *Rocket* cover came out, it was kind of like the Posies exploding upon the scene. I think it kind of mystified a lot of people who were actually in the Seattle music scene. It was like, 'Who are these guys and where are they coming from and why are all these kids showing up to their all ages concerts.' At the time, too, there was this thing called the NAMA awards which was like Northwest Area Music Awards and I think the year that *The Rocket* cover came out, the Posies won like 13 awards at this ceremony and we got accused of stuffing the ballot and doing all these crazy things like hiring kids to fill out forms to vote the Posies into every category — none of which was true, of course."

— Jon Auer, Posies

After Green River broke up in late 1987, Mark Arm and Steve Turner formed Mudhoney, while Jeff Ament, Bruce Fairweather, and Stone Gossard along with 10 Minute Warning drummer Greg Gilmore and ex-Malfunkshun vocalist Andrew Wood formed Mother Love Bone. The new band combined the glam-inspired rock of Green River with the flamboyant style of Andrew Wood. Wood was grunge's Freddie Mercury; while in Malfunkshun, he went by the name L'Andrew the Love Child. Mother Love Bone quickly became a draw in Seattle and signed to Polygram in early 1989.

On March 16, 1990, only days before the debut of their album *Apple*, Andrew Wood was found dead, overdosed on heroin. Wood was beloved, and his passing was a shock. Soon after, Soundgarden's Chris Cornell (Wood's former roommate) approached Ament and Gossard, and with the addition of Stone's friend Mike McCready, Soundgarden drummer Matt Cameron, and vocalist Eddie Vedder, formed Temple of the Dog, to record songs in tribute to Wood. In April 1991, they released an eponymous album, named after a Wood-penned Mother Love Bone lyric. Andrew Wood's death ended one of the brightest lights in the Northwest scene. It also brought together a group of musicians who would change the musical landscape as Pearl Jam.

STAGE BANNER PAINTED BY JEFF AMENT AND USED BY MOTHER LOVE BONE, CA. 1989
GIFT OF BRUCE FAIRWEATHER. **PHOTOGRAPH BY LANCE MERCER**

"Chris Cornell wrote two songs after Andy died and wanted to put out a single. He wanted me and then the members of Mother Love Bone to work with him on this single — I think it was going to be on Sub Pop or something. Then we wrote a bunch of songs together and went into a studio, recorded it, and it was at the time when Eddie Vedder had just moved up to Seattle, and he was just kind of getting worked into Pearl Jam. So he got to sing on a song with us. That was one of his first experiences with working in a big studio, so it was really good for Eddie at the time. But it was just a lot of fun. We were feeling the loss of a really good shining talent that OD'd. Andy was a huge part of the scene — like Malfunkshun, the group he was in, was bitchin'. That was a rockin' group, man, they were one of my favorite local bands ever. So we definitely were feeling the loss."

— Matt Cameron, Soundgarden, Pearl Jam

"There's this intersection on Bainbridge Island — Sportsman Club and High School Road — and in those days it didn't have stop signs or stop lights, it just had this crazy intersection, two different directions of traffic. So I'm riding with the bass player on the way to [our March of Crimes] gig and he goes 'WHOA!' and there's a car wreck in front of us. And we stop and get out. We notice that there were two girls and they go, 'Yeah, our car's over there, Andy's in the back. All of the sudden, the back door opens up, this guy who's wearing a huge kimono, this amazing kimono thing, and gigantic hair, all ratted out, starts rubbing his eyes — 'What happened? I was asleep?' That's how I met Andy Wood: at that car wreck, on the way to that gig. Lo and behold, of course he's asleep — the Love Child."

— Ben Shepherd, Soundgarden

OCTOBER 21 1989   60p

SOUNDS

WIN!
VER £1,000
RI-FI GEAR
ENTER SOUNDS
READERS' SURVEY

EINSTÜRZENDE NEUBAUTEN
AMERICAN MUSIC CLUB
CLAYTOWN TROUPE
DANIEL LANOIS
PALE SAINTS

LIVES: THE STONE ROSES ● LUSH
● MARC ALMOND ● THE CHILLS
● BITCH MAGNET ● THE LA'S

LOSER

TAD & NIRVANA
GRABBING AMERICA BY THE BALLS
INTERVIEWS INSIDE

ALBUMS: ALL ABOUT EVE ●
THE WEDDING PRESENT ●
MUDHONEY ● ERASURE ●
THE TELESCOPES ●

42

9 770144 577003

TAD AND NIRVANA PHOTOS BY IAN T TILTON.

By October 1989, the Sub Pop hype machine was in full swing. The nine combined members of TAD and Nirvana, plus crew, toured together in a small Fiat van across the UK and Europe on the "Bleach God's Balls" tour, supporting TAD's *God's Balls* and Nirvana's *Bleach* albums. TAD was fronted by Tad Doyle, a sweet-as-pie but ferocious guitarist/vocalist. Sub Pop took pleasure in noting that Tad was once a butcher from Idaho. He formed TAD in 1988 with bassist Kurt Danielson, from the ashes of H-Hour and Bundle of Hiss, and from the start they created some of the heaviest grooves Sub Pop would ever release. After Mudhoney, TAD was considered one of Sub Pop's biggest priorities.

TAD and Nirvana had a grueling month-and-a-half tour, which took a toll on the band members. Days were marked by the cramped quarters of the van, lack of sleep, and endless travelling; nights featured shows erupting with sweaty, moshing kids. At the end of the tour, the bands met up with Mudhoney, who had been criss-crossing the UK to similar fanfare. The Sub Pop Lame Fest UK was held at the Astoria Theater in London on December 3, 1989. Like the Seattle version in June, it was packed. Halfway around the world from Seattle, people were starting to tune in.

SOUNDS MAGAZINE, OCTOBER 21, 1989

"We co-headlined with [Nirvana] all across Europe – Germany, Switzerland, England, France, Belgium, Italy and even Budapest, Hungary while it was still a communist state. We were all in a Fiat minivan which seats probably nine people and there was ten or eleven of us in the bands with our equipment and t-shirts. And y'know I'm a pretty big fella and Krist Novoselic is pretty tall. And so it was like every day we'd be in the van just hating life, freezing our buttocks off. We were in a strange new land, all of us Americans who never even thought of traveling outside of our own state, let alone a foreign country. The food was strange, the drink was strange, the hotels were strange, everybody was speaking a foreign language. It was just kinda like a really weird bad dream, except when we were on stage doing what we like to do."

— Tad Doyle, TAD

"I think the most memorable moment was probably going into East Germany and seeing the line of East German cars leaving and it was like forty kilometers long and at the border they were being greeted by flowers and bottles of champagne and fruit and what not. We didn't know [the Berlin Wall had fallen] because we were cut off from the media — our whole world was this van and we kinda thought, 'Wow, what a nice reception. These East Germans really know how to lay out the red carpet.' But we soon realized that it had nothing to do with us. The tragedy

about it was we didn't have time to go down to the Wall. We played Berlin that night and left that night as well."

— Kurt Danielson, TAD

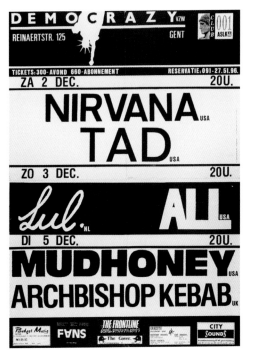

NIRVANA AND TAD AT DEMOCRAZY, GHENT, BELGIUM, DECEMBER 2, 1989

Love Battery was led by guitarist/vocalist Ron Nine, along with Kevin Whitworth on guitar, Tommy Bonehead on bass, and ex-Skin Yard member Jason Finn on this Gretsch drum kit. Their first single, released by Sub Pop, was the shimmery, psychedelic "Between the Eyes" / "Easter." During their career, the band went through numerous lineup changes, at times counting ex-U-Men bassist Jim Tillman and ex-Mother Love Bone guitarist Bruce Fairweather among their ranks. The several albums they made for Sub Pop – including *Between the Eyes* (1991), *Dayglo* (1992), and *Far Gone* (1993) – were steady sellers, but the band never gained the recognition that many of their compatriots did.

Jason Finn quit in 1995 and assumed full-time drummer duty with the Presidents of the United States of America (with whom he'd been playing since 1993). He played this Gretsch kit for the first few dozen shows with PUSA. They released their self-titled debut on Seattle's Popllama label in 1995, and their infectiously goofy power pop tunes became an instant Seattle favorite during the city's grunge hype hangover. Columbia Records signed the Presidents shortly thereafter, and re-released the record, which climbed the charts with the hit singles, "Lump," "Kitty," and "Peaches."

GRETSCH DRUM KIT, PLAYED BY JASON FINN WITH LOVE BATTERY (1989 – 1995) AND THE PRESIDENTS OF THE UNITED STATES OF AMERICA (1993 – 1995)

"Jason Finn saw the band Go that Chris and I had and he begged me for the next two or three years, 'If you ever start a band with Chris again I want to be in it.' Jason joined the band and, y'know, once you've got the Pope of Pike Street you can write your own ticket in this town, so then we got more shows and people liked us and the next thing we knew all these record companies were chasing us around. That all happened within like six months, nine months."

— Dave Dederer, the Presidents

"After Skin Yard, I started this band called Love Battery with Ron Rudzitis – Ron Nine as we called him 'cause he was in this band called Room Nine that was one of the very popular mid '80s Seattle bands. So we started this band and it was about that time that other bands were getting signed. The Sub Pop label started and Mudhoney started to do really good, so we weaseled our way onto Sub Pop 'cause Ron worked with Bruce Pavitt at Muzak. Then there was the Sub Pop explosion. Journalists all over the country and in Europe were 'Seattle,' 'Seattle,' 'Seattle,' and there was definitely a sense that, 'Wow, we are on this wave right now. Why don't we just grab on and maybe we'll get huge too.' We were still playing the Vogue and the Central and stuff, but people were talking. And you believe the hype! Everybody was talking about my city like we were mutantly good musicians or something. Like there's something in the water that makes us better bands. And if people are saying that, of course it's just a total load, but hey, if there saying it about you it's, 'Sure! Yeah, yeah we're better 'cause we're from Seattle.'"

— Jason Finn, Skin Yard, Love Battery, the Presidents

MELVINS
NIRVANA
DWARVES
DERELICTS

SAT 22 SEPT

ALL AGES! $8/$10

TEAT HORN Flyer Corps

Motor Sports Int'l Garage
Stewart & Vale

The Motorsports International Garage was a massive space near downtown Seattle. In 1990 and '91, it hosted several concerts, including this celebrated show headlined by Nirvana (despite the order listed on this poster designed by renowned Seattle illustrator Jim Blanchard). The show was a watershed moment: it drew Nirvana's largest hometown audience, over 1500 people, and foreshadowed the scene's future explosion. Nirvana played a high-energy set that included new songs they had recorded with producer Butch Vig the previous spring. The band ended the set with an improvised spoken-word piece from bassist Krist Novoselic, followed by an impromptu guitar destruction jam, with Kurt Cobain swinging his guitar around his head before smashing it to pieces on stage.

This concert was the only Nirvana show to feature Dan Peters on drums, who was on hiatus from Mudhoney. Kurt Cobain and Krist Novoselic had just parted ways from Chad Channing, and the Melvins' Dale Crover had been filling in on drums. Peters was asked to join the band, and the trio began writing songs, including "Sliver," which they recorded with Peters and released as Nirvana's last single of original material with Sub Pop in 1990. While the Motorsports show was the last for Peters, there was someone in the audience who would soon change fortunes for the band: Dave Grohl.

MELVINS, NIRVANA, DWARVES, AND DERELICTS AT THE MOTORSPORTS GARAGE, SEATTLE, SEPTEMBER 22, 1990. ORIGINAL ARTWORK BY JIM BLANCHARD

"The Motorsports International Garage was essentially an old garage, I think they'd been storing cars there or repairing them. And this was sort of a no-man's land in downtown Seattle by the freeway and it held almost 1500 people or something, which was at the time a really big space. And they filled it up. That's the point to me where the scene really had taken off."

— Charles Peterson, photographer

"That show was so exciting because Nirvana was head-lining the show, and I felt like they were finally getting the credit that they deserved for how good of a band they were. And they delivered the goods, too. I remember being airborne most of the show and just jumping up and down and dancing, and thinking this is the greatest show ever. And then after the show, I remember walking home, just thinking, 'They're too good, they're going to break up.' This is probably one of the best bands in America right now.

And I felt like, it was like seeing a young Springsteen or Prince, or one of these young geniuses that you see in their prime. I really felt that way about Kurt — he was this incred-ible talent, and I thought that this is just terrible, because in America right now, this stuff will never fly, will never get big. It can never break through what's going on right now. I remember walking home and just thinking that this'll be one of these bands we talked about that came and went and never broke through."

— Earnie Bailey, guitar tech, Nirvana, Foo Fighters

"The Motorsports show was the first time they played where you realized they were finally getting bigger and they were finally catching on. Before then it seemed like a smaller community of people. But now Nirvana was getting a lot bigger, and I was recognizing people from high school that I never would have expected to see at a Nirvana show."

— Rob Kader, Nirvana fan

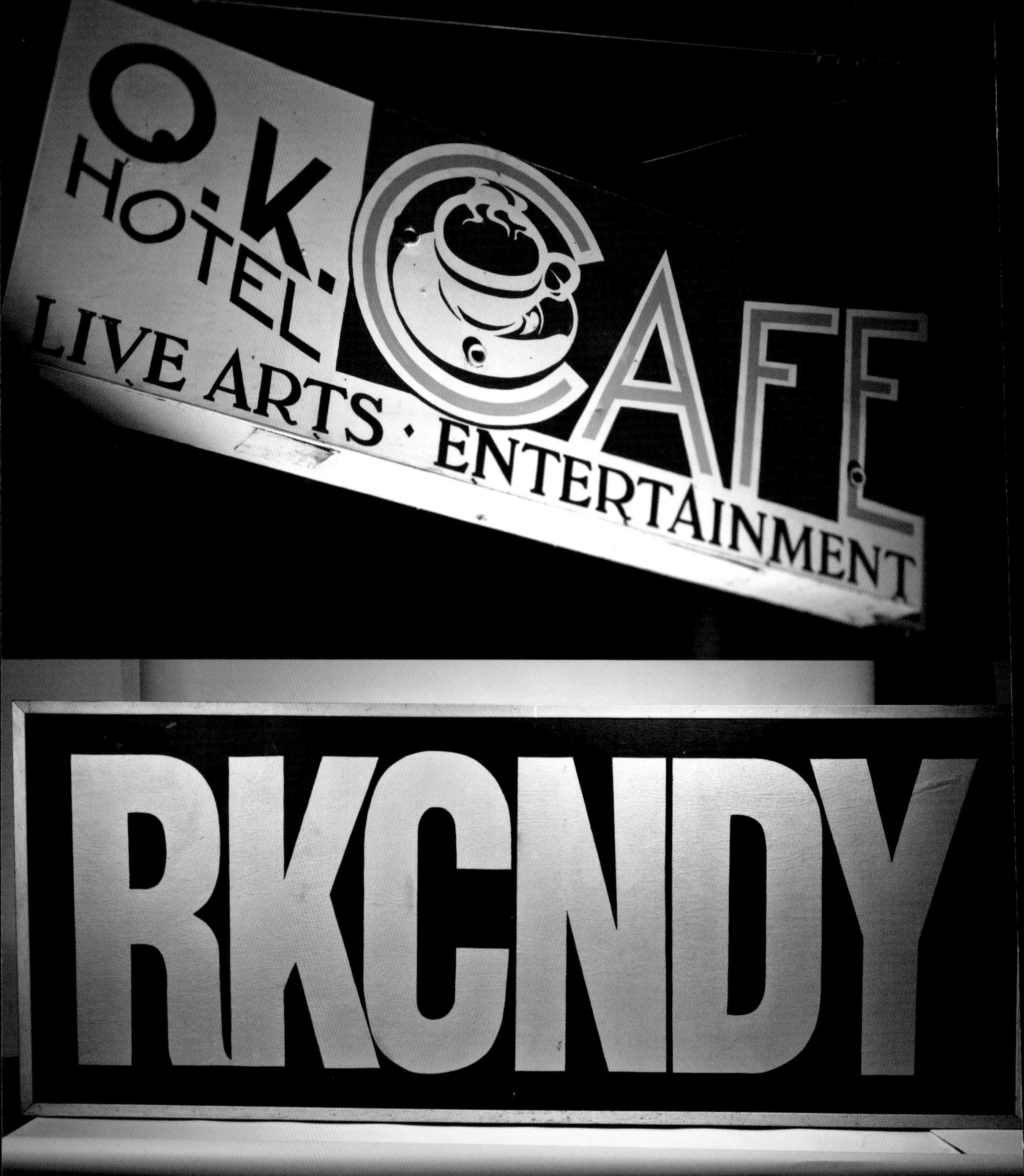
O.K. HOTEL
CAFE
LIVE ARTS · ENTERTAINMENT
RKCNDY

In 1990, the scene in the Northwest was reaching a boiling point. By year's end Nirvana, Pearl Jam, Soundgarden, Alice in Chains and Screaming Trees had been signed by major labels. Gone were the days of Sub Pop Sundays at the Vogue or intimate shows at the Central Tavern. Now shows were big, and a new crop of venues sprang up to accommodate them.

The Off Ramp and RKCNDY were located near each other between Seattle's downtown and the Capitol Hill neighborhood. In 1990 and 1991, they were the hip clubs in town. Pearl Jam, then known as Mookie Blaylock, played their first show at the Off Ramp on October 22, 1990. The OK Hotel was located near Pioneer Square, and quickly became popular as one of the few all-ages venues. Mother Love Bone played their first show there in April 1988, Nirvana debuted "Smells Like Teen Spirit" at the venue on April 17, 1991, and the club was prominently featured in the 1992 grunge romance film *Singles*. As the scene was expanding, a new group of bands started playing in these venues and others, including the Crocodile Café, the Weathered Wall, and the Colourbox. Bands like Treepeople, Hammerbox, Silkworm, 7 Year Bitch, Alcohol Funnycar, the Gits, Gas Huffer, and others initiated the vibrant indie rock scene that would follow grunge's collapse.

SIGNS FOR THE OFF RAMP, RKCNDY, AND OK HOTEL

"When they were filming that *Hype!* movie, Love Battery's set was at the Off Ramp and the place was just packed because there was this rumor that Soundgarden was gonna play the show too. Of course they weren't and we're the last band of the night and setting up and this girl grabs my leg from below, y'know, 'Are they here yet?' And we're like, 'Oh god' — we're gonna start and actually have bottles thrown at us. But they didn't throw any bottles. It was a fun show."
— Jason Finn, Love Battery, the Presidents

"For whatever reason this state has some weird laws and really harsh liquor laws. These days, there sure are a lot of kids that go out to shows. When I was under 21 there just wasn't a lot of kids into that kind of music at that point. Punk rock was really new. And now everybody knows what punk rock is, y'know? Those RKCNDY shows always seem to sell out, and there's tons of kids that want to go see that stuff."
— Kim Warnick, Fastbacks

"I started playing bass and a month and a half later, we had our first performance at the OK Hotel. The first song was one I used to sing. I just remember being so petrified, just completely scared. But it was addicting, y'know? I really wanted to do it more and more."
— Elizabeth Davis, 7 Year Bitch

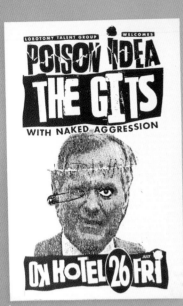

POISON IDEA, the Gits, with Naked Aggression, at the OK Hotel, Seattle, July 26, 1991. Poster by Jeff Kleinsmith; SPITBOY, 7 Year Bitch, and Ruination, at the OK Hotel, Seattle, May 25, early 1990s. Poster by Jeff Kleinsmith; THE GITS, Alcohol Funnycar, Officer Down, and Christdriver, at the Weathered Wall, Seattle, December 19, 1992. Poster by Jeff Kleinsmith; TREEPEOPLE, 7 Year Bitch, Gnome, and Nubbin, at RKCNDY, Seattle, May 15, 1992. Poster by Jeff Kleinsmith; HOLE, Adickdid, Sourpuss,

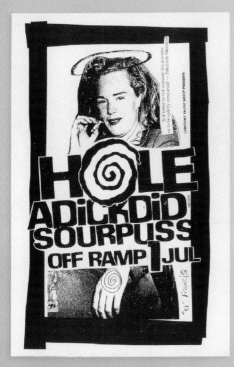

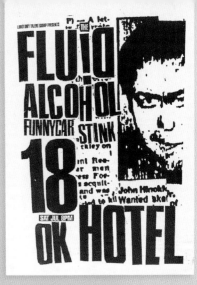

at the Off Ramp, Seattle, July 1, 1993. Poster by Jeff Kleinsmith; THE FLUID, Alochol Funnycar, and Stink, at the OK Hotel, Seattle, July 18, 1992. Poster by Jeff Kleinsmith; THE GITS, M-99, Sunshine Miner, at the Colourbox, Seattle, July 3, ca. 1993. Poster by Jeff Kleinsmith; HAMMERBOX, the Gits, and 7 Year Bitch, at the Off Ramp, Seattle, January 17, 1992. Poster by Jeff Kleinsmith

After Chad Channing left Nirvana in May of 1990, Kurt Cobain and Krist Novoselic were left without a drummer just when they were talking to several major labels. Driving back from a label meeting in Los Angeles, the two stopped in San Francisco to visit their pals from the Melvins, Dale Crover and Buzz Osbourne. During the visit, they checked out a show by the hardcore band Scream at a club called the I-Beam. Scream's drummer Dave Grohl was a powerhouse and Kurt and Krist were duly impressed. In a twist of fate, Scream broke up soon after, leaving Dave stranded in LA. Buzz Osbourne, who was friends with Grohl, called up Cobain and Novoselic, since he knew that they needed a new drummer and both had been impressed with Grohl's hard-hitting style. The band immediately agreed to meet with Dave and he flew up to Seattle, rehearsing for a few weeks, and playing his first show with Nirvana on October 11, 1990, with Witchypoo, a band put together by Slim Moon, formerly of the bands Lush and Nisqually Delta Podunk Nightmare.

NIRVANA AND WITCHIPOO AT THE NORTH SHORE SURF CLUB, OLYMPIA, OCTOBER 11, 1990
PHOTOGRAPH BY JON B. SNYDER

"The show was plagued by technical difficulties. The power and lights went on and off and a few songs stopped and started a couple times. Long stretches of waiting. I was doing a video shoot with borrowed tape and equipment that came free from the Evergreen State College Media Loan — old gear even by 1990 standards. I made the mistake enlisting hardcore Nirvana fans to help me do a multi-camera shoot, and the resulting footage shows they were more interested in rocking out rather than getting a good shot. The venue was a cave. The North Shore was a flat wide box with low ceilings and black walls — easily the least appealing place I ever saw Nirvana play. By fall of 1990 the band was heavily attracting 'jock-crossover.' Kurt was becoming a Pied Piper leading rock fans away from Guns N' Roses. This made for a culture clash with the Evergreen/K Records crowd at the show. And the show was packed beyond capacity. Despite all of this the band just rocked and rocked some more. The version of 'Love Buzz' they played that night was the best I ever heard. Dave Grohl's drumming added urgency and menace to that song in a way I'd never heard before. Once they were in a groove the place went nuts. It was several hundred people in a group throb waiting for the floor to give out. I didn't realize it at the time but this would be the last Nirvana show I would ever see."

— Jon B. Snyder, photographer/Evergreen student

"We were driving back from LA and we thought, 'Let's go see Buzz and Dale, our old buddies,' and so we went to San Francisco. And Buzz is like, 'Hey, Scream's playing in North Beach.' 'Oh, let's go to the show.' So we saw Scream play and they were great, and what a great drummer. We need a drummer. We don't have a drummer. What are we gonna do? You know, we drove back — and then we got the call from Buzz. Scream broke up. They made it as far as LA and the bass player quit. And Dave needed to get out of there, so he came up to our place."

— Krist Novoselic, Nirvana

"Skin Yard was playing a show in San Francisco at this place called the I-Beam, which was this big, cavernous rock club right on Haight-Ashbury. We got there a day early and Kurt and Krist from Nirvana were in town to go see this drummer that they were gonna audition for the band. Me, Jack and Ben McMillan met Kurt and Krist at the I-Beam to go see this punk band called Scream, whose drummer was Dave Grohl. And they said, 'Yeah, we're just checkin' out this drummer. I think we're gonna audition him for the band.' Dave was just a monster on the drums and we all said, 'Uh, I think that's your audition.'

— Barrett Martin, Screaming Trees

Dinosaur Jr's guitarist/vocalist J Mascis played this Jazzmaster, decorated with bright happy-faces and animal stickers, throughout much of the band's career, from 1984 – 1993. The guitar's whimsical decoration belied Mascis's often melancholy, distorted, classic rock-influenced punk. The band, comprising of Mascis, bassist/singer Lou Barlow, and drummer Murph, formed in 1984 after the breakup of the hardcore band Deep Wound. Mascis's college friend Gerard Cosloy, manager of Homestead Records, offered to release anything that Mascis could pull together. The resulting band, dubbed Dinosaur (later Dinosaur Jr), released their eponymous debut on the label in 1985.

New York tastemakers Sonic Youth became early fans and asked Dinosaur to tour the following year. The band's 1987 release, *You're Living All Over Me*, received significant press in underground circles, largely due to the band emphasizing their loud-soft dynamics, virtuosic solos, feedback and distortion. 1989's *Bug* continued in this vein, and brought the band to the top of the UK indie charts. Dinosaur Jr's inroads into college radio and the UK scene, along with their ability to merge pop music's structure and rhythm with layers of distorted guitar and vocals, helped to set the stage for the mainstream success of bands like Nirvana.

1965 FENDER JAZZMASTER, PLAYED BY J MASCIS OF DINOSAUR JR, 1984 – 1993

"I met J Mascis when I was maybe 15 years old. J went to a lot of the shows that I went to. He lived in Amherst at the time, and he would drive into Boston. J always wore the same t-shirt, it was a 'Trix are for Kids' shirt, it's the only one he ever wore. And he looked like a fuckin' train wreck. We called him Chemo Boy because he had all these long strands of hair shooting out and then there'd be chunks that were just shaved to the scalp, and he just looked like a weird-ass slug that got run over by a car."

— Megan Jasper, Sub Pop Records

"I had saved money all summer painting the next door neighbor's house. I got like 500 bucks for painting the house. I wanted to get a Strat and there's this place that would advertise called Slimy Bob's Guitar Rip Off in Connecticut, and they advertised Strats for $450. So I went down there and he was like, 'Oh yeah, those are gone but we have all these Strats for $550 or something.' I didn't have the money to buy the Strat at that point, but they had a Jazzmaster which looked all right. I'd only seen

Elvis Costello play it and he was, y'know, kind of a dweeb, so it seemed like a nerdy guitar. I liked the neck on the Jazzmaster — it was long and it had all the finish worn off, and it had Grover tuning pegs on it which I always thought were cool, like Peter Frampton in Humble Pie or something. And yeah between the neck and the Grovers I went for the Jazzmaster."

— J Mascis, Dinosaur Jr

"All through the late '80s and early '90s, the idea was for us to use whatever helping hand we could to shine a spotlight on bands that we thought were of note and that we felt really were giving and taking with what we were doing. Dinosaur was an early example. They went with us on our first couple US tours, at the time when they were a brand new band. But we'd already felt like there was so much interesting stuff that they were doing, stuff that we were going to try and lift from them, and it was obviously mutual at that point. We just wanted people to see them."

— Lee Ranaldo, Sonic Youth

the off ramp goes friday !

Alice in Chains

MOOKIE BLAYLOCK

SWEET WATER

FRI FEB 1
OFF RAMP

Throughout 1990, Alice in Chains had toured down the West Coast and across the country by themselves and in opening slots for Extreme and Iggy Pop. Their debut, *Facelift*, had been selling moderately well, but by the time of this show at Seattle's Off Ramp, MTV had added the "Man in the Box" single to its daytime rotation, which increased *Facelift* album sales by a factor of ten. The disc went gold and became the first dose of grunge to reach a widespread mainstream audience. From there it was straight to the top – the acoustic *Sap* EP (1992), *Dirt* (1992), *Jar of Flies* (1994), and *Alice in Chains* (1995), all went gold or platinum, cementing Alice in Chains' reputation as superstars in the pantheon of grunge.

Mookie Blaylock played their first show at this same venue three months earlier, and soon were signed to Epic on the strength of their promising songs, along with the cachet of ex-Mother Love Bone members Jeff Ament and Stone Gossard. The band toured with Alice in Chains for the rest of the month down the coast to San Diego and back and by March 10, Mookie Blaylock (a name chosen to show their admiration for the star NBA basketball player) had become Pearl Jam, entering Seattle's London Bridge Studios the next day to begin recording their game-changing debut album *Ten*.

ALICE IN CHAINS, MOOKIE BLAYLOCK, AND SWEETWATER AT THE OFF RAMP, SEATTLE, FEBRUARY 1, 1991

"After Andrew Wood died, I got a call from Stone out of the blue, who I had known back in the Shadow days. I kind of knew him for many years. He was saying, 'Do you want to get together and jam?' And I said, 'Shit yes, I do.' It seemed like a really good opportunity at the time. Mother Love Bone had just broken up and I didn't have really anything going on. We started jamming. I couldn't believe all the songs the guy had. And we both had a very cynical sense of humor, so we kind of touched off on that level."

— Mike McCready, Pearl Jam

"I remember sitting there at the Central, and Alice in Chains was just a bar band at the time, and we were just hanging out and I heard them play and I just went up to those guys after and I go, 'You're rock stars. You're going to get a deal.' I remember not too long after that we played the Community World Theater with Alice in Chains. They were going, 'Yeah man, we got this deal, like 150,000 dollar advance.' And I'm going, 'I told you, dude. Told you.'"

— Tony Benjamin, Forced Entry

"As we were making *Dirt*, we'd all been into Nirvana and Love Bone and then Pearl Jam, and we knew it was really good and we were like, 'God, I hope this stuff's gonna do well,' but we had no idea it was gonna do as well as it did. It just eclipsed anything we could even imagine."

— SEAN KINNEY, ALICE IN CHAINS

NIRVANA

ALL AGES $8

FITS OF DEPRESSION
BIKINI KILL
WED APRIL 17
OK HOTEL
212 ALASKAN WY. PH.621-7903

After Nirvana debuted their new drummer Dave Grohl at the North Shore Surf Club on October 11, 1990, the band went on a brief UK tour with L7, along the way playing a show with one of Kurt Cobain's favorite bands, the Scottish group the Vaselines (their tunes "Molly's Lips" and "Son of a Gun" were common additions to Nirvana's set list). In spring of 1991, the band took a short tour of Canada, and on April 17, 1991, played a show with Olympia friends Fitz of Depression and Bikini Kill at Seattle's all-ages OK Hotel – a show that has since become legendary among fans.

The show opened with rousing sets by riot grrrls Bikini Kill and punk rockers Fitz of Depression, Cobain opened Nirvana's set with a solo version of a new song, "Pennyroyal Tea." The band then kicked in with a rousing set of songs from their previous releases; covers of Devo, the Troggs, and Naked Raygun; as well as songs that they had been writing for their next record. Toward the end of the set, they played for the first time a song that they been working on called "Smells Like Teen Spirit." At that point, it was just one of many solid songs in Nirvana's set; by the end of the year, the song's pop hooks and enigmatic lyrics would enthrall listeners around the globe, almost instantaneously changing the face of popular music.

NIRVANA, FITZ OF DEPRESSION, AND BIKINI KILL AT THE OK HOTEL, SEATTLE, APRIL 17, 1991

"I went with my friend Jim Jones down to the OK Hotel in Pioneer Square, and I think that was the first time I ever saw Bikini Kill play. They were brand new. I knew the gals in Bikini Kill from college in Olympia at Evergreen, then they all moved to Washington DC for like a year, then they came back and they'd started this band. So they had come back from DC and I saw them playing at the OK Hotel, and then Nirvana played and someone told me later that that was the first night they played, 'Smells Like Teen Spirit,' but you know, it was just all a blur. It was so much fun."

— Alice Wheeler, photographer

"I had a cassette copy of *Nevermind* because friends that booked them during the *Bleach* era were sent the advanced cassette of the album months before it came out. I put that thing on my tape player in my apartment and I cried. I invited every single person over and said, 'Listen to this. The world is changed.' Life changed at that moment. I heard it in the songs, and I played it on auto-reverse for a whole week. I was like 'Nobody is going to listen to anything but this record because now the world has changed.'"

— Melissa Auf der Maur, Hole, Smashing Pumpkins

"The first time I heard 'Smells Like Teen Spirit' definitely was at the OK Hotel. Everyone was having a good time and then this song started and it was like the room just exploded. You just can't help it, it was a visceral response, and people were saying, 'What was that? What was that? What was that?' It was an immediate favorite."

— SUSIE TENNANT, DGC, SUB POP RECORDS

riot
grrrl

a free weekly
mini-zine.

please
read and dis-
tribute to your
pals.

riot grrrl was a zine created by Molly Neuman, drummer for Bratmobile, with contributions by her bandmates, vocalist Allison Wolfe and guitarist Erin Smith, as well as Bikini Kill's vocalist Kathleen Hanna and drummer Tobi Vail. It was self-published and distributed in Washington DC and Olympia, the two initial homes of the movement. Zines like *riot grrrl*, *Girl Germs* (by Bratmobile's Allison Wolfe and Molly Neuman), and *Jigsaw* (by Bikini Kill's Tobi Vail) were an important way for like-minded women to get involved in underground music, network and provide support for one another, and were a primary catalyst for the transformation of riot grrrl from an idea into an identifiable community.

Riot grrrl was less of a musical style (though most of the self-identified riot grrrl groups played music grounded in punk) and more of a rallying point to bring awareness to the perception of women in society and specifically in music. Women in mainstream music were typically pigeonholed into the role of sex object or overly-sensitive and ineffectual songstress. The underground, from the days of hardcore onward offered scant relief: the bands were often male-dominated and the messages frequently misogynistic. The women involved in riot grrrl started their own bands that were aggressively pro-girl and confidently carved out a scene of their own.

RIOT GRRRL ZINE, JULY 1991

"In observing the indie underground scene I noticed that at least in the late '70s, there tended to be more women involved in the scene. The music tended to be a little more diverse. There was an emphasis on creativity, and then by '82, '83, the scene really shifted in a lot of ways towards the hardcore scene, which was very masculine, so there were fewer women involved, and that really set the tone for the American underground for a while. And in this context, Olympia really stood out because it embraced a different feel, a different aesthetic, and there were some women in Olympia that to this day hold a lot of influence. Stella Marrs, with her graphic sensibility and her graffiti in downtown Olympia and her postcards — she was an amazing influence. Also Heather Lewis from Beat Happening, Candice Pedersen who was co-managing K Records. Of course you had the riot grrrl scene that came out of Olympia. I thought it was a very healthy counterpoint to a lot of the hyper-masculine hardcore punk energy that was dominating a lot of the indie scene, especially in the early-to mid-'80s."

— Bruce Pavitt, Sub Pop Records

"One of the first instances of that was pre-riot grrrl was actually in 1988. There was a fanzine called *Maximumrocknroll*, and they were a very political punk magazine, and they decided to do a women's issue. They asked me and Cynthia Connelly, who was another woman who was really active in the Washington DC punk scene, to submit something. Cynthia and I looked at each other and we said, 'A women's issue? Why do we have to have one issue to ourselves? Every issue should be a women's issue.'"

— Sharon Cheslow, Chalk Circle and *Interrobang?!*

"My zines were really mostly pop culture, they weren't really riot grrrl zines. But I guess it was a big deal at that time for a woman to be doing a zine at all, which seems really weird, to think of it now. But back then in '87, '88, the only people I ever heard who were girls doing zines were Tobi Vail and Donna Dresch. So to me just doing any kind of DIY thing was revolutionary."

— Erin Smith, Bratmobile

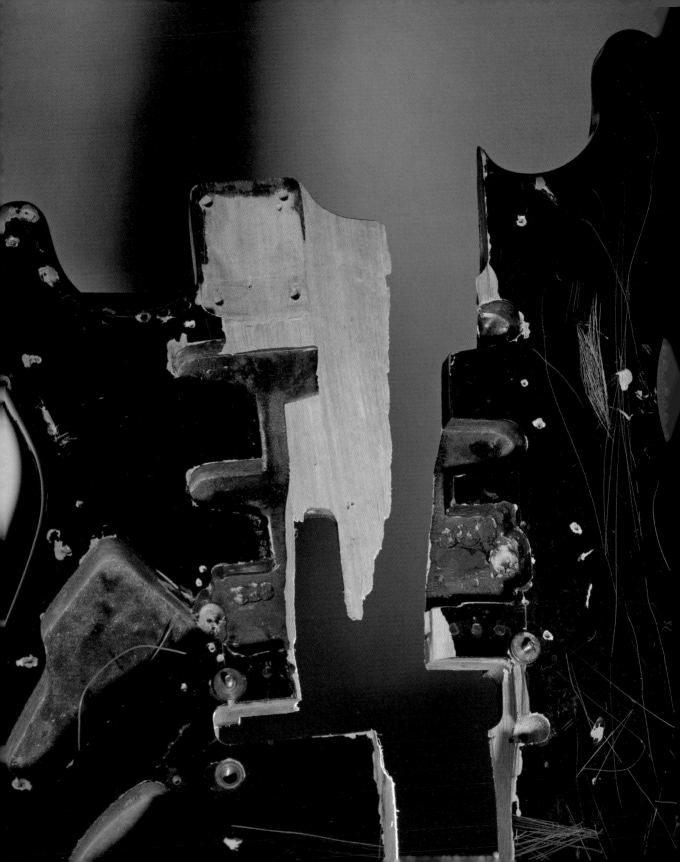

Soon after Nirvana's concert at the OK Hotel in Seattle on April 17, 1991, Nirvana drove down to Los Angeles to begin recording sessions for the *Nevermind* album. The sessions took place at Sound City Studios, with Butch Vig in the producer's booth. Nirvana had recorded with Vig a year earlier at Smart Studios in Madison, Wisconsin. They were introduced by Bruce Pavitt, who suggested they record with Vig in 1990 after hearing his production of Killdozer's growling wall of sound on the *Twelve Point Buck* album.

Now Nirvana had a generous recording budget from DGC Records, allowing them to take their time in the studio, and record over several sessions. Vig overdubbed vocals and guitars on several tracks, an embellishment the band couldn't consider with the limited budget they had during the *Bleach* sessions with Jack Endino. Kurt Cobain used this black Fender, among other guitars, during the sessions. After spending several hours recording "Lithium," they started in on a feedback-laden jam and Cobain, letting off steam, smashed the guitar, while Vig kept the reels running. The cut, later titled "Endless, Nameless," appeared as a hidden track at the end of *Nevermind*.

BLACK FENDER STRATOCASTER, SMASHED BY KURT COBAIN DURING THE RECORDING OF "ENDLESS, NAMELESS" DURING THE *NEVERMIND* SESSIONS, APRIL 1991

"This was Kurt's first black Stratocaster, and it was modified at some point to have a Gibson type tail piece and bridge on it, which is very unusual for a Strat. It was present during the recording of *Nevermind* and smashed during the recording of 'Endless, Nameless.' There's a photograph of it sitting on the mixing console. From there, it was rebuilt over and over. It's one of the longest running guitars of Kurt's guitars. And the reason why you don't see a lot of these smashed guitars complete is because we would recycle almost everything on them to use later on down the road."

— Earnie Bailey, guitar tech, Nirvana, Foo Fighters

"Nirvana was just such a force. They took all the ideas that we had, the bands that I worked with like Mission of Burma and the bands of my time, the Minuteman and Hüsker Dü and Black Flag and Meat Puppets. Nirvana seemed to take the elements that worked for those bands and make just one final explosive statement. It brought it all together — the attitudes, the sound and somehow Kurt Cobain and Butch Vig were able to distill it with *Nevermind*. Bleach was more like one of our records. *Nevermind* seemed to be the perfect storm of everything that had happened over the last 10 or 15 years. And it just exploded. And I don't think anything's been the same ever since."

— Rik Harte, producer and owner, Ace of Hearts Records

"We recorded *Nevermind* in May of 1991 in Los Angeles with Butch Vig and then we went and did this tour with Dinosaur Jr. The record came out in September, but we had already been touring for a month. We were still kind of on our Sub Pop reputation. We would be somewhere in Texas and then a label person would show up and say, 'Hey man, you just got added on K-whatever radio station.' It was starting to pick up. And then we were over in Europe and that's when the 'Smells Like Teen Spirit' video was on heavy rotation. And then Nirvana was a phenomenon. Geffen had printed up 50,000 copies of our records, and that was supposed to last us for a while. 50,000 copies is a lot of records for an underground independent band. And you couldn't buy the record. People were going to the record store and you couldn't buy it."

— Krist Novoselic, Nirvana

The release of Nirvana's *Nevermind* on September 24, 1991, and its rise to the top of the *Billboard* charts signified not only the mainstream ascendance of grunge and alternative rock, but also the deposing of glam metal as the rulers of rock 'n' roll. At the time, bands such as Skid Row, Winger, Ratt, Britny Fox, and others reigned over the rock charts, and reveled in spandex, big hair, flashy solos and easy women. Sales of *Nevermind* and MTV's constant rotation of the "Smells Like Teen Spirit" video changed all that, breaking down a wall that divided underground punk culture and mainstream tastes.

Nirvana was the culmination of a long line of underground bands that began making inroads into mainstream culture – Black Flag, Hüsker Dü, the Replacements, Sonic Youth, R.E.M., and the Pixies were all prepping mainstream audiences and leading them toward the DIY, independent, unique and innovative music coming from the underground. Nirvana's *Nevermind* brought the punk message and ethos, wrapped in pop's clothing, to the masses.

BUTT-ROCK QUILT, DESIGNED BY JULIANNE PETERSON, CA. 1992

"The *Butt-Rock Quilt* came about when I was in college and no longer felt cool wearing a Skid Row shirt! I didn't want to get rid of the shirts, because they were all important to me in high school, so I decided to make them into a quilt. I designed it so that the shirt back would be in the same spot as its corresponding front when the quilt was turned over. All of the shows were from concerts that I went to in the Midwest, and most have the tour dates on the back. The band Nemesis was from my hometown of Beloit, Wisconsin and were a favorite among the high school kids. I thought it would be funny to include them with all of my other favorite butt-rock bands."

– Julianne Peterson, Metal Fan/Quilter

"I think grunge in a lot of ways was aesthetically kind of a populist embracing of blue collar culture. You have to remember that at the time that the sound really broke, we were going through economic hard times, and what was going on in popular culture — you had shows like *Lifestyles of the Rich and Famous*, you had pop stars with names like Prince and Madonna, so there was this elitist aristocracy. Duran Duran, cruising around in their yacht. There was this real glorification of aristocracy, and a lot of people felt

really shut out of that, so when you have some young kids who are just wearing flannel shirts that they picked up at the thrift store, recording with Jack Endino who's charging $50 an hour, it was a huge inspiration to young people who didn't necessarily have access to resources, saying, 'Wow, I can create my own career out of my own cultural environment.'"

– Bruce Pavitt, Sub Pop Records

"I kind of look at indie rock as an evolution. They were a series of experiments. You started out with Black Flag, and that hits a certain amount of popularity. Then you get Hüsker Dü who take roughly the same thing and put a little spin on it — a little faster, a little bit more melodic. That makes it a little bit more commercial. Then you get Dinosaur Jr elaborating on that a little bit. They slow it down, more melodic, still kind of aggressive and noisy. And then Nirvana comes along and that's the next evolution. And meanwhile all these bands are selling progressively more and more records, and finally *Nevermind* comes out and quote unquote perfects the formula — very aggressive, more melodic than all those previous bands combined, very hooky, and that was the winning formula."

– Michael Azerrad, music journalist/biographer

BIG GIRLS are GO!!

Miss Maggie Murphy	you know it
Heavens to Betsy	xo xo
Wonder Twins	powers activa
Margaret/Stella/Maureen	fool proof
Jean Smith	scandaliciou
Kreviss	count 'em
D.C. Girls	monumenta
Bratmobile	Kiss & Rid
Lois Maffeo	bellyacher
Suture	self
Nikki McClure	girl scienc
Tobi Vail	0069
I Scream Truck	stone cold f
Spinanes	Reb-els
7 Year Bitch	erch

This set list was used at the kickoff show for the International Pop Underground Convention in Olympia, August 20 – 25, 1991. The show was dubbed "Love Rock Revolution Girl Style Now," otherwise known as "Girl Day," a showcase dedicated to women in underground music. It was a watershed moment in riot grrrl history, an energizing concert featuring sets by Bratmobile, members of Bikini Kill, Kreviss (featuring eight girls with guitars), Lois Maffeo, Nikki McClure, 7 Year Bitch, the Spinanes, Mecca Normal's Jean Smith, along with the first performance by Heavens to Betsy, whose guitarist Corin Tucker would later co-found Sleater-Kinney.

Candice Pedersen and Calvin Johnson of K Records sponsored the IPU Convention, with a goal of uniting disparate elements of the underground scene without involvement from the "Corporate Ogre," which is to say, the major label music industry. This stance excluded some, like Nirvana, who had signed to DGC Records, even though Cobain had a strong affinity for the Olympia scene. At direct odds with the grunge hype that would soon envelop the nation, the IPU Convention was conceived, organized, and attended by people invested in the idea that a vibrant music community can be created without corporate involvement, and still become meaningful to the world.

SETLIST FOR GIRL DAY AT THE INTERNATIONAL POP UNDERGROUND CONVENTION, AT THE CAPITOL THEATER, OLYMPIA, AUGUST 20, 1991

"As the corporate ogre expands its creeping influence on the minds of industrialized youth, the time has come for the International Rockers of the World to convene in celebration of our grand independence. Hangman hipsters, new mod rockers, sidestreet walkers, scooter-mounted dream girls, punks, teds, the instigators of the Love Rock Explosion, the editors of every angry grrrl zine, the plotters of youth rebellion in every form, the midwestern librarians and Scottish ski instructors who live by night, all are setting aside August 20-25, 1991 as the time."

— Poster for the IPU Convention

"On Girl Day, the first day of the convention there was only women playing. I had never seen anything like that happen. And I just had the chills the whole day. Everyone was really supportive, they acted like there was nothing silly about it, or goofy about it, which was weird, because all the time when I started playing guitar in high school,

I was just nothing but discouraged the whole time. I didn't have any network of other girls that were playing instruments. I think that's what really got me so fired up about doing something about it."

— Erin Smith, Bratmobile

"My friend Michelle Noel was organizing this thing called Girl Day for the IPU Festival, and she said, 'Oh, you started a band? Come play this Girl Day thing.' And we were like, 'Well we've never played a show before, we barely have any idea how to play our instruments.' But she said, 'Come play it.' And we went and played it, and there were over a hundred people watching us on the huge Capitol Theater stage, and we were so nervous that I thought Tracey [Sawyer, Heavens to Betsy's drummer] was going to pass out. But we got up and played, and it was really amazing. People really responded to it."

— Corin Tucker, Sleater-Kinney, Heavens to Betsy

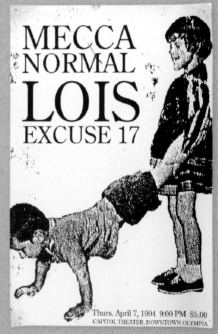

INTERNATIONAL POP UNDERGROUND CONVENTION, Capitol Theater, Olympia, WA, August 20 - 25, 1991; HEAVENS TO BETSY, Fleabag, at Red House, Olympia, WA, May 24, 1994; MECCA NORMAL, Lois, Excuse 17, at the Capitol Theater, Olympia, WA, April 7, 1994; HEAVENS TO BETSY, Control, Bratmobile, at the Capitol Theatre Backstage, Olympia, WA,

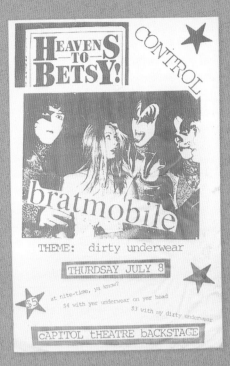

July 8, 1993; BEAT HAPPENING, Bratmobile, Stuart Moxham, Lois, Heavens to Betsy, at the Capitol Theater, Olympia, WA, May 30, 1992; GIRL GERMS #1; BIKINI KILL, Phranc, Team Dresch and Mary Lou Lord at the Sailors Union of the Pacific, Seattle, March 3, 1995

Steve Turner, lead guitarist for Mudhoney, produced some of the most distinctive fuzzed-out guitar sounds of the Seattle scene, and one of his favorite instruments was the Fender Mustang. Turner played this Fender "Competition" model (named for its stripes) from 1992 to 1999, during Mudhoney's tenure at Reprise Records.

After the release of Mudhoney's eponymous full-length in November 1990, the band spent the next year extensively touring the US, Australia, the UK and Europe. They also cut tracks for their sophomore album, but due to money troubles at Sub Pop, *Every Good Boy Deserves Fudge* wasn't released until July 1, 1991. The album, considered by Turner to be their best, was especially important to Sub Pop – the label's dire financial straits had come to a head, bringing it to the verge of collapse. With former labelmates Soundgarden, Screaming Trees, and Nirvana already signed to majors and gaining popularity, Sub Pop was banking on Mudhoney's new record to pull them back into the black. The record sold well, but not well enough. By the next year, Mudhoney, despite being extremely loyal to their long-time label, began shopping around for a new deal. By 1992, a share in royalties from Nirvana's DGC Records album *Nevermind* put Sub Pop back on solid financial ground, but Mudhoney was long gone.

1973 FENDER "COMPETITION" MUSTANG GUITAR, USED BY STEVE TURNER OF MUDHONEY, 1992 – 1999. GIFT OF STEVE TURNER

"If there could be said to be one pivotal record that saved the label, I would say that *Every Good Boy Deserves Fudge* was it."
— JONATHAN PONEMAN, SUB POP RECORDS

"It was a real funny period to watch this transpire. Don't forget this came on the heels of the big Sub Pop mania thing. That was all dying down, and they were just about bankrupt. *The Rocket* ran stories on their impending bankruptcy, and you know, Mudhoney saved their ass by basically giving them *Every Good Boy Deserves Fudge* in exchange for a broken down van. And you know that's what saved them from bankruptcy. And then that Nirvana record came out and shit hit the fan, it was the weirdest feeding frenzy I've ever seen."
— Art Chantry, graphic designer

"Mudhoney's *Every Good Boy Deserves Fudge* came out after we'd essentially laid off the entire staff. Jonathan and I were down in the basement boxing up records and shipping them to Japanese stores hoping to get $800, y'know, through Federal Express or whatever. But Mudhoney's *Every Good Boy Deserve Fudge* came out and sold 100,000 copies, which for an indie label at that time was amazing. It was like having a platinum record."
— Bruce Pavitt, Sub Pop Records

Kurt Cobain wore this sweater on the cover of *SPIN* magazine in January 1992, with a headline that read, "Nirvana: Knockin' on Heaven's Door." The title was apropos, given that by that time *Nevermind* was outselling *Use Your Illusion I* and *II*, the new albums by metal gods Guns 'N Roses (who had recorded a popular version of Dylan's "Knockin'"). "Smells Like Teen Spirit" was in steady rotation on MTV, and the band had overtaken the King of Pop, Michael Jackson, by dethroning his *Dangerous* album from the #1 spot on the *Billboard* Top 200 chart. Kurt Cobain was being touted as the "voice of his generation," and the band was reeling from the overnight success. The indie scene had finally broken through to mainstream audiences, and major labels were taking advantage – initiating "alternative" departments to scoop up any promising bands in the underground scene, outcompeting independent labels with hard cash. "Grunge" and "alternative" were now household words.

SHORT SLEEVE SWEATER, WORN BY KURT COBAIN ON THE COVER OF *SPIN*, JANUARY 1992

"Nirvana is the first thing to make Seattle front page news since Mount St. Helens erupted."
— Lauren Spencer, *SPIN*, January 1992

"Once *Nevermind* broke in the fall of 1991, and the whole Seattle scene got international attention, that label was suddenly stamped on everything from Seattle: Grunge, Grunge, Grunge, Grunge."
— Charles R. Cross, music journalist/biographer/
The Rocket publisher

"I remember a lot of people talking about the expectations for *Nevermind* and what people thought that record could do, and what we used to all just say is, 'That record's gonna be huge, that record's gonna be huge.' But nobody knew what huge meant. At that time, 'huge' for a band in our community — weirdly huge, was 250,000 records. Well, that ended up being a sliver of what they ended up selling. And that's what was strange about that time in Seattle — this was happening with Nirvana, it had started happening with Soundgarden, it started happening with Pearl Jam, it started happening with Alice in Chains, and nobody knew what 'huge' was. At some point, you just kind of throw your arms up and go, 'I don't fuckin' know what the hell is goin' on here!' It's crazy, it's weird, it's surreal, you can't wrap your head around it and you kind of just have to go for the ride and see where it all lands."
— Megan Jasper, Sub Pop Records

In March of 1991, Pearl Jam started recording their landmark debut *Ten*, which was released on August 27, 1991. By mid-1992 when grunge was exploding, sales of the album took off and the band went from playing mid-sized venues to huge amphitheaters. In September, the band worked with the city of Seattle to sponsor a free outdoor concert – a "Drop in the Park" for the fans – at Seattle's Magnuson Park. Tickets were given away by radio station KNDD, which had switched over to an alternative radio format a month earlier in light of the changing musical landscape.

Nearly 30,000 people showed up to see the Jim Rose Circus Sideshow, Seaweed, Shawn Smith, Cypress Hill, Lazy Susan, and of course, Pearl Jam. Rock the Vote registered 3,000 new voters, evidence of the strong sense of social responsibility and activism Pearl Jam have embraced throughout their career. The band has long used their influence and popularity for good causes; here, through entirely grassroots means, they arranged a massive and free festival, outside of the corporate system. Pearl Jam has since remained one of the most important rock bands of the last two decades, selling more albums than any other Seattle band from the grunge scene.

PEARL JAM AT MAGNUSON PARK, SEATTLE, SEPTEMBER 20, 1992
PHOTOGRAPH BY LANCE MERCER

"I had no idea Pearl Jam was growing as fast as they were and becoming the big band that they have become. They were trying to do a free show in Seattle and I remember they were trying to do it at Gasworks Park and it got nixed by the city, so it worked out to where they were able to do Magnuson Park and they had to get buses to bus people in and it was huge. Like, amazing. They had Seaweed and Lazy Susan and Cypress Hill and these bands that they had kinda gotten to know and it was free. It was – I don't know, humungous. When you're that close to it, you don't know how historic these things are. I'm just there. I'm just thinking, 'Wow, this is a big crowd.'"

– Lance Mercer, photographer

"We played with Pearl Jam quite a bit and they've always been extremely cool to us. Besides knowing Jeff and Stone and Matt Cameron for a long time, I've known Mike McCready since he was in Shadow. At some point in the Green River days we sort of like crossed paths with those guys in Shadow and actually kind of hung out with that band and became friends with those guys. They definitely handled their success in a reasonable way. They didn't freak out, they didn't just close off from each other like Nirvana did. They were smart enough to surround themselves with really good people in terms of management and crew. I think that's one of the reasons that Pearl Jam is here as a band and as people whereas those other bands have broken up or killed themselves."

– Mark Arm, Mudhoney, Green River

This Slingerland drum kit was played by two of the best drummers in the scene, Barrett Martin and Mark Pickerel. Martin bought the kit in 1986 when he was a music student at Bellingham's Western Washington University. In 1990, he joined Skin Yard, employing his hard-hitting poly-rhythmic style on 1991's *1000 Smiling Knuckles* and 1993's posthumous *Inside the Eye*. When Skin Yard broke up in 1992, he joined the Screaming Trees, whose original drummer, Mark Pickerel, had just left after playing with the band since their formation in 1985.

Later that year, the Screaming Trees shot up the charts with the song "Nearly Lost You," from their 1992 album *Sweet Oblivion*, primarily due to the popularity of the *Singles* movie soundtrack, where the track was also included. Martin can be seen playing the Slingerland kit in the band's iconic video for the single. With the newfound success of the Trees and the ensuing lengthy tour, Martin felt that he needed a bigger, more durable kit. He traded in the Slingerland for a new Tama kit. A bit later in a strange twist of fate, Mark Pickerel bought the Slingerland, which he used in his band Truly, which he formed in 1989 with ex-Soundgarden bassist Hiro Yamamoto and guitarist/vocalist Robert Roth.

SLINGERLAND DRUM KIT, PLAYED BY BARRETT MARTIN IN SKIN YARD AND THE SCREAMING TREES (1986 – 1992) AND MARK PICKEREL IN TRULY (1992 – 1999)

"The Slingerland drum set is a Buddy Rich signature series. I bought that in Olympia at Music 6000 in my second year of college in '86. I had a cheap, factory-made Pearl drum set that was kind of my rock drum set when I was playing in the Thin Men, but I ended up going back to the Slingerland because it sounded so good. It's a late '60s model with a big 26 inch kick drum which was the jazz style of that time. One rack tom, two floor toms. I would always use that in the studio because it sounded so good. When the Screaming Trees got big, I didn't want to take it on the road because I felt like it would just get destroyed. I traded it in for what became my first Tama drum set. That tour was two years long, and we went all over the world and you needed a drum set that could just survive. And then Mark Pickerel bought it, which is funny because, y'know, he's the original drummer in the Screaming Trees."

— Barrett Martin, Screaming Trees

"I was always enamored with the drummers of the big band era (Gene Krupa, Buddy Rich, Louis Bellson, Art Blakey, etc.) and not only did I have a hard time recreating their signature drum sounds from behind my modern Yamaha kit but I didn't like the way I looked behind it either. I ended up selling the kit to Dan Peters of Mudhoney and

I went off to search for the perfect kit. Later on, I was in a drum shop around the corner from where Truly was recording and came across the most beautiful set of Slingerland drums. I had no idea that they'd been left there on consignment by Barrett a few weeks earlier. A couple of years later I was working on my first solo album and Barrett came in to drop off a payment for a Tuatara session when out of the blue he screamed, 'Those are my drums!'"

— Mark Pickerel, Screaming Trees, Truly

"World music started appearing in jazz, like with what Dizzy Gillespie was doing with his United Nations band later in his career, you start to hear African drumming and Cuban drumming. What Art Blakey was doing with his records. You can hear it in all of the jazz drummers — you can hear an Afro-Cuban, Afro-Brazilian, sometimes just direct African rhythmic influence in the drumming. So that was kind of always with me as a rock drummer. I always had that desire to kind of play tribal rhythms and use the toms more than the cymbals — play rhythms on the toms, so that when you do go to the cymbals, you get this more dynamic effect than if you're just constantly on a cymbal."

— Barrett Martin, Screaming Trees

Nirvana kicked off 1992 with a spot on *Saturday Night Live*, during which they played "Smells Like Teen Spirit" and "Territorial Pissings," and closed out the credits with the band in a mock make out session. The band then set out on a stadium tour of Australia, Japan, the UK and Europe. On August 30, Nirvana headlined the Reading Festival amidst rumors about Cobain's poor health and battle with heroin. To spoof the gossipers, music journalist Everett True pushed Cobain on stage in a wheelchair dressed in a patient's smock and shaggy blonde wig. Cobain sang a bit of Bette Midler's "The Rose" before the band launched into their set. If Nirvana were struggling at the time to accept their sudden rise to fame, the 50,000 people at Reading could hardly notice.

This left-handed Sunburst Stratocaster, which Cobain played during the Reading Festival, was customized by guitar technician Earnie Bailey and was one of Cobain's main guitars beginning in the spring of 1992. Cobain smashed it at the Morocco Shrine Temple in Jacksonville, Florida on November 26, 1993 (it was later reassembled for display by Bailey). After the show, Cobain, Novoselic, Dave Grohl, and Pat Smear (who had joined the band two months earlier) signed the guitar.

FENDER STRATOCASTER, PLAYED BY KURT COBAIN AT THE READING FESTIVAL, UK, AUGUST 30, 1992

"The 1992 Reading Festival, the famous one that Nirvana headlined, was a three-day festival and the third day was the day that Nirvana headlined and it was 'the Seattle day' because Kurt kinda curated it. The opening band was the Melvins, then the Screaming Trees, and I think it was L7 after us, Mudhoney, Nick Cave and the Bad Seeds were on it, I think TAD was on it, and then Nirvana headlined. I can't remember what the order was exactly. And you know, even those of us in the opening bands, we were playing to 50,000 people. It was pretty remarkable to see that happen."

— Barrett Martin, the Screaming Trees

"When you've got to go through the thing of like 'You're famous,' it's all of a sudden: 'Oh.' And I knew I didn't really have the skills to deal with it. But one thing that I did do was that, we would be on *Saturday Night Live* and would be wearing Melvins or L7 t-shirts. We were true believers, saying, 'OK, so punk rock has gone mainstream. People are listening to this music now.' And so there's a cultural change

— rock 'n' roll music used to be about like Harleys and fifths of Jack Daniels, y'know, those clichés about hair metal bands, right? And then the grunge movement or the alternative music scene — there was a different consciousness there. Like all of a sudden there could be an Amnesty International booth at a concert, you know what I mean? Whereas before it just didn't really go together."

— Krist Novoselic, Nirvana

"When EMP acquired that guitar, it was missing most of the internal electrical components. I received a phone call, asking if I might have anything that they could use to complete the guitar. I went looking through my stuff and I had a small box taped up and it was dated from the time that the parts were removed off of it. So it was just perfect. I said, 'Yeah, you should take 'em. I'll be glad to put 'em on there for you. They belong back on the guitar. So I rebuilt the guitar and put it all back together. It was kind of nice to see."

— Earnie Bailey, Nirvana guitar tech

Since the early 1980s, the indie scenes in Olympia, WA and Washington DC have maintained strong sister-city connections, fostered in part by the early friendship of Calvin Johnson and Ian MacKaye. The two iconoclasts' record labels, K and Dischord, had similar independent outlooks, and bands like Fugazi (from Dischord) and Beat Happening (from K) toured together. This intercity link grew stronger as riot grrrl flourished, with band members of Bratmobile inhabiting both cities for a time. Tight friendships developed between bands such as Bikini Kill and Nation of Ulysses.

Bikini Kill, the quintessential riot grrrl group, toured with Nation of Ulysses, an all-male ensemble of sharply dressed, leftist punk revolutionaries, on a West-to-East coast tour in the summer of 1991, as riot grrrl was gaining steam. Steve Gamboa played this Bradley "P" bass throughout his time with Nation of Ulysses. When Bikini Kill was in DC following year, they borrowed Gamboa's bass for their show with Fugazi and L7 at the Sanctuary Theatre on April 4, 1992. A photograph from the show, by punk shutterbug Pat Graham, was used on Bikini Kill's self-titled EP, released later that year.

BRADLEY ELECTRIC BASS, PLAYED BY STEVE GAMBOA OF NATION OF ULYSSES, 1988 – 1992

BIKINI KILL AT THE SANCTUARY THEATRE, APRIL 4, 1992. PHOTOGRAPH BY PAT GRAHAM.

"There was a band on Dischord at the time, Nation of Ulysses, which came through and blew my mind. All these guys wore suits, the singer had a broken leg but was still thrashing around the dance floor and I couldn't believe he didn't break his leg again. He broke it onstage, I heard, from a previous show that tour. Nation of Ulysses was an amazing band."

— Jeremy Enigk, Sunny Day Real Estate

"The spring of '91, I think, we met the Nation of Ulysses, a boy-band in Washington DC, because Molly Neuman, the drummer in Bratmobile, is from Washington DC, so we would sometimes spend spring breaks out there together. At the same time, Bikini Kill was very active and they were friends with Nation of Ulysses. So they had planned a US tour from the West Coast to the East Coast with Nation of Ulysses. So they toured across the country ending up in DC that summer."

— Allison Wolfe, Bratmobile

"I moved to Olympia and I started really getting interested in Bikini Kill and Bratmobile. I was just overwhelmed by their, y'know, their power and how great they were. And also how they seemed very accessible to people. And I was kinda like, 'I can do this!'"

— Corin Tucker, Sleater-Kinney, Heavens to Betsy

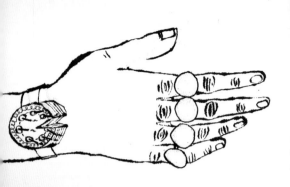

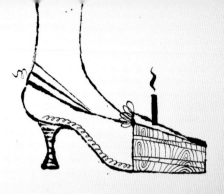

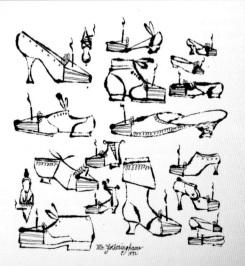

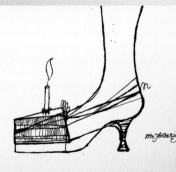

In 1992, Mudhoney left Sub Pop and signed with Reprise. They were now on a major label, but the sound of their next record, *Piece of Cake*, was classic Mudhoney garage punk, recorded by Popllama's Conrad Uno. Nevertheless, the mainstream didn't latch on as readily as they'd accepted many other grunge bands. Mudhoney rode out grunge's heyday on Reprise with 1994's *My Brother the Cow* and 1998's *Tomorrow Hit Today*. In 2000, they returned to Sub Pop, where they remain. While they never reached the commercial heights of some, Mudhoney always maintained their influential swagger and snarl – in prototype and production, the embodiment of the Seattle Sound.

This artwork for *Piece of Cake* was created by Ed Fotheringham, who used a blotted line technique employed to popular effect by Andy Warhol in his early commercial work. Fotheringham's sophisticated art ran counter to his hilariously infantile antics as the vocalist for the Thrown-Ups, the band he fronted in the late '80s with Mudhoney's Mark Arm and Steve Turner. Throwing raw oysters and wearing a "zit suit" that would spray shaving cream on the crowd were among his many audience gifts. Nevertheless, Fotheringham went on to critical acclaim, illustrating children's books, magazines, and such posh publications as the Neiman Marcus catalog.

ORIGINAL ARTWORK FOR MUDHONEY'S *PIECE OF CAKE* ALBUM, BY ED FOTHERINGHAM, 1992

"Everyone was sort of looking at these jazz covers, these old Blue Note covers and David Stone Martin and all this stuff and everyone was really into it because it hadn't yet been aped fully. I started looking a little, well, not elsewhere. It was very similar in time and almost in intent, but it was from a different source. I was looking at Andy Warhol, and I talked to Art Chantry about Andy Warhol, and he knew a lot about the mid-'50s illustration work Warhol was doing, and he knew this guy named Nathan Gluck who used to work with Andy as an assistant and did handwriting and would help him out. And so I read about how to do this blotted line technique. It was immediate and looked cool, and Warhol had passed away, so it seemed kind of appropriate and inappropriate to appropriate him, especially for a punk rock record. And so I just drew a bunch of drawings for that record cover and since it was called *Piece of Cake* and I have the mind of a 16-year-old boy, I wanted everything to be about cake, and so I thought, 'urinal cake,' and that's what I drew for the cover."

— Ed Fotheringham, illustrator

"Luckily because of Nirvana and Pearl Jam blowing up we had a couple of really good years there. And because of that we all have houses now. We had our deal with Reprise structured so that we got an advance for recording and whatever we didn't use for recording just went directly to us and we didn't have to pay that money back to them. I think they thought they'd eventually get that out of royalties, which they probably never have or will. Our first two albums with Reprise cost maybe 20 or 30,000 dollars, and that allowed us to keep the back end, which was probably about 120 more dollars to divide up amongst ourselves. I remember watching other bands spending months in the studio, going through their entire recording budgets and that whole idea just baffled us. It's as if they thought that if they spent all this money that they were more likely to win the lottery somehow. And the chances of winning the lottery are so slim to none that I wasn't going to count on that."

— Mark Arm, Mudhoney

The New York Times

MONDAY, NOVEMBER 16, 1992

LAMESTAIN

Lexicon of Grunge: Breaking the Code

WACK SLACKS: Old ripped jeans

FUZZ: Heavy wool sweaters

PLATS: Platform shoes

KICKERS: Heavy boots

SWINGIN' ON THE FLIPPITY-FLOP: Hanging out

BOUND-AND-HAGGED: Staying home on Friday or Saturday night

SCORE: Great

HARSH REALM: Bummer

COB NOBBLER: Loser

DISH: Desirable guy

BLOATED, BIG BAG OF BLOATATION: Drunk

LAMESTAIN: Uncool person

TOM-TOM CLUB: Uncool outsiders

ROCK ON: A happy goodbye

C/Z records

During Sub Pop's financial troubles in 1991 and '92, most staffers were laid off, including receptionist Megan Jasper (who today virtually runs the label as vice president). One day she got a call from her old boss Jonathan Poneman, saying a *New York Times* Style section reporter was planning to interview her about the grunge lifestyle. When reporter Rick Marin called, he asked if people involved in the grunge scene had any particular lingo. Jasper, who thought the incessant media interest for anything grunge was hilarious, bizarre, and ultimately annoying, began feeding the journalist fake terms she fabricated on the spot. "Harsh Realm" was the fictitious grunge term for "bummer." "Swingin' on the flippity-flop" was another phrase for hanging out. "Lamestain" was an uncool person.

The *New York Times* trusted the terms were genuine and ran a piece called "Lexicon of Grunge: Breaking the Code" on November 16, 1992. Paroxysms of laughter rippled throughout the Seattle scene. C/Z Records, run by ex-Skin Yard bassist Daniel House, printed up "Lamestain" and "Harsh Realm" t-shirts with a facsimile of the *Times* article on the back, commemorating the best grunge joke ever told.

"LAMESTAIN" T-SHIRT, CA. LATE 1992. DESIGN BY ART CHANTRY

"Well, y'know, there is no lexicon — there never was. There was no secret language or weird slang that was just unique to the Northwest. But I was psyched. I wasn't quick enough to just start rattling stuff off, so I told the reporter to just give me words and I would give him the grunge translation, because that bought me a couple of seconds. But honestly, I was raised an Irish Catholic kid and all of a sudden this guilt is starting to come in, and so I decided to make it as absurd and retarded as I possibly could so that he would go, 'D'oh! This doesn't really exist! Come on. This is all a joke!' But he just kept typing — tic tic tic tic. And I thought, 'That'll never make its way to print. There's no way. It's too absurd. Someone's gonna catch it. The sayings are too retarded.' And then my mom called me up about maybe a week or two later and said, 'You're not gonna believe it, you need to go pick up a *New York Times* right now.' I'm like, 'What the fuck?' And she said, 'You're in the *New York Times*, the Lexicon of Grunge!' I was like, 'Oh. My. God.' I ran down and I picked up the paper, and I was like, 'You are fucking kidding me!' Word for word! Printed! In the most prestigious newspaper! I couldn't believe it. I was psyched! And I felt a little bit bad."

— Megan Jasper, Sub Pop Records

"I was sitting in my office and the *New York Times* called. And so I pick up the phone and they go, 'Hello, this is so-and-so from the *New York Times*, and I'm doing an article. I want to know about the language that you grunge people speak to each other.' I mean, this is said completely earnestly, y'know? I thought it was a prank at first and I kind of realized that it was legitimate. And anybody who knows Megan, would know that she would be able to handle this far better than anybody else."

— Jonathan Poneman, Sub Pop Records

By 1993, the grunge hype was getting to be a bit much. For the first time in history, bands were moving to Seattle, not away, in order to get signed to a major label. Grunge hair gel and comic books detailing the careers of Nirvana and Pearl Jam were available at 7-Eleven. Even *Vogue* magazine capitalized on the "grunge movement" in December of 1992, featuring numerous photos of high-fashion models wearing flannel and work boots, with designer Donna Karan lauding the collection as having "a natural, just thrown together feeling that's all about spirit, attitude and individuality."

Seattle cartoonist Peter Bagge, best known for his Gen X slacker comic series *Hate*, which had poked fun at the absurdity of the grunge media frenzy, used his acid pen to create this artwork for a poster featuring a mythical Seattle grunge band, the Trying-Too-Hards. A stoner Jonathan Poneman and tripped-out Bruce Pavitt are illustrated on the bottom left and right, ready to pull out the pocketbook. The scene was ready for a change.

FLANNEL FEST '93!: FASTBACKS, POND, VELOCITY GIRL, AND HAZEL AT THE BRIDGE, SAN FRANCISCO, FEBRUARY 13, 1993. ORIGINAL ARTWORK BY PETER BAGGE

"I remember when bands started coming to town. They moved here and they had the whole grunge rock look and sound. And then the joke was, 'I moved to Seattle to get a record deal and all I got was this lousy heroin habit.'"

— KRIST NOVOSELIC, NIRVANA

"I was making fun of the grunge scene because it was ripe for ridicule — almost designed to be so. Anybody that took all that stuff seriously was crazy, because to me it was very much a repeat of what I saw firsthand with the whole punk/new wave thing. Of getting away from taking all that stuff seriously, and stop politicizing all of it. It should just be fun. Fun, wacky, crazy, entertainment. Dare to be stupid."
— Peter Bagge, cartoonist

"Grunge! Grunge! But what is that anyway? The way I always looked at it, people can call it whatever they want and I don't care. If they listen to it, go to the show, and make their own minds up, they can call it whatever the hell they want, and that's fine with me. It's just rock 'n' roll, y'know? Just another tag, and people need to have that to make themselves feel good. No problem. Rock on, y'know?

Do I think we were a grunge band? No, but on the same token, do I think most bands that were categorized grunge were grunge? Probably not, y'know? But hey, it's a good term. Rolls off the tongue. And if it gets Dieter to come out and check out the grunge band from Bellingham, I'm all for it, y'know? Not a problem."
— Dave Crider, Mono Men, Estrus Records

"Who made money? Stone Temple Pilots. Y'know? They're not bad people, and they've been through some really shitty times and all of that, but they used to be at the top of my shit list. There used to be some Seattle bands that had copped the grunge thing and the flannel, and I would just say all those people are idiots. They were a metal band a year ago, y'know, and now they're grunge."
— Steve Fisk, recording engineer/producer/musician

GIBSON RIPPER BASS, PLAYED BY KRIST NOVOSELIC with Nirvana, 1993 –1994. Novoselic had three black Ripper basses that he played in Nirvana from 1990 – 1994, including this one, which was purchased in December of 1993. From the collection of Krist Novoselic.

MOSRITE GOSPEL GUITAR, PLAYED BY KURT COBAIN with Nirvana, August 1990 – April 1991. One of Cobain's favorite guitars, he played it at key shows such as the Motorsports Garage, Seattle, September 22, 1990 and at the OK Hotel, Seattle, April 17, 1991, where Nirvana first publicly played "Smells Like Teen Spirit." It is also likely that most of the songs on *Nevermind* were written on this guitar. Courtesy of the Karsh Family Collection.

Donna Dresch is best known as the powerful bassist behind queercore group Team Dresch and the founder of the zine-turned-label Chainsaw. Formed in 1993 in Portland, Ore., Team Dresch earned a loyal following in queer and feminist punk circles for their aggressive sound and unflinching lyrics that addressed gay rights, bigotry and self-worth. Dresch's Chainsaw label championed influential women-led acts such as Excuse 17, the Frumpies, the Third Sex, Heavens to Betsy, and Sleater-Kinney, and became a powerful advocate for a constituency that had been underrepresented.

Dresch has been involved in the Northwest scene since the mid-'80s, playing in and touring with numerous bands, including Olympia's Dangermouse, Ellensburg's Screaming Trees, Amherst, Mass.'s Dinosaur Jr, and others. Dresch played this early 1980s Fender Precision bass with those bands and customized the instrument with the neck from a Fender Jazz model that Soundgarden bassist Ben Shepherd had smashed onstage. She later added a Badass bridge given to her by Minutemen bassist Mike Watt. As a finishing touch, she changed the bass color from red to green and applied the AIDS activism sticker "Action = Life." Given her storied career, it's no wonder she's affectionately known as the Queen of Grunge.

FENDER PRECISION BASS, PLAYED BY DONNA DRESCH WITH DANGERMOUSE, SCREAMING TREES, DINOSAUR JR, TEAM DRESCH, AND LOIS, MID-1980S – 1996

"Jody Bleyle from Team Dresch started her own label called Candy Ass Records. And she got this idea about women being able to defend themselves in tough situations, on the street where they're being harassed or attacked, which was a perfectly natural segue from riot grrrl. A lot of it at first seemed to be mentally oriented, like how to be strong internally, and then it led to how to be strong externally. So, Team Dresch, which also had Donna Dresch in it, started this project called *Free to Fight*. They would have shows where they would have workshops from their friends performing self-defense moves and martial arts. Feminist and self-defense training people would come and they would do mock situations that you might need to get out of. And that way a lot of girls would show – which caused a lot of problems in one way, because the boys couldn't come watch. They needed a safe environment, so that would happen before Team Dresch shows."

– Sue P. Fox, spoken word artist

"I started a band called Eights and Aces and we played a couple of shows with this band called Dangermouse, and they were from Olympia. We got to actually talking to the other bands, and I met Donna Dresch, who was the bass player of Dangermouse, and there's a whole long story about dropping out of high school, and getting in an argument with my mom and stuff like that, but the time was ripe for me to do something. And Donna was like, 'Well, I have a vacancy in my house.' So I just ended up moving down here. And the funny thing was the week before I moved in, she moved out. So I ended up moving in with these three guys who I didn't know, and moving to Olympia, not really knowing anybody."

– Slim Moon, Kill Rock Stars

Underground movements stay underground, die out, or make the transition to mainstream culture. At the height of grunge in 1992, new scenes were already percolating, '90s indie rock among them. One band that epitomized the new indie sound was Built to Spill, brainchild of Doug Martsch. Built to Spill was decidedly beyond grunge – melodic and lyrical, quirky and introspective, driven by Martsch's Neil Young-esque vocals and playfully dominant guitar. The band's sophomore record, *There's Nothing Wrong With Love*, was a breakthrough album of indie pop perfection, released on Seattle's Up Records. Up would quickly champion this new scene, which would come to dominate Seattle, with bands like Modest Mouse, 764-HERO, Quasi and others.

Graphic designer Jeff Kleinsmith created this artwork for an early Built to Spill show. While in college, Kleinsmith was drawn to the design aesthetic of Sub Pop Records (he later became the label's art director), posters by Portland, Oregon designer Mike King, and the Seattle music magazine *The Rocket*. He got a job at *The Rocket* working under designer Art Chantry, whose collage techniques heavily informed Kleinsmith's early work. Since that time, Jeff Kleinsmith has created thousands of posters, record covers, and other works that have put an indelible, visual mark on Seattle's music scene.

BUILT TO SPILL, THIRTY OUGHT SIX, SILKWORM, AND VIOLENT GREEN AT THE CROCODILE CAFÉ, SEATTLE, NOVEMBER 15, 1993. ORIGINAL ARTWORK BY JEFF KLEINSMITH

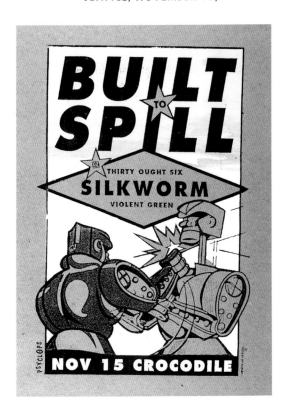

"Doug Martsch was in the Treepeople when I first moved to Seattle. Chris Takino for a short time managed the Treepeople, and he eventually worked with Doug putting out Built to Spill records. Up ended up signing bands like Quasi and 764-HERO and just so many other incredible bands. It was Up Records that was able to breathe a new life into what Seattle was, and it was this fresh air that kind of replaced the stale grunge. It felt exciting and new and creative and it didn't feel like a desperate solution to something that people were hungry for. It felt like a real solution. And it was great that it was able to happen in Seattle twice, back to back. Meaning, what had happened at Sub Pop in the late '80s and early '90s and then what was happening in Seattle from the early- to mid-'90s. And I think Up Records was lucky enough to really document that time."

— Megan Jasper, Sub Pop Records

"I think that Built to Spill in particular is brilliant. And I think their sensibility has really carried over and influenced other groups, like Modest Mouse, for example. Just their approach to songwriting and the way their music sounds. And I think those two groups in particular are really talented."

— Bruce Pavitt, Sub Pop Records

After years of battling heroin addiction, depression and other ailments, Kurt Cobain ended his life on April 5, 1994 with a shotgun blast to the head. In that moment, the life of an incredible and talented soul was gone, Nirvana was over and the death knell for grunge had sounded. It was a blow to Seattle and the world. Cobain had unwittingly become a role model and icon for disaffected youth, and they grieved his loss. On April 10th, a candlelight vigil was held at Seattle Center and 7,000 people came to offer their respects, while millions around the world watched.

Photographer Alice Wheeler was a friend of Cobain's, capturing the band for the cover of their "Love Buzz" / "Big Cheese" single among other beautiful shots. At the height of grunge, Wheeler became fascinated with fans' relationship to the band, and to Cobain specifically. She took this photograph at the Lollapalooza festival on August 31, 1994, four months after Cobain's death. Through his music, lyrics, lifestyle, and departure, Cobain managed to strike a chord that resonates as strongly today as when he was alive.

BOY WEARING KURT COBAIN T-SHIRT, LOLLAPALOOZA, GORGE AMPHITHEATRE, GEORGE, WA, AUGUST 31, 1994. PHOTOGRAPH BY ALICE WHEELER

"He should have just stuck around. He just shouldn't have done that. That's all I can really say. I mean, it's a huge understatement. He could have done anything he wanted to do. He could have been a painter or a sculptor or anything. And for years after Kurt died, I had this habit — if I'd walk by a pawn shop, I'd look in the window and I'd always look for a left-handed guitar. One day it was like, 'Oh, I don't need to do that anymore,' y'know?"

— Krist Novoselic, Nirvana

"I remember vividly when Kurt Cobain died. I was a sales rep at ADA, the distributor that sold Sub Pop and so many other great independent labels. This guy Don was the main buyer for Fred Meyers and he had no time for me, he hated the shit that I sold and he didn't love dealing with me. As I sat in Don's office, he had [KNDD] The End on the radio and he said to me, 'Did you hear about Kurt Cobain?' 'No.' 'Kurt Cobain killed himself.' And he put the volume up on the radio and I heard that there was a body that was found in the house that had not been identified, and I sat there and I was in complete shock. But to be brutally honest, I didn't think it was Kurt's body. I thought it was [Kurt's friend] Dylan Carlson, because I had heard that Kurt was in rehab in California, and Dylan was over there so much anyway, had a lot of guns, and was just not in a great space. And Dylan was a good friend of mine. I kept thinking, 'This is awful.' Because someone had died, and it was either Kurt or Dylan. Don ordered more Nirvana CDs than I'd ever sold, ever. I walked out with the sales slip and it was the grossest moment of my working life."

— Megan Jasper, Sub Pop Records

This clown-faced archway guarded the bar entrance at Moe's Mo'Roc'n Café, one of Seattle's top venues between January 1994 and June 1997. The club staged shows with thousands of alternative and indie acts that were big on the local scene or beginning to gain national attention. The Presidents of the United States of America, Bush, Radiohead, Oasis, Built to Spill and Modest Mouse all played Moe's. One famous, last-minute show had Pearl Jam and Neil Young performing together for Young's 1996 *Mirror Ball* tour. Moe's was also a champion of screen-printed rock posters. An ill-conceived Seattle law prevented bands from posting Xeroxed flyers on telephone poles, but cafés and restaurants would often hang nicer prints on their walls and in their windows. Moe's commissioned posters by many talented Seattle artists.

Local artists Graham Graham and Spike Mafford designed the arch, using chain saws and rough lumber to make it look as if it had been taken from an old fun house or circus. The venue was filled with wiry metal sculptures and art exhibits that accompanied emerald green plastic seats; clown faces riddled Moe's room for extra whimsy. Another highlight was the "Rose Room," which showcased objects that grunge-era performer Jim Rose had passed through his digestive system.

ENTRY ARCH FOR MOE'S MO'ROC'N CAFÉ, SEATTLE, 1994

"We had a deal with Moe's to produce screen printed posters for like every show. The guys in the shop would print for days to make posters and then they would get free lunch. We started bringing in Art Chantry and then Ed Fotheringham and Ellen Forney and Todd Lovering and Justin Hampton and a bunch of other people that I should remember. I didn't get paid for them but I got posters out of them. And I didn't care because I had a job and I just wanted to have posters. So Moe's got all these really cool designed posters for all these shows and all these designers had this opportunity to do screen printed posters that they didn't have before. I don't remember any of those people making screen printed posters for rock shows before that. I know Art Chantry did some long before that, but before Moe's happened I don't think there were really that many screen printed posters being made."

— Jeff Kleinsmith, Sub Pop Records

"Jane Nolan, that great statesman that we're all so thankful for in Seattle, her one great accomplishment as city councilman was making it illegal to post a poster on a public telephone pole or construction site wall or anything like that, and if you did it was a $500 fine. Five-hundred-dollar fine per poster, for everybody associated, so the band, the venue, the designer, the printer, the guy who stapled it up there, everybody would get a $500 fine

per poster. Basically when that happened it killed off the single most effective form of communication among the Seattle underground."

— Art Chantry, graphic designer

L7, TEEN ANGELS, 66 SAINTS, AT MOE, SEATTLE, AUGUST 29, 1995. POSTER BY ELLEN FORNEY

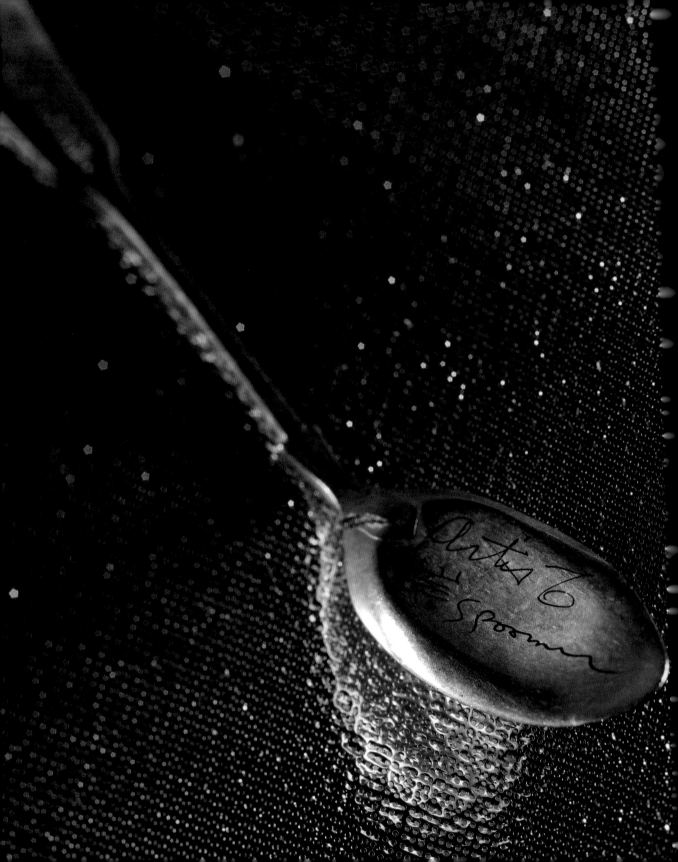

Soundgarden's *Badmotorfinger*, released in 1991, was a heavy, intricate record, on which the Led Zeppelin influences of *Louder Than Love* were outpaced by aggressive thunder and dissonance. Through the strength of the singles "Jesus Christ Pose," "Outshined" and "Rusty Cage," the band received widespread exposure on MTV and a growing audience. In 1994, *Superunknown* shot up the charts with "Black Hole Sun." The song's pop inflections illustrated Soundgarden's ever-broadening range and influence. From that point on, they were mega rock stars.

"Spoonman," the lead single on *Superunknown*, featured Seattle street musician Artis the Spoonman, a master of the musical spoons. Artis played his frenetic percussive instruments, such as this spoon, on the recording and video for the Grammy award-winning single. 1996's *Down On the Upside* expanded their sound further, incorporating banjo and other eclectic instrumentation. It produced the hits "Pretty Noose" and "Blow Up the Outside World," among others. But the following year they suddenly disbanded due to internal strife. Throughout their career, Soundgarden were instrumental: in the launch of Sub Pop Records to the popularization of grunge. Soundgarden's musicianship and diversity of sound has inspired untold musicians to pick up instruments in their wake.

ARTIS THE SPOONMAN'S SPOON, MID 1990S

"Artis the Spoonman was as a local street musician/poet/philosopher — just all around amazing guy. We used to see him perform at Pike Place Market and were amazed at his agility and his speed. The sort of thing he could do

with these spoons — he sounded like he was playing jazz or something. Chris [Cornell] wrote this song about him and we got him to play some spoon solos on the tune and it came out really cool. We were really happy with it. And it was good for him. After that song came out, he would be signing autographs down at the Market and all these kids would go up to him and go, 'You're Spoonman!'"
— Matt Cameron, Soundgarden, Pearl Jam

"Artis is one of those characters that busks at the Pike Place Market. And he plays the spoons. He's traveled all over the world and he's got the keys to many different cities by playing the spoons. There's an on switch or an off switch in people — his is welded on. The song came from Chris having a setlist in the movie *Singles*, right? Matt Dillon's character had this band Citizen Dick. In the background during a scene you can see this setlist. And Chris knew Cameron from working on the movie, and he grabbed the set list and wrote a song to every one of those fake songs that Citizen Dick did. Chris has a great home recording of all those songs and 'Spoonman' was on there. So I brought it up, 'Wow, did you know that I know Artis?' 'Yeah? Cool, man!' So we got to actually bring him in for the recording."
— Ben Shepherd, Soundgarden

BUTTERFLIES
WINNEBAGO
FLOAT
    BIG ME
    WATERSHED
FOR ALL THE COWS
I'LL STICK AROUND

ALONE + EASY
PODUNK
EXHAUSTED

Several months after Nirvana's sudden collapse in April 1994, Dave Grohl entered Seattle's Robert Lang Studios to record songs he had been writing on his own during his time in Nirvana. He recorded 12 songs, singing and playing all the instruments himself. That demo tape soon gained interest from several major labels, who saw gold in both Grohl's catchy, anthemic songs and his association with Nirvana. Grohl invited former Nirvana bassist Krist Novoselic to join, but they scuttled the idea to avoid the obvious comparisons to Nirvana. Instead, Grohl invited drummer William Goldsmith and bass player Nate Mendel, both from the recently-defunct Seattle emo giants Sunny Day Real Estate. To complete the band, he asked former Germ and Nirvana touring guitarist, Pat Smear, to join on second guitar. The Foo Fighters were born.

This setlist was from the fourth show in the Foo Fighters' career, at the Velvet Elvis Arts Lounge, an independent theater space that masqueraded as one of the only all-ages venues in Seattle during the mid-1990s. With the release of their first single "This is a Call," from the band's self-titled debut album, the band found instant fame. Dave Grohl went from being the drummer of the biggest band in the world to being the frontman of another group that could compete for that title.

FOO FIGHTERS SET LIST FROM THE VELVET ELVIS ARTS LOUNGE, SEATTLE, MARCH 4, 1995

"At one point Dave phoned me and said that he had this demo tape, y'know, that he wanted me to hear. I remember feeling awkward about that, y'know, it's really tough when friends present you with their demo tape. So he said he was going to swing by. I remember him ringing the doorbell. I think I told him on the phone, 'If I'm not here, just pop it through the mailbox.' And so I waited for him to pop it through the mailbox and then after he drove off, I went and got it and popped it into my cassette deck and listened to it. And I wanted to phone him right away and say, 'Hey, this is really good!' It sounded almost as good as Teenage Fanclub. It was a lot of complex harmonies on there that I didn't realize that he had down to that degree. There was stuff that was almost Beach Boys-esque, y'know? I was really impressed by it."

— Earnie Bailey, guitar tech, Nirvana, Foo Fighters

"When Sunny Day had broken up the first time Nate Mendel and William Goldsmith were approached by Dave Grohl to play in the Foo Fighters. That was really exciting for me because I had in a way felt that I had been pulling the rug out from underneath their feet by quitting Sunny Day, but yet Dave approaches and you know it's going to be successful if Dave's a part of it. So this was really exciting and they made amazing records. And still do."

— Jeremy Enigk, Sunny Day Real Estate

"Foo Fighters" VELVET ELVIS, SEA, WA   Photo By Alanna J. Alvarez 1995©

CROCKSHOCK, at the Crocodile Cafe, Seattle, May 25, 27, 28, 1994. Poster by Art Chantry; BOTTLE SHOCK, the Mono Men, the Oblivians, the Empty Bottle, Chicago, IL, August 11, 12, 1994. Poster by Art Chantry; MONO MEN, Kim Salmon and the Surrealists, Dura-Delinquent, at the 3B Tavern, Bellingham, WA, May 10, 1996. Poster by Art Chantry; GARAGESHOCK, at the 3B Tavern, Bellingham, May 25-28, 1995. Poster by Art Chantry; CROCKSHOCK, at the Crocodile Cafe, Seattle, May 26,

27, 1995. Poster by Art Chantry; TEENGENERATE, Satan's Pilgrims, and the Statics, at the Crocodile Café, Seattle, December 9, 1995. Poster by Art Chantry; THE MAKERS, with the Huntington Cads, at Double Down Saloon, Las Vegas, NV, February 17, 1996. Poster by Art Chantry

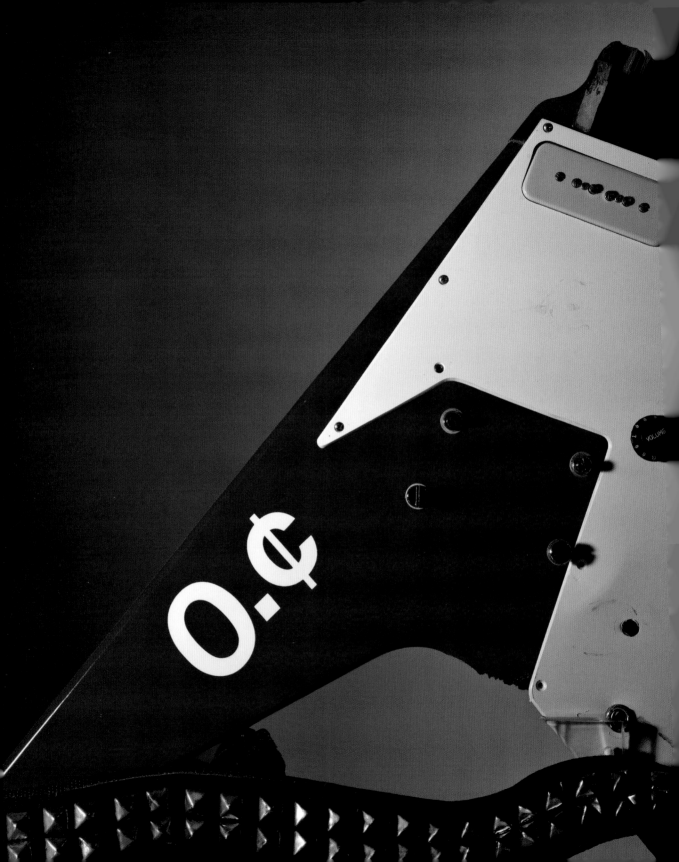

This "basitar" was played by Chris Ballew of the Presidents of the United States of America from 1997 to '98. In the Northwest tradition of Hendrix and Nirvana, Ballew smashed it at the end of what was to be their final performance, at Seattle's Paramount Theatre on January 31, 1998.

The Presidents of the United States of America formed in late 1993 by Chris Ballew and Dave Dederer, who had attended high school together in Seattle. In college, Ballew had been in a band with Mark Sandman of the band Morphine, where he developed a modified two-string bass, a "basitar" which became integral to the Presidents' music. Dederer played a three-string guitar – a "guitbass" – while former Love Battery drummer Jason Finn played an unusually normal drum kit. Despite Seattle's obsession with grunge, the band became known for their goofy pop tunes. The Presidents signed to Seattle's PopLlama in 1994, and released a self-titled debut the next year. After it quickly became a local favorite, Columbia Records re-released the disc pulling hit singles from it in "Lump," "Kitty," and "Peaches." Although that Paramount Show was billed as their last, the band soldiered on to release five more albums, with Andrew McKeag replacing Dederer in 2004.

FLYING V-STYLE GUITAR, PLAYED BY CHRIS BALLEW FROM THE PRESIDENTS OF THE UNITED STATES OF AMERICA, 1997 – 1998. GIFT OF THE PRESIDENTS OF THE UNITED STATES OF AMERICA

"In terms of what was happening in Seattle from 1987 or '88 to 1994 we were anomalies, but really the whole grunge thing to me was more of an anomaly than we were. To me, y'know, the Northwest is Sonics, the Wailers, the Kingsmen, Paul Revere and the Raiders. And then moving into the '80s and '90s you had bands like the Heats and the Cowboys and then the Young Fresh Fellows. Basically the real long term rock 'n' roll tradition in the Northwest is like crazy-get-loose-party-down rock 'n' roll. And we're certainly squarely in the middle of that tradition. Grunge is really just an extension of that. It's more sort of taking the Sonics scary element of it and expanding on that. It still has the same abandon and the same don't-give-a-shit attitude. So that's the commonality. But I didn't see us being very different. I felt firmly rooted in the Fastbacks, Young Fresh Fellows, Wailers, Kingsmen kind of thing. People playing fun songs for fun.

– Dave Dederer, the Presidents of the United States of America

"I had seen Chris and Dave play in this band called Go at the Crocodile Café with like ten people there and it really was great. I knew Dave from this Tuesday night poker game at my house and Dave would come by 'cause his sister Claire was dating Ed Fotheringham. I'd always say, 'Well,

y'know, if you wanna play in a band with me that would be great sometime' and he'd just blow me off politely – he's a master at that. So Love Battery's making this record and we had all this downtime all of sudden and so I started playing with Dave and Chris. I think we rehearsed like twice and then we got a 'big' show at the Romper Room on Acoustic Monday night and I think maybe six months after that we had gotten pretty popular in Seattle, but I was still doing Love Battery. The Presidents was getting more and more popular and it really started to feel like something special was happening. Like these crowds were just getting insane. At one point I was kind of booking the band and I said, 'I'm just going to book us into the biggest clubs in Seattle every single weekend. I just want to see how big our draw is. I want to see at what point it taps out.' Well it didn't tap out. It was BANG – sold out, sold out, sold out. I'd been touring around and playing for a long time in a lot of bands and I just I knew something was definitely happening. The Love Battery record was about to come out and I just quit. It was really hard. Some of the rock people said that it was a really bad move. But within a couple months we were flying to LA all the time and meeting Madonna and stuff. That started our meteoric rise to superstardom."

– Jason Finn, the Presidents of the United States of America

Recorded by Calvin Johnson at his Dub Narcotic studio in 1994, *Sad Sappy Sucker* was a follow-up to Modest Mouse's debut EP *Blue Cadet-3, Do You Connect?*, released in 1993 on Johnson's K Records. This demo tape was given to Meg Watjen, who booked Seattle's all-ages Velvet Elvis Arts Lounge, to secure shows for the band.

Hailing from the Seattle suburb of Issaquah, Modest Mouse quickly became Northwest darlings, releasing a series of acclaimed records on both Up and K Records. The band's appeal hinged on leader Isaac Brock's seemingly endless stash of quirky indie rock tunes. Over skeletal guitar, he proffered earnest and melancholy lyrics, sung in a voice that could stretch from a near-falsetto whisper to throaty yowl. The band eventually supplanted Built to Spill as the Northwest's flagship indie rock band. Many regard their 1997 album, *The Lonesome Crowded West*, as one of the best indie rock albums of the '90s. Modest Mouse signed to Epic in 1999, and released three more albums and several EPs, including 2004's *Good News for People Who Love Bad News*, which contained the hit "Float On." In the post-grunge era, Modest Mouse and other bands like Death Cab for Cutie helped define Seattle as one of America's capitals of indie-rock.

SAD SAPPY SUCKER, MODEST MOUSE DEMO TAPE, 1994

"I ended up hanging out in Olympia. Some friends lived down there and they were in this band called Lync. They all moved down there and I'd go down and visit them and lurk around. I took pictures of shows — really terrible pictures, and traded them with Calvin Johnson for records. Took more records than I think he thought I was gonna, for the trade. He was like 'Take some records for these pictures.' I did. Oh, I did. I never quit takin' records. I haven't stopped. I'd take 'em today if he were here."

— Isaac Brock, Modest Mouse

"When Chris Takino started Up Records, this was at a time when Nirvana were already huge, they had taken over the world, there was a real quiet lull in Seattle. There were so many bands that were still doing well, some that were still try-ing to ride on what had happened years ago. And it didn't feel new and exciting really. But Chris had found some people that he was really interested in working with, and one of those people was Isaac Brock who was 14 when Chris met him. Isaac was like no other kid — he had a wisdom that was beyond his years, he had a craziness that was more fun than anyone else, he was spontaneous, he was bright, he would speak his mind and not give a fuck, and Chris loved, loved, loved Isaac Brock. And it turned out, Isaac was not only a lover of great music but he made great music, and Chris was psyched to work with him, with the new band he'd put together: Modest Mouse."

— Megan Jasper, Sub Pop Records

Elliott Smith owned and played this Cable piano from 1997 – 1999 on some of his most recognizable songs: "Miss Misery" from the *Good Will Hunting* soundtrack, "Baby Britain" and "Amity" from his 1998 album, *XO*, all of which were recorded by Larry Crane or Joanna Bolme at Portland's Jackpot! Recording Studio.

In 1991, Smith formed the band Heatmiser with Neil Gust at Hampshire College. The two moved to Portland, Oregon, after graduating and released three indie rock albums of ever-widening scope, culminating in their 1996 release, *Mic City Sons*. During his tenure in Heatmiser, Smith's solo career bloomed. He had a gift for melancholy songs, which he revealed on *Roman Candle* (1994), *Elliott Smith* (1995), and *Either/Or* (1997). That same year, he was featured on the *Good Will Hunting* soundtrack. The film was nominated for an Academy Award for Best Song with Smith's "Miss Misery." Smith played the song during the awards broadcast – a huge triumph, even if he didn't win. He went on to sign with Dreamworks Records and *XO* (1998) and *Figure 8* (2000) soon followed. In October 2003, Elliott Smith passed away under still-unclear circumstances, ending the life of one of the most talented musicians of his generation.

CABLE UPRIGHT PIANO, PLAYED BY ELLIOTT SMITH, 1997 – 1999
GIFT OF LARRY CRANE AND JACKPOT! RECORDING STUDIO

"The thing about Elliott is... well, here's the thing. I didn't have a particular expectation about Nirvana, but I knew that Kurt was a really, really talented guy. I had just thought that he can take this talent wherever he wants to take it. And that was the same way I felt about Elliott Smith. Mainstream or underground, y'know, wherever Elliott wanted to take it. So to me, it wasn't that surprising. And we had really been behind Elliott for that reason. When his first record on Kill Rock Stars came out, it sold really poorly. And I really believed in it. I would call people up and I would be like, 'You need to take a listen to this," and they would say 'Oh, that's that folk music, I've heard that before.' And three years later the very same people who wouldn't even listen to the record are calling me up telling me how great it is. I really worked hard with the Elliott Smith records, because I knew that all it would take was for people to listen. And an Oscar nomination, that was pretty trippy. But if there's one thing that I've noticed is that I don't get surprised by the unexpected anymore. Because that's what usually happens."

– Slim Moon, Kill Rock Stars

"I'd seen Heatmiser playing shows around Portland, and initially (in 1993) didn't enjoy them, but by 1996 I was becoming a fan. I'd only heard Elliott's *Roman Candle* once, and had never heard his second solo record, but in summer 1996 I found myself tracking vocals with him for a new song entitled 'Pictures of Me' in my home studio. I was blown away by the song's arrangement, lyrics and sound. By the end of 1996 we were scouting locations for what would become Jackpot! Recording, and in early 1997 we put together a studio for both of us to work out of. It always seems helping him record and eventually becoming a good friend happened accidentally – like it naturally fell into place. Working with him in the studio was never difficult – ideas were already in his head and he'd lay down instruments with apparent ease. When 'Miss Misery' – what we thought was 'just a demo song' that we'd knocked out – became the closing music for Gus Van Sant's *Good Will Hunting* and was nominated for an Oscar, things seemed surreal but Elliott took it all in stride and was ready for the challenge of following it up with a great album. I got to watch him work on *XO* in Hollywood for a week in 1998, and on the final day I watched as they laid down strings for all the songs. I'd never heard something so beautiful in the studio in my life, and had to hold back tears as layers of strings filled the songs and the room. I still miss the guy. I was supposed to fly to LA and stay with him and work on his next record. Helping his family with his archives and overseeing releases is rewarding, but there isn't a day I don't think about Elliott, and wish we could once again wrap a recording session up and go grab a beer down the street."

– Larry Crane, Jackpot! Recording, *Tape Op* Magazine

Carrie Brownstein played this guitar from 1993 – 1999 with her band Excuse 17 and more prominently with indie-rock powerhouse Sleater-Kinney. Named after a road outside of Olympia, Sleater-Kinney formed in 1994 as a side project for Brownstein and Corin Tucker, guitarist for the riot grrrl band Heavens to Betsy. From the beginning, the band merged their riot grrrl roots with a stripped-down, frenetic punk sound. While both women sang and played guitar, Sleater-Kinney was best known for Tucker's piercing vocal vibrato and Brownstein's staccato guitar leads. Grounding the maelstrom was the rock-solid, innovative drumming of Janet Weiss.

Donna Dresch's Chainsaw Records issued Sleater-Kinney's first two albums. Their next record, 1997's *Dig Me Out*, released on Kill Rock Stars, expanded their audience considerably. Though Sleater-Kinney could have easily jumped to a major, they remained loyal to Kill Rock Stars, which began as an early supporter of the riot grrrl scene and had grown by the mid-1990s into one of the most respected indies in the nation. The band released three more albums for Kill Rock Stars, and one for Sub Pop. They went on hiatus in 2006, having achieved the remarkable goal of becoming a critical and commercial success while remaining true to their independent ideals.

EPIPHONE SG GUITAR, PLAYED BY CARRIE BROWNSTEIN WITH EXCUSE 17 AND SLEATER-KINNEY, 1993 – 1999. PHOTOGRAPH OF EXCUSE 17 BY PAT GRAHAM, SAN FRANCISCO, 1994

"I was in between universities – Western Washington University and Evergreen State College. I was about to move to Olympia but was living in Seattle and working a telemarketing job. Every day during my lunch break I would go to this guitar store on University Avenue in Seattle and would just stare at the guitars. Finally one day I just went in there and bought that one. I don't even think I played it, I just liked the color. I knew that SGs meant something in rock. I felt like I didn't need to try it out – I knew it was going to suit me, and it did. I used it for many years. I love that guitar, it's really a guitar I grew up on."

— Carrie Brownstein, Sleater-Kinney, Excuse 17

"There was a period where if you were a woman singer/songwriter you were taken less seriously and you couldn't rock because you weren't a guy, and your songs were probably going to be all sensitive and you probably played an acoustic guitar. It was this thing that women had to live under and when women started getting angry, when you get bands like Sleater-Kinney, they just proved that you can scream and rock and be female and there's just no question about it."

— Penelope Houston, the Avengers

The Mono Men formed in 1989 in Bellingham, WA. Founding members Dave Crider (guitar/vox), Ledge Morrisette (bass), and Aaron Roeder (drums), along with John Mortensen (guitar/vox), were more interested in the raucous garage punk played by Australia's Lime Spiders, Boston's Lyres, or Sweden's Nomads, than the heavy, Sabbath-inspired sound brewing in Seattle. As the Mono Men entered the 1990s, their popularity grew, especially outside of the Northwest. The band released an incredible 11 albums and 28 singles before disbanding nine years later.

Crider launched Estrus Records in 1987, releasing *Pound Bound*, a cassette by the Roofdogs, a band that morphed into the Mono Men. The label grew and became a garage rock powerhouse, releasing records from garage, trash, surf, and punk bands from across the globe. By the mid-'90s, tiny Bellingham, near the Canadian border, became a mecca for the garage-minded, with the label hosting annual Garageshock festivals. On January 16, 1997, the label's warehouse – which held master tapes, their entire catalog, plus Crider's personal record collection and the Mono Men's equipment – burnt to the ground. This drum kit, played by Aaron Roeder, was one of the casualties. It was a huge blow, but the legacy of Estrus lives on, delivering garage rock to true believers around the world.

LUDWIG 1960'S REISSUE DRUM KIT, PLAYED BY AARON ROEDER OF THE MONO MEN, 1989 – 1997, AND BURNT DURING ESTRUS RECORDS WAREHOUSE FIRE, JANUARY 16, 1997

"It's just shit, it's just stuff that burned. And it really was never an option to me to stop. I mean, if I'm going to stop doing this, it's because I decide. It's not because some asshole plugged in a refrigeration unit full of turkeys next to a can of paint thinner. That was the cause of the fire. Had to keep them turkeys cold! They raised wolves! Talk about the Northwest! 'I've got to keep the turkeys cold for my wolves!' I mean, can't argue with that, plus you don't really want to piss him off too much. Fuckin' raises wolves and feeds 'em turkeys! It's part of the Northwest experience, y'know? Come and visit! You'll love it in the Northwest! Bring a turkey."

– Dave Crider, Mono Men, Estrus Records

"Dave Crider and I found out we were practically the same guy. We both wanted to be archaeologists, went to college, ended up going into something else, we had the same love of crap culture, and we both collected the same crap, so we just started working on projects. Estrus was more smartass than bonehead, and it was very

sophisticated, very knowledgeable about pop culture and underground culture and crap in America. And so the Mono Men's style was kind of that bonehead, bachelor pad, hot rodder, garage rock style. I like to think that if Ed Norton and Ralph Kramden had a rock band they would have been the Mono Men."

– Art Chantry, graphic designer

"I know from the very beginning when I started playing music, what made Bellingham different to me was that I really wasn't paying attention to what was going on in Seattle. It's 84 miles away. Now, in the United States, that's not a big deal. In Europe, that's a country. It's quite a distance. And so I think people would look at it and say that a lot of what happened in Seattle was because they were isolated. Well, a lot of what happened, at least with us, is that we weren't paying that much attention. We really didn't care."

– Dave Crider, Mono Men, Estrus Records

ACKNOWLEDGE-MENTS

This book, in many ways, is the end-product of a 16-year educational journey that I've experienced since joining the proto-EMP team during the summer of 1994, at the tender age of 21. At the time, my concept of underground or alternative culture was non-existent, unless listening to lots of Jethro Tull and growing an Abe Lincoln beard counted. I was able to witness firsthand the growth of EMP's collection, alongside the original curators, **Peter Blecha** (from who I gained a huge appreciation for "Louie Louie"-era Northwest) and **Jim Fricke** (who hired me – *twice!* – and introduced me to the Gang of Four, the Pixies, Charles Ives, and all sorts of weird jazz). Soon the objects that we were acquiring evolved in my mind, taking on cultural meaning as I began to see patterns and connections between the bands, artists, and musicians that these objects represented. As we began to collect material from the Pacific Northwest, I started to feel more connected to the region, a feeling that evenutally erupted into a deep personal obsession with local music. Over the years, EMP opened my eyes up to whole worlds of unexplored culture, and for that I will be ever grateful.

I've had the great fortune of being able to tap into a large infrastructure of amazing people, without whom I wouldn't have been able to complete this tome. Thanks to **Gary Groth**, **Kim Thompson**, and **Eric Reynolds** at Fantagraphics for their excitement about the project. For the stellar look-and-feel and for investing so much of himself and his time making this project shine, I'm eternally indebted to designer **Jacob Covey**, who is always an inspiration to me. Thanks to photographer **Lance Mercer**, who did so much more than was required, infusing an air of beautiful mystery to the artifacts. **Krist Novoselic** is a literal and figurative rock star for being excited about the project and committing his time and thoughts to the Foreword, as well as his considerable contributions to the *Nirvana: Taking Punk to the Masses* exhibition. Much thanks to **Michael Meisel** for his advice and considerable power for good. **Jasen Emmons**, as always, provided much-appreciated structural, narrative, and editorial insights. I'm incredibly grateful to **Erin Wheeler** for her amazing attitude, efficiency at quote-finding, bio and index-assembling, and organizational wizardry, and **Malcolm Sangster** for doing all of the little (and big) things that I never seemed to have time for – this would be a shambles without their help. **Chris Nelson** was stellar at dotting my "i"s and crossing "t"s. **Bridget Jennings**, you kept this on the rails! I can't thank enough our collections team of **Melinda Simms, Ariane Westin-McCaw, Rosa Castaneda**, and **Aaron Hart** for tirelessly pulling, tracking, and re-housing all of the artifacts that I selected. Thanks to **David Wulzen** and **Nik Perleros** for making the DVD happen, under the tightest of timelines, and for being patient with my inability to deliver a monologue. Eternal thanks to **the Karsh Family,** for access to their collection and their generous financial support, without which this book would only be an idea. I owe my wife **Sara Guizzo** and daughter **Isobel McMurray** infinate thanks and an untold number of family outings and vacations for their patience and support. I love you!

Thanks to the following people for their incredible advice, knowledge, and insight – this couldn't have happened without you: **Mark Arm, Liam Barksdale, Traci Carman, Art Chantry, the Cobain Estate, Patricia Costa Kim, Larry Crane, Dave Crider, Tomi Douglas Anderson, Donna Dresch, Ed Fotheringham, Fab 5 Freddy, Jim Fricke, Addy Froehlich, Jeff Gilbert, Pat Graham, Keith Griffith, Patty Isacson-Sabee, Rich Jensen, Jeff Kleinsmith, Chris Maresca, Barrett Martin, Diona Mavis, Lance Mercer, Andrew McKeag, Christina Orr-Cahall, Bruce Pavitt, Charles Peterson, Mark Pickerel, Tom Price, Larry Reid, Jon Snyder, Kris Sproul, Chris Stein, Alice Wheeler, Mark Wittow**, and **Mark Yarm.**

Special thanks to **Michael Campbell, Larry Crane and Jackpot! Recording Studio, Devo, Steve Fisk, Jack Endino, Bruce Fairweather, John Foster, David Gulbronson, the Presidents of the United States of America, Kim Thayil**, and **Steve Turner** – the artifacts that you have donated to the EMP collection and knowledge you have shared have enriched this book immeasurably. Thanks as well to the **100+ individuals** that we have interviewed as part of our Oral History Program – without you this book would be much less, in every way.

— J.M.

ORAL HISTORY NOTES

The Experience Music Project Oral History Program is a continually growing collection of interviews with musicians and other key figures who have shaped popular music. Conducting these oral histories is a principal focus of EMP's curatorial and educational mission, and the collection currently includes more than 800 recorded interviews.

Interview segments referenced in this book were quoted from the following individuals, and are listed with the date of interview:

Albini, Steve, recording engineer and guitarist/vocalist for Big Black and Shellac, Mar 27 2007

Alvin, Dave, guitarist for the Blasters and X, Jul 31 1999

Arm, Mark, guitarist/vocalist for Mr. Epp and the Calculations, Green River, Thrown-Ups and Mudhoney, Mar 5 1998, Mar 16 2007

Auer, Jon, guitarist/vocalist for the Posies and solo musician, Dec 2 1999

Auf der Maur, Melissa, bass guitarist for Hole and The Smashing Pumpkins, Sep 24 2010

Azerrad, Michael, music journalist/ biographer, Nov 7 1998

Bag, Alice, vocalist for the Bags, Oct 14 1999

Bagge, Peter, cartoonist, Apr 30 2010

Bailey, Earnie, guitar technician for Nirvana and Foo Fighters, Dec 11 2008

Barrett, K. K., drummer for the Screamers, Apr 29 1998

Basnight, Jim, guitarist/vocalist for the Meyce and the Moberlys, Mar 9 2010

Benjamin, Tony, vocalist and bass guitarist for Forced Entry, Jan 4 2000

Biafra, Jello, vocalist for the Dead Kennedys, Mar 26 1998

Bingenheimer, Rodney, radio DJ for the Los Angeles rock station KROQ, Oct 19 1999

Bloch, Kurt, guitarist for the Cheaters, Fastbacks and Young Fresh Fellows, Dec 6, 1999

Bolles, Don, drummer for the Germs, Nov 19 1999

Brock, Isaac, guitarist/vocalist for Modest Mouse, Nov 19 1999

Brownstein, Carrie, guitarist/vocalist for Sleater-Kinney, ca. 1999

Burrill, Bud, drummer for Culprit, Jan 20 2000

Cameron, Matt, drummer for Skin Yard, Soundgarden and Pearl Jam, Dec 18 1999

Cantrell, Jerry, guitarist/vocalist for Alice in Chains, Sep 23 2009

Case, Peter, guitarist/vocalist for the Nerves and the Plimsouls, Sep 3-6 1999

Casale, Gerald, vocalist/bass player for Devo, Jul 13 2006

Cervenka, Exene, vocalist for X and the Knitters, Apr 29 1998

Channing, Chad, drummer for Nirvana, Jan 21 2009

Chantry, Art, graphic designer, Mar 6 2000, Mar 30 2007

Cheslow, Sharon, author of *Interrobang?!* zine and multi-instrumentalist for Chalk Circle, Dec 3 1999

Childish, Billy, guitarist/vocalist of Thee Headcoats, Feb 3 2000

Connolly, Cynthia, photographer and promotions for Dischord Records, Nov 2 1998

Cosloy, Gerard, author of *Conflict* zine, manager of Homestead Records and co-owner of Matador Records, Nov 6 1998

Crider, Dave, guitarist/vocalist for Mono Men and owner of Estrus Records, Feb 3 2000

Cross, Charles R., editor/publisher for

The Rocket, music journalist and biographer, Aug 25 2009

Danielson, Kurt, bass guitarist for TAD, Mar 4 1998

Davis, Elizabeth, bass guitarist for 7 Year Bitch, Jan 18 1996

Dederer, Dave, guitarist/vocalist for the Presidents of the United States of America, Mar 4 1998

De Janeiro, Rio, guitarist/vocalist for the Tupperwares, ca. 2000

Doe, John, bass guitarist/vocalist for X, Apr 29 1998

Doyle, Tad, guitarist/vocalist for TAD, Mar 4 1998

Earl, Mari, Kurt Cobain's aunt, Aug 18 2009

Endino, Jack, guitarist for Skin Yard and recording engineer/producer, Oct 5 2009

Enigk, Jeremy, guitarist/vocalist for Sunny Day Real Estate and solo musician, Mar 23 2007

Fields, Danny, music industry executive responsible for signing the MC5, Stooges, and the Ramones, Oct 2 2006

Finn, Jason, drummer for Skin Yard, Fastbacks, Love Battery and Presidents of the United States of America, Mar 4 1998

Fisk, Steve, recording engineer/producer, solo musician, and multi-instrumentalist with Pell Mell and Pigeonhed, Dec 11 1999, Feb 11 2010

Foster, John, publisher of *OP* magazine, music librarian and music director at Evergreen State College radio station KAOS-FM , Oct 29 2009

Fotheringham, Ed, illustrator and vocalist for the Thrown-Ups, Nov 11, 2009

Fox, Sue P., spoken word artist, Dec 3 1999

Ginn, Greg, guitarist for Black Flag and owner of SST Records, Nov 20 1999

Hart, Grant, drummer for Hüsker Dü, Jun 7, 1998

Harte, Rick, producer and founder of Ace of Hearts Records, May 2 2006

Houston, Penelope, vocalist for the Avengers, Mar 26 1998

Inez, Mike, bass guitarist for Ozzy Osbourne and Alice in Chains, Sep 23 2009

Jasper, Megan, vice president of Sub Pop Records, vocalist for Dickless, and perpetrator of the famed Grunge Lexicon Hoax, Jul 17 2009

Jesperson, Peter, co-founder of Twin/Tone Records, Sep 22, 1998

Johnson, Calvin, owner of K Records, vocalist and guitarist for Beat Happening and Dub Narcotic Sound System, Dec 9 1999

Kader, Rob, avid Nirvana fan, Oct 25 2008

Kaye, Lenny, guitarist for the Patti Smith Group, Mar 13 2006

Kinney, Sean, drummer for Alice in Chains, Sep 23 2009

Kleinsmith, Jeff, Art Director for Sub Pop Records, Mar 8 2007

Kramer, Wayne, guitarist for MC5, May 1 2000

Lanegan, Mark, vocalist for Screaming Trees and solo musician, Feb 16 2000

Martin, Barrett, drummer for Skin Yard, Screaming Trees, Tuatara, and Mad Season, Jan 20 2010

Mascis, J, guitarist/vocalist for Dinosaur Jr, Nov 6 1998

McCaughey, Scott, guitarist/vocalist for Young Fresh Fellows and Minus 5, Dec 6 1999

McClellan, Steve, manager of the First Avenue in Minneapolis, MN, Jun 6 1998

McCready, Mike, guitarist for Shadow, Temple of the Dog, Mad Season and Pearl Jam, Oct 20 1995

Mercer, Lance, music photographer, Apr 7 2010

Moon, Slim, spoken word artist, vocalist for Lush, Witchypoo, and owner of Kill Rock Stars, Dec 9 1999, Nov 16 2010

Mueller, Karl, bass guitarist for Soul Asylum, Sep 22 1998

Mullen, Brendan, founder of the Masque in Los Angeles, CA, Apr 29 1998

Novoselic, Krist, bass guitarist for Nirvana, Nov 18 1999, Jun 27 2008, Feb 26 2010

Pavitt, Bruce, co-founder of Sub Pop Records, Dec 14 1999, Jul 10 2008, Mar 3 2009

Peterson, Charles, music photographer, Dec 9 2008

Peterson, Julianne, metal fan/quilter, email correspondence

Pickerel, Mark, drummer for Screaming Trees, Truly, email correspondence

Pierson, Kate, vocalist for the B-52s, Apr 14 2006

Pirner, Dave, guitarist/vocalist for Soul Asylum, Sep 22 1998

Plunger, Trudie, Los Angeles early punk scenester, Apr 29 1998

Poneman, Jonathan, co-founder of Sub Pop Records, Jul 10 2008

Price, Tom, guitarist for U-Men and Gas Huffer, Nov 23 2009

Ranaldo, Lee, guitarist for Sonic Youth, Sep 3-6 1999

Reid, Larry, manager for the U-Men, owner of Rosco Louie and Graven Image galleries, Mar 8 2007

Roche, Mike, bass guitarist for T.S.O.L., Oct 13 1999

Rollins, Henry, vocalist for Black Flag, Feb 24 1998

Satz, vocalist for Ze Whiz Kids and the Lewd, Oct 25 2008

Shepherd, Ben, bass guitarist for Soundgarden, Jan 25, 2009

Shumway, Alex, drummer for Green River, Nov 14 2009

Sinsel, Brad, vocalist for TKO, Dec 4 1999

Smith, Erin, guitarist for Bratmobile, Dec 4 1999

Smith, Jean, vocalist for Mecca Normal, Dec 2 1999

Snyder, Jon B., photographer/Evergreen student, email correspondence

Stein, Chris, guitarist for Blondie, email correspondence

Stringfellow, Ken, guitarist/vocalist for the Posies and solo musician, Dec 1 1999

Tennant, Susie, promotions for Geffen/DGC Records and Sub Pop Records, Feb 25 2009

Thayil, Kim, guitarist for Soundgarden, Jun 2000

Tucker, Corin, guitarist/vocalist for Sleater-Kinney and Heavens to Betsey, Dec 3 1999

Turner, Steve, guitarist for Mr. Epp and the Calculations, Green River, Thrown-Ups, Mudhoney, Mar 5 1998

Uno, Conrad, recording engineer/producer and owner of PopLlama Records, Jan 26 2000

Vanderhoof, Kurdt, guitarist for Metal Church and bass guitarist for the Lewd, Jan 4 2000

Warnick, Kim, bass guitarist/vocalist for the Fastbacks, Mar 8 2007, Dec 1 1999

Wayne, David, vocalist for Metal Church, Jan 4 2000

Weiss, Janet, drummer for Sleater-Kinney and Quasi, ca. 2000

Wheeler, Alice, music photographer, Aug 7 2009

Wiedlin, Jane, guitarist for the Go-Go's, Oct 14 1999

Wolfe, Allison, vocalist for Bratmobile, Dec 2 1999

INDEX

**DO NOT BE BITTER,
DECEPTIVE OR PETTY**

SWEDA